# Real Estate Office Desk Book for APPRAISING RESIDENTIAL PROPERTY

John E. Green

Prentice-Hall, Inc.
Englewood Cliffs, NJ

Prentice-Hall International, Inc., *London*
Prentice-Hall of Australia, Pty. Ltd., *Sydney*
Prentice-Hall of Canada, Ltd., *Toronto*
Prentice-Hall of India Private Ltd., *New Delhi*
Prentice-Hall of Japan, Inc., *Tokyo*
Prentice-Hall of Southeast Asia Pte., Ltd., *Singapore*
Whitehall Books, Ltd., *Wellington, New Zealand*



**Library of Congress Cataloging in Publication Data**

Green, John E
Real estate office desk book for appraising residential property.

Includes index.
1. Real property—Valuation. I. Title.
II. Title: Appraising residential property.
HD1387.G73 333.33'7 80-14630
ISBN 0-13-764951-7

*Printed in the United States of America*

# The Practical Value This Book Offers

The ability to appraise residential property has become increasingly important for the successful completion of transactions in this type of real estate. Requests for a practical, down-to-earth, "how to" guide on residential appraising for use by *all* types of real estate professionals have come from a wide occupational range of persons whose livelihoods depend on evaluating residential property. The purchase of a residence is normally the largest single investment a family will make and these purchasers are entitled to the best appraisal possible to assist them in making a decision.

The demand for residential appraisals far exceeds the capabilities of available professional appraisers. This conclusion is shared by many leading firms, and to solve this problem an "in-house" program of training, for persons who are presently engaged in related occupations, has become essential. While the use of reading materials alone will not substitute for broad experience and formal training, efficient use of this book and a generous helping of common sense will permit you to become a competent residential appraiser while engaged in other real estate activities. It contains all the information required and outlines necessary steps toward developing a reliable and defensible estimate of value.

The *Real Estate Office Desk Book for Appraising Residential Property* is written for the broker, the salesman, the lender, the investor, the developer, the insurer, the beginning fee appraiser, and the staff appraiser—in both government and private enterprise. I will focus on the need of professional real estate people to acquire a working knowledge of the real property valuation process and the techniques of professional appraising. These are people who realize that a practical appraisal program, based on sound principles and on techniques proven in the marketplace, will lead to a more successful real estate operation. Such knowledge is essential, for example, in arriving at the most probable conclusion regarding how the greatest benefit can be derived from a particular property—its highest and best use.

An understanding of the principle of "highest and best use" is indispensable to the valuation process. The greatest benefit accrues from the best use made of a particular property. Whether these benefits represent profits or amenities of ownership, clients and the general public are better served when the property's fullest potential is realized. The determination of highest and best use provides a basis for arriving at an estimate of any type of value sought in regard to a specific property.

The client needs to know that the information provided to him is the best available when he asks such questions as: *What should I ask for my property? What can I rent it for? How much insurance should I carry on it? What would it cost to replace it? How can I best use it to protect my investment? How much money can I borrow on it? How much can I safely lend to the buyer of a certain property?* All these questions call for appraisal information. Proper use of the principles and techniques outlined in this book will provide accurate and realistic answers to most questions which may arise from an appraisal standpoint.

Knowledge of the appraisal process is frequently important in determining whether or not it would be worthwhile to accept a listing or other contract. Many clients expect unreasonable results because of the value they place on a particular property. Why waste valuable time in presenting real estate that will not sell? Time spent in appraising the property and in counseling the client as to the best listing price more often than not will help turn a profit on what would otherwise be a useless venture. A value estimate based on verifiable data becomes a source of confidence in the handling of sensitive and potentially explosive situations. Only the professional real estate person can be expected to know all the factors that create, change, and influence value in residential property. In this regard, the professional should be aware of growth or declining trends in neighborhoods and what they offer. *Are the homes beginning to look drab? Do they reflect design and construction preferences of a past era? Does lack of pride of ownership come through in poorly trimmed lawns and shrubs? Have the streets begun to crumble?* He must know how to assess the ability of a particular property to satisfy the needs of the typical buyer in the current market. (For example, today's family of four normally needs three bedrooms and two baths. A cottage with a good potential for resale in the future may be preferred by the young executive on his way up.) He should be aware of the restrictions and services available in the neighborhood. He should be aware that older homes are sometimes located too near the street to conform with recent zoning laws. Frequently, fire and police protection are not adequately available in certain neighborhoods, particularly new developments on the fringes of a municipality. Perhaps the most important requirement of all is the ability to recognize social and economic trends. This book provides invaluable, practical help in all these areas.

External factors affecting the value of a subject property must be considered by the appraiser; however, no dollar figure can be assigned before dealing with the physical unit itself. This requires the application of one or more of the accepted approaches to value. The three most common and universally used approaches to value in residential appraising are identified as: (1) the Comparable Sales or Market Data Approach, (2) the Reproduction Cost or Cost Approach, and (3) the Rent Multiplier or Income Approach. Normally, all three of these approaches are used for each appraisal, thereby insuring that no consideration of value is overlooked. Each approach may quite naturally result in a figure that differs from the other two, and the final dollar value assigned will be more closely related to the approach that supports the *purpose* of the appraisal—the type of value being sought.

The *Real Estate Office Desk Book for Appraising Residential Property* presents a detailed step-by-step process to guide you through the techniques of defining the appraisal problem, planning for maximum efficiency in the use of time, gathering and analyzing data, applying the data to each of the approaches to value, arriving at a value estimate, and writing the appraisal report.

The understanding of this practical program will lead to better business practices as well as greater profits. For example, appraisal reports rendered by others may be reviewed with confidence. Indications of the appraiser's integrity and reliability are revealed in his reports, the thorough and adequate appraisal is easily spotted, and the defensibility of report content is readily apparent.

This *Real Estate Office Desk Book for Appraising Residential Property* is written in laymen's terms and shows by practical example how appraisal principles are applied in the day-to-day operation of an appraisal and/or general real estate business. It should be remembered that a mere review of basic theory will not make anyone an experienced residential appraiser. However, understanding and applying the detailed guidelines in this book will enable you to take a very important step toward becoming an outstanding professional in the residential appraisal field.

The truly successful person in the field of real estate is the one who strives to do a professional job in the most efficient manner. Careful use of the techniques outlined in this book can reduce the typical overhead cost of doing each residential appraisal by approximately one-half, resulting in the proper pricing of listings and the maximum number of sales and profits.

*John E. Green*

# Contents

# 1

# How to Establish an Efficient Residential Appraisal System

The essential ingredient in providing any type of professional service is efficient utilization of time. This is true whether we are speaking of an attorney, engineer, accountant, doctor or real estate professional. There are only 24 hours in any given day, and none of us is capable of manufacturing additional time. It is therefore vital that we budget our time very carefully, and that we effectively utilize the skills of individuals working under our supervision. For anyone to achieve financial success in the appraisal of residential property, an efficient system must be developed so that this particular type of appraisal assignment can be completed in a minimum of time. This chapter is devoted to procedures for establishing an efficient residential appraisal system.

## THE NEED FOR AN EFFICIENT APPRAISAL SYSTEM

In many appraisal assignments, other than the appraisal of residential property, the problem to be solved is usually unique enough to allow the appraiser to do research limited to the appraisal of that particular property. The limited fee and time involved in the appraisal of residential property, however, does not permit the appraiser to engage in this type of individual research. If it were necessary for the appraiser to individually research each residential appraisal problem, there is no doubt that the appraisal fee would be many times more than the amount which can be charged under normal circumstances. Thus, if the appraiser is to be successful from an economic standpoint in operating a residential appraisal practice, he has no choice except to establish an efficient system so that the residential appraisal assignment can be completed in a minimum amount of time. Time is the only stock-in-trade of a residential appraiser, or indeed of any real estate professional.

During the first two years after I established my appraisal practice, the major portion of my appraisal assignments were for single-family residences. These appraisals were for mortgage lending purposes, for advising buyers or sellers, for real estate departments of corporations that were transferring employees, and for condemnation purposes for various agencies of the government. During my first few months of operating an appraisal business, I attempted to do individual research on each appraisal assignment. I found that the volume of work which could be completed under these circumstances was extremely low, thus producing adequate income only when I worked approximately 70 hours per week.

It soon became evident that there was no choice except to establish some type of residential appraisal system which would allow me to earn an adequate return for my services and to serve my clients promptly enough to satisfy their needs. Following the steps outlined in this book will result in a simple, yet readily useable, appraisal system for residential properties. If the appraiser isn't careful, he will end up with such a complicated system that it will partially defeat the ultimate goal of efficiency and speed in completing residential appraisal assignments.

## HOW THE SYSTEM EVOLVED: THE FOUR KEY ELEMENTS

As I said earlier, during the first few months of my practice, each appraisal assignment was individually researched. It soon became obvious that it would be necessary to establish a source consisting of four key elements of data for residential properties:

1. Comparable sales of improved properties.
2. Construction cost data.
3. Residential rentals.
4. Residential lot sales.

Each comparable sale which was researched during the process of making an appraisal assignment was recorded on a 4″ × 6″ card. This card contained a substantial amount of information about the sale property. In many instances, a photograph of the sale property was attached to the back of the comparable card. Comparable sales cards were arranged alphabetically by street name, ranging from the lowest street address to the highest street address. This is a simple yet practical way of arranging comparable sales cards. If the appraiser receives an assignment to appraise a residential property at 216 Main Street, he simply has to refer to the comparable sales cards, and he can usually find those sales which have occurred in the subject block, or the blocks adjacent to it on Main Street. If no sales have occurred on that particular street, a simple reference to a map will show those streets which are immediately adjacent to Main Street.

Details regarding data sources, along with their verification and proper utilization, for all four of the essential elements of the system will be found in the appropriate chapters of this book.

It is essential for the appraiser to maintain a file of residential construction costs within the city in which he is making appraisals. There are many sources of construction cost data. Many of the appraisal assignments will be for new residences. It is possible to obtain construction costs on these new residences and convert this construction cost to either cubic-foot or square-foot units. It is also possible to contact builders of various classes of residential structures to obtain cost data for a wide range of structures. An essential tool in establishing and maintaining a file of construction costs is a cost service. It will be necessary to adjust this cost service for local construction costs and to keep this data current. If it is found that the cost service is reasonably accurate when compared with actual, recent, local construction, then it will lend itself readily as a reliable cost reference. It is essential that this construction cost data be kept current, particularly during periods of rapid construction cost changes. It is suggested that construction costs be kept in separate files for the various classes of residential property. This would require maintaining a file for a substandard home, a standard home, an above-standard home, and various additional classes ranging through the high-priced, luxury home. This will allow the appraiser to quickly locate the appropriate construction cost for the particular class of property that he is appraising. The use of construction cost data will be explained in detail in Chapter 10.

I found that, in some appraisal assignments, it was necessary to consider the rental value of the particular structure. It is usually true that residential structures ranging from slightly above-average cost through the luxury category are not rented. While making appraisals of residential structures which are part of the rental market, it is easy to obtain the amount of monthly rent for any particular structure. It is then necessary to establish a file showing rent per month, rent per room per month, and details as to any items which may be furnished by the lessor. This information should be kept in separate files by class of structure, in the same manner as explained for construction costs. This permits the appraiser to quickly obtain data on the probable rental value of any particular residential structure he is appraising.

I have also found it necessary to maintain a file of comparable sales for all types of residential lots. This file of lot sales evolved through the process of obtaining the sale price of a lot for any appraisal assignment in which the lot was sold separately. In many instances, the builder will purchase several lots at wholesale from the developer, and will price the lot at retail to arrive at the selling price of the dwelling and the lot. The validity of the alleged lot sale price can be determined by subtracting the normal construction cost of the improvements from the total sale price to arrive at the indicated value contribution of the lot. Lot sales data may also be obtained from developers of residential subdivisions. Once the lot sales have been obtained, it is relatively simple to convert them to a price per front foot and a price per square foot. These lot sales can then be maintained either on a subdivision basis or by neighborhoods within the city. The use of comparable sales data will be discussed in more detail in Chapter 8.

## MAINTAINING A USEFUL CROSS-REFERENCE FILE

If a residential appraisal system is to function efficiently, there are certain essential files which must be maintained. One very important element is a complete file of completed residential appraisals. These appraisals should be filed alphabetically by street, ranging from the lowest street number to the highest street number, so that if an appraisal assignment occurs within any given area, the appraiser can readily determine if he has previously made appraisals in that area. This will allow him to use the same neighborhood data, zoning information, rental data and comparable sales and construction cost information in the present appraisal assignment, assuming that the previous appraisal was made recently. It may be necessary to establish a cross-reference file for the appraisals which have been completed so that if the owner of the property is known, but the street address is not, information on the street address and thus the location of the appraisal file can be quickly obtained. In such a cross-reference file, the second card would contain only the owner's name and street address

I mentioned earlier the importance of maintaining a comparable sales file. The following information describes some of the mechanics of maintaining such a file. It is necessary that those sales which become part of the comparable sales file must have been verified as to selling price, age of the structure and construction details. Unless the comparable sales data are verified, the appraiser can be greatly misled in using this information in the process of making residential appraisals. The appraiser will find that the maintenance of a comparable sales file is rather expensive, regardless of whether this file is maintained by the appraiser's own employees or furnished by someone who is in the business of supplying comparable sales data for a monthly fee. The amount of time which can be saved by the use of a good sales data file, however, will pay for the cost of maintaining this file many times over.

It is also important for the appraiser to maintain a readily available copy of the zoning ordinance and a current zoning map for each city in which he accepts appraisal assignments. A copy of all new subdivision plats is also helpful.

## HOW TO MAINTAIN SUCCESSFUL CLIENT RELATIONS

One of the problems in operating a residential appraisal practice is that most clients want their appraisals "yesterday." These clients are unaware of the fact that the appraiser may have a substantial number of appraisal assignments ahead of theirs. Clients also tend to feel that all the appraiser has to do is ride by, look into his crystal ball, and immediately arrive at a value estimate! The solution to this problem is to educate the clients about the steps required in arriving at a supportable value estimate. For the appraiser to keep a client on a continuing basis, he must furnish prompt service. This is a major reason for maintaining as complete and efficient an appraisal system as possible. When the client asks you to simply ride by and give him a quick value conclusion, you might explain to him all the steps that must be followed in order to arrive at a meaningful value estimate. I have found that the client will appreciate your sincere interest in providing an appraisal which will really meet his needs.

I have had clients who requested a simple letter opinion of value, one which would be of no use whatsoever for submission to a lending institution. An explanation to the client that you must fully document a value estimate in your own file, and that the only saving to him is in the time required to actually write the report, will usually eliminate requests for short letter-type reports. The client should be told that a meaningful appraisal report must be fully documented and should support the value estimate; thus, there are really no shortcuts available. A brief explanation of the steps to be followed in making an appraisal, perhaps in the form of a letter, will usually be worthwhile. Such an educational process, combined with prompt service within the framework of the actual work effort required, will eliminate some of the problems that might normally arise in any relationship with a client.

A further problem that may be encountered in the client relationship is the concern on the part of your clients that you know the sale price or the value which they established for loan purposes, in the hope that it will influence your value estimate. It is recommended that you explain to the client that you wish to arrive at an independent value estimate, totally uninfluenced by any extraneous factors. If a client insists on your knowing the contracted sale price or the value desired for loan purposes, you will simply have to receive this information and promptly put it out of your mind in order to render an independent professional opinion. I have found that the totally independent approach, together with prompt service and the very best appraisal effort, will maintain the proper client relationship and will assure you of a successful residential appraisal practice.

## DEFINING THE APPRAISAL PROBLEM

When you receive a request to make an appraisal, the first thing you must do is determine the problem involved. It is necessary to understand the purpose of the appraisal, as well as to obtain specific information about the subject property, prior to assembling and analyzing the data. Most of the appraisal assignments will be for simple residential properties in stable residential neighborhoods, with no tendency toward a change to some other use. If you have operated a residential appraisal practice for some length of time within a particular city, it will be rather easy for you to define the problem and assemble the necessary data prior to leaving the office to make the appraisal. In situations where there is a pending change in use, it will be necessary to thoroughly study the zoning which is present within the area, the probability of the demand for change in use, and the probability of a change in zoning, if such is necessary, in order to accomplish this change in use.

It should be readily apparent that, by putting in the time required to define the problem, the appraiser will avoid much duplication of effort when he carries out the actual appraisal assignment. The following steps should be taken in defining the appraisal problem:

1. Identify the type of property to be appraised.
2. Identify the property rights involved (usually fee simple).
3. Determine the date of the value estimate (usually last date inspected).
4. Determine the purpose of the appraisal (purchase, sale, loan, taxes, etc.).

5. Define the value sought (usually market value).
6. Determine the data needed, data sources, and personnel needed.
7. Determine the time required and the fee for the appraisal assignment.

Detailed explanations of each of these steps will be furnished in the following chapters.

## COLLECTING DATA

If the appraiser has maintained an adequate comparable sales file, comparable residential lot sales file, construction cost file, and rental data, he is well on the way toward promptly completing the appraisal assignment. An additional major source of data is to check the file of recently completed appraisals to see whether neighborhood data and much of the comparable information may be obtained directly from a previously completed report. Assuming that all of the necessary data, other than that particularly relating to the subject property, are available in the appraiser's file, then the additional data required can be obtained through inspection of the subject property.

## CORRELATING DATA

In the process of appraising residential properties, the appraiser will have obtained data on the subject site, sales of other residential sites, details of the subject improvements, cost data on similar improvements, sales data on similar residential properties, plus an analysis of the neighborhood in which the subject property is located. All of the data which have been gathered should be very carefully checked for accuracy and pertinence to the particular appraisal problem. An ultimate value estimate can be no better than the accuracy of the underlying data.

## CURRENT TRENDS IN RESIDENTIAL APPRAISING

For many years, there was an almost mandatory requirement that the appraiser of residential property use all three of the recognized approaches (cost, direct sales comparison, and gross rent multiplier or income) in every appraisal. Many clients still have the same requirement today. The American Institute of Real Estate Appraisers and the Society of Real Estate Appraisers currently require their professionally designated members and candidates to use all three approaches where possible and to explain reasons for lack of applicability in instances where one or more of the approaches is not utilized. The current trend is toward giving almost total emphasis to the direct sales comparison approach in most residential appraisals.

There is also a movement toward giving the client a range of probable selling prices rather than a specific figure as a value estimate. The introduction of the computer, with its application of regression analysis, has tended to speed up residential appraisals, not necessarily resulting, however, in an improvement in the accuracy of value estimates. A word of caution here to those who are prospective or present members or candidates in one of the appraisal organizations, is that the use of computers or any of the modern techniques does not exempt you from the ethics or standards of professional practice.

The sections which follow will offer a discussion of each approach and how it applies to residential appraising today. It should be remembered that we must know how to properly apply each approach to meet client requirements, in addition to the ethics and standards of professional practice of the various appraisal organizations.

## APPLICABILITY OF THE COST APPROACH TO RESIDENTIAL APPRAISING UNDER CURRENT TRENDS

There is no doubt that the cost approach is of secondary importance in appraising residential property when adequate sales data are available. Most mass appraisals which are done for tax purposes place primary emphasis on the use of computer-generated value estimates, using the cost approach as the major indicator with a halfhearted attempt to cross-check the result by making some sales comparison. This method of estimating value may suffice for mass appraisal purposes, but it certainly is not acceptable for use in general appraisal practice.

My suggestion is that you use the cost approach—carefully applied—as a check against your value estimate derived from the direct sales comparison approach. There will also be an occasional situation where you simply will not have adequate sales data available, and in such circumstances the cost approach will assume more importance. If you are going to use the cost approach in appraising a particular residential property, I would suggest that your own reasoning be applied rather than blind acceptance of a computer printout or a result obtained from a rigid cost and/or depreciation table.

## APPLICABILITY OF THE DIRECT SALES COMPARISON APPROACH TO RESIDENTIAL APPRAISING UNDER CURRENT TRENDS

In most residential appraisals, you will find that there are an adequate number of good comparable sales available. Under these circumstances, you can and should give the most weight to the value indicated by the direct sales comparison approach. The use of a computer provides the capability of making a larger number of adjustments for differences between each sale and the subject property than would be possible otherwise. The point to be remembered is that the computer does not possess judgment or reasoning capability and is thus dependent upon the reliability of the data fed into it. Use the computer as a tool when it is available to you, but use your own judgment in evaluating the answer it gives you.

If your client wants a range of probable selling prices rather than a single figure as a value estimate, you should accommodate him while also maintaining data in your file to support your reasoning. If your client requires that you furnish him with data and a value conclusion from the direct sales comparison approach, only then can you and should you do so. If this occurs, remember to retain in your files adequate documentation of your testing of the other approaches against the result obtained from the direct sales comparison approach, or an explanation of why the other approaches did not apply.

## APPLICABILITY OF THE GROSS RENT MULTIPLIER APPROACH TO RESIDENTIAL APPRAISING UNDER CURRENT TRENDS

Even under the best of circumstances, the gross rent multiplier approach is the least meaningful of the three approaches in appraising residential property. It should be applied only when the property you are appraising is part of the rental market and when adequate rental data are available, in addition to adequate sales of residences which were rented at time of sale. A value estimate derived from imputed rents and imputed multipliers is meaningless. It is possible to use this approach in appraising a single condominium or cooperative unit if it is within the rental pool in the complex and if similar units within the rental pool have recently sold. It is important to know how to apply the gross rent multiplier approach to those circumstances where it is applicable. The current trend is for many appraisal clients who formerly required the use of this approach to abandon this requirement for most appraisals.

## THE SYSTEM IN ACTION

The following chapters are arranged in the normal sequence that should be followed by the appraiser in making an appraisal of a residential property. A systematic approach is vital to the appraisal of any property, particularly a residential property. The appraiser is usually limited in the amount of time he can devote to the appraisal of a residential property, and must therefore use his time efficiently.

The steps outlined in the coming chapters will lead to the establishment of a practical system for appraising residential property for any real estate professional.

It is my intention to present the material in this book in simple terms so that it can be applied in the day-to-day operation of a residential appraisal practice and/or general real estate business. The techniques presented herein, when applied in the actual operation of a residential appraisal practice, have proven to be effective in permitting the appraiser to perform appraisals in the minimum amount of time. An appraisal practice specializing in residential properties can be quite successful when, and if, the business is operated in an efficient manner.

# 2

# The Essential Elements in Evaluating Property Rights

Every appraisal assignment requires the appraiser to estimate the value of the property based upon certain rights to be considered and included in the appraisal. Many unfortunate errors that occur in making appraisals result from the fact that the appraiser has not adequately informed himself of the rights involved in appraising the property. The purpose of this chapter is to provide some guidelines which will help you avoid many of the common mistakes arising from a lack of understanding of property rights. For example, there is a substantial difference between the value of a property when it is encumbered by an easement or a lease, and a property which has no such encumbrance. Later chapters in this book will follow the actual steps which you, as the appraiser, will take during the process of estimating the value. This chapter will lay a proper foundation for you, toward becoming a competent appraiser.

## KEY TERMS AND HOW THEY ARE USED

The average person tends to confuse the terms *real estate, real property* and *realty,* often using the terms interchangeably. There is a basic difference in their meanings, and it is very important for you to know this difference. The term *real estate* includes the land and all improvements which are permanently located thereon—the physical thing. This includes structures as well as walks, drives, fences, landscaping and other such items. *Realty* also refers to the physical entity, and may be used interchangeably with *real estate.* What is most important for the appraiser to understand is that *real property* means the *rights in real estate.* Real estate is fixed in location and cannot be physically picked up and moved away; therefore, you do not sell real estate or realty. The thing that is sold is the *rights* which the owner may possess with regard to the real estate. In many instances, these rights are almost absolute and are known as *fee simple interest.* In some instances, the rights are restricted due to encumbrances such as leases and easements, and under those circumstances the rights which are transferred are not equivalent to fee simple. The most important thing for you to understand here is that the thing which you are appraising in all circumstances is *real property,* that is, *rights in realty,* and not the physical thing itself.

## IMPORTANT PHYSICAL ASPECTS OF REAL ESTATE

A major physical aspect of real estate is that it is *durable.* It does not wear out quickly, as does an automobile or other short-lived asset. Structures that are placed upon the land do tend to wear out and to that extent are not as durable as the land itself. We are dealing with a long-life asset and must keep this in mind in appraising the property. There are certain things which might bring the physical life of an improvement to an end long before it actually wears out. This particular characteristic will be dealt with in some detail in the depreciation and obsolescence sections of this book.

Another distinguishing physical feature of real estate is that it is *immobile,* and for that reason it must be valued as it sits, where it sits, with all of the good or bad characteristics taken into consideration. There is no way that you can change the environment of a property other than by the gradual process of a change in use within the immediate area. Because real estate is immobile, it requires particular effort on your part to evaluate the property's surroundings so that you fully understand any positive or negative characteristics that may affect the present value and future economic life of any improvements located on the property. For example, a single-family residence located in an area which is changing to substandard boarding houses will usually suffer a loss in value.

One more distinguishing physical characteristic of real estate is that *no two properties are identical.* The improvements, which are located on the property, may be identical and the land size, shape, topography and all other elements may be identical, but there is still the distinguishing characteristic of location. Any parcel of real estate can be described with such precision that there is no doubt whatsoever about the property involved in the appraisal. In appraising any property, it is essential for you to understand the unique characteristics of the particular site and the improvements located thereon. This understanding will enable you to compare the subject with properties that have sold in arriving at a supportable and defensible estimate of value.

## PROPERTY RIGHTS OR LEGAL ASPECTS OF REAL ESTATE

As I explained earlier, that which is sold in a real estate transaction is the real property or property rights. The basic rights in real estate have been defined as the "bundle of rights." This bundle of rights consists of the right to possess the property, control it, enjoy it, dispose of it, use it, exclude others from using it, or the right to do none of these things. On occasion, the owner of real property may bargain away a portion of the bundle of rights. One example is when the owner of the property allows a person to have an easement for right-of-way across a portion of his land, thus eliminating his right to exclusively use this portion of the property. Another instance in which a portion of the rights is bargained away is a lease situation in which the owner disposes of the right to use all or a portion of the property for a specified period of time in exchange for the lessee's payment of a certain stipulated rent. In this case, the owner still owns the real property, but the ownership is encumbered with certain restrictions. It is very important for you to be fully aware of any outstanding encumbrances in the nature of leases, easements, assessments or any other items which would tend to place a limit on the property rights possessed by the owner.

### PUBLIC LIMITATIONS ON PROPERTY RIGHTS

I have described some of the voluntary restrictions, such as leases and easements, which would limit the bundle of rights. In addition to such voluntary restrictions, there are several basic public limitations on the exercise of the bundle of rights. These are eminent domain, police power, taxation and escheat. All real property has these basic limitations imposed upon it, and it is incumbent upon you, as the appraiser, to be fully aware of how restrictive these limitations are. In order to have a thorough understanding of the zoning part of police power limitation, which may apply to a particular parcel of property, it is necessary to study the local zoning ordinances, to be aware of the ease with which changes in zoning may be accomplished, and also to understand other police power restrictions, such as the local building codes and any restrictions which may be placed on the property by local health department regulations. Police power also includes the obligation of the local governmental agency to provide police protection, fire protection and other services of the government.

The limitation on the property which is imposed by the right to tax can be very important. The property tax burden may be so prohibitive that it will basically make it unprofitable to own and operate any type of property. As the appraiser, you must investigate the tax burden that applies to the area in which the subject property is located and compare it with the other alternatives available to prospective buyers of property. In some taxing jurisdictions, the assessing personnel do an outstanding job in properly appraising and equalizing the tax burden, while in other areas there is no equalization whatsoever, and any particular property may be called upon to bear much more than its normal share of the tax burden.

The limitations of escheat generally apply in most areas of the United States. Escheat occurs when the property owner dies without a will or any known heirs. Under these circumstances, after a reasonable period of time, the property does revert to and is owned by the State. This occurs fairly infrequently in most areas, since there are usually some heirs around; however, if the appraiser has some doubt as to this element of the property, he certainly should investigate.

The limitation of eminent domain provides that private property may be condemned and put to public use when such use is in the public interest. There are circumstances in which the condemnation and acquisition of only a small portion of a property will almost destroy the value of the remaining property that has not been acquired. I know of instances where pending urban renewal acquisition programs have placed severe limitations on residential sales prices and have also caused them to be very difficult to rent. The property owner must be compensated for the market value of the property acquired under eminent domain, and for any damages arising from the acquisition. The appraiser should determine any present plans to acquire part or all of any property he is appraising. This information can usually be obtained by contacting the City Housing Authority and/or the local Urban Renewal or Community Development Agency.

## HOW TO EVALUATE DIFFERENT TYPES OF OWNERSHIP

The various types of property ownership are classified as *estates*. The most common type of estate is known as *fee simple* or *fee simple absolute*. This is the most complete type of private property ownership possible. There are still the public limitations which have been previously discussed, as well as some private limitations such as mortgages and easements which may apply to a particular property and still not affect the fact that it is a fee simple estate. It is very important for you to thoroughly understand any limitations or encumbrances which may affect the value of this type of ownership.

Another type of estate is known as a *fee tail estate,* where the property can be disposed of only to the owner's descendants or heirs. This property cannot be sold and can simply be handed down to certain descendants as specified by the grantor of the estate in his will. Another type of limited estate is known as a *life estate,* which provides that a person may use the property for the remainder of his life, at the end of which the property will vest in some other person. Another type of estate is a *community property estate,* in which the husband and wife jointly own a particular property. All of the preceding types of estates are known as *freehold estates.*

There are certain types of non-freehold estates which may contain some ownership interest. These are, however, always of a specific, determinable length of time. One type of non-freehold estate is from *year to year,* or *month to month,* and under these circumstances renewal terms are usually clearly spelled out in a contract. If there is no contract, the local area probably has a governing statute. Another type of non-freehold estate is one known as an *estate for years,* which sets a definite contractual term with renewal terms being also set by the same contract. Another non-freehold estate is one known as *at will,* and this is for an indefinite term with the termination of the estate occurring at the point in time in which either party desires it to end. A final non-freehold estate is known as an *estate at sufferance,* which means the wrongful or illegal continued use of possession of a property by a person until such time as the owner dispossesses him. This type of estate is usually not enforceable by the tenant.

## THE EFFECT OF DIFFERENT TYPES OF TENANCY ON VALUE

The most common type of tenancy is known as a *tenancy in severalty,* and, in these circumstances, there is only one owner of the property. Another type of tenancy is a *joint tenancy,* in which two or more owners have an undivided ownership interest in the property, usually with the right of survivorship. For example, a husband and wife may have joint tenancy with a survivor receiving full ownership at the death of the other party. Another type of tenancy is a *tenancy in common,* where two or more owners each have an undivided fractional interest in the real estate, but without the right of survivorship that would apply under a joint tenancy. An additional type of tenancy is *tenancy by the entireties,* and this is a situation in which husband and wife own the property with survivorship rights if one dies. This is a voluntary arrangement, as opposed to being required in community property states. *Community property* is another type of tenancy which is a joint interest of husband and wife, each with survivorship rights. This type of ownership is involuntary in community property states.

*Condominium tenancy* is becoming very common. This is a situation in which fee ownership exists for certain individual units in a multi-unit property, with each owner of a specific unit having an undivided interest in certain common areas. If you plan to do any type of condominium appraisal, it is essential that you obtain a copy of and carefully study the condominium agreement. It is also very important for you to fully understand the condominium laws in the state in which you are doing the appraisal. As this type of ownership becomes more common, it will be a major portion of the practice of an appraiser specializing in residential properties, and it certainly demands his full attention to every detail prior to making the first appraisal. The subject of appraising condominiums will be covered at some length in a separate section in the Appendix portion of this book. There are also separate sections there which relate to luxury homes, cooperatives and apartments.

The appraiser of residential property should pay particular attention to the type of tenancy involved. The interest being appraised may have an important bearing on the value estimate.

## HOW TO DETERMINE THE VALUE EFFECT OF LEASES IN RESIDENTIAL APPRAISING

As I explained earlier in this chapter, one of the bundle of rights permits the owner to use a particular property. Quite frequently, the owner chooses not to exercise this particular part of the bundle of rights, and instead bargains away the right to use the property to someone for a specified period of time, in exchange for the payment of rent. This is known as a leasing of rights in real property. A *lease* is defined as a contract for the use of specified premises in exchange for the payment of rent. The person who owns the property and enters into an agreement to allow someone to use his property is known as a *lessor* or landlord. The person leasing the property, thus obtaining the right to use the property, is known as the *lessee* and his interest is known as a *leasehold estate*. Leasehold is identified as a non-freehold estate, and this is an item which can cause problems in appraising a property subject to a lease. There are circumstances in which the tenant has the right to use and enjoy the property for a specified rent that is less than the market rental for the particular property. Under these circumstances, the tenant acquires a leasehold interest in the leased property due to the advantage which is present in the rent. Furthermore, under many circumstances, the tenant will erect certain improvements upon land owned by the lessor, thereby acquiring an interest in these improvements over the life of the lease, at the end of which the improvements will revert to and become the property of the lessor.

There are several types of leases which the appraiser may encounter. One of the more common leases is known as a *gross lease,* which requires the lessor or landlord to pay all of the taxes, insurance, maintenance and other expenses of operating the real estate. Another type of lease is a *net lease,* in which the tenant pays some or all of the operating expenses of the real estate. There are some circumstances in which the tenant pays all expenses, taxes, and maintenance of the property; thus, in effect, the lessor landlord would have no expenses to charge against the rental income. Another type of lease is a *percentage lease,* and under these circumstances the amount of rent is based on some percentage of gross receipts from a specified business activity. This type of lease can vary, but it generally provides for a specified minimum rental plus a certain percentage of all sales over a specified amount, thus giving the lessor or landlord an interest in the outcome of the business operation. A fairly common leasing method is a *step lease,* wherein the rental payments are increased or decreased at certain fixed intervals according to terms that have been carefully spelled out in the lease contract. You, as the appraiser, should be very careful in appraising a property subject to this type of lease, since the amounts of income may be substantially different from one period to another. Occasionally, you will encounter a type of lease known as a *ground lease,* in which the landlord owns only the ground on which the improvements are built, with the lessee owning all improvements with said improvements reverting to the lessor at the end of the lease term. A rather common type of commercial lease is a *sale/leaseback* type of situation in which the owner of a parcel of real property will sell the property to a buyer with a specific contract specifying that he will immediately lease the property back from the buyer at some certain fixed rental. This occurs in circumstances where the owner needs immediate cash and feels that there is a tax advantage to him in having rental payments fully deductible, rather than charging depreciation on the improvements over some specified period of time.

The type of lease, lease terms, amount of rent and method of payment, as well as the financial strength of the tenant, can affect the value of a rental property. You should carefully examine all economic factors when a rental property is being appraised.

## TYPES AND VALUE EFFECTS OF VARIOUS KINDS OF REAL ESTATE CONTRACTS

There are certain types of common real estate contracts which you should understand. One of the most common types of contracts for persons engaged in real estate brokerage is a *listing contract,* which may be an open listing, exclusive agent listing, exclusive right to sell listing, or a multiple listing agreement in which any one of the many members of the local multiple listing agency may sell the property. A very common real estate contract is a lease, and this document is of extreme importance in appraising any type of property which is encumbered with a lease.

You will quite frequently encounter another common type of real estate contract known as a *land contract.* This document may cause you some problems in attempting to analyze sales in arriving at a value estimate for a property. This type of contract simply provides that the buyer does not receive title to the property until either all of the payments, or at least a specified percentage or portion of the payments, have been made. In many instances, the consideration shown in the land contract has encompassed interest income which is really not a part of the market value of the real property. You should carefully analyze this type of sale and frequently you will find that you cannot use it for comparison purposes unless you are appraising a property which is also being sold under this type of agreement.

Another type of contract is a *sales contract.* This a document where the buyer and seller both agree to all terms and specify that they are agreeable to transferring ownership of the property after certain acts have been accomplished by each of the parties. This document must be in writing to be enforceable.

There is another type of contract that is encountered quite often by the appraiser of any type of property, and it is known as an *option agreement.* This type of agreement occurs when the purchaser pays a fixed sum for the right to purchase the property at a stipulated price within a specific period of time. One item to be given careful consideration with the option agreement is that, in many instances, an uninformed property owner will encumber his property with an option agreement for a substantial period of time at a very low option price. This allows speculators to control the land within a given area with the expenditure of a small sum of money until such time as he has acquired the exact property he is seeking and allows him to sell or develop his particular property while effectively holding all other properties in the area off the market. It is advisable not to consider the specified purchase price in an option agreement as being the ultimate sum for which the property will sell unless you are very familiar with the parties to the option agreement and you have also exhausted every other possibility of acquiring comparable sales of actually completed sales transactions, rather than having to rely on something as uncertain as an option agreement.

## TYPES AND VALUE EFFECTS OF VARIOUS KINDS OF REAL ESTATE DEEDS

One of the most important documents in real estate is the *deed*. As an appraiser, you will be studying the property owner's deed to determine an accurate legal description, the type of interest owned in the property, and any encumbrance which may be of record. It is essential that you have an understanding of the various types of deeds. A deed is defined as a document which transfers title to real estate. As explained earlier in this chapter, the item which is transferred is actually the rights in real estate, otherwise known as real property. There are several types of deeds, and each has its specific place in the real estate market and in the appraisal profession.

The type of deed which is most binding on the grantor is a *warranty deed*. This is the type of deed usually desired by the buyer. Under a warranty deed, the seller warrants that he has a full and clear merchantable title to the subject property other than as specifically outlined in the instrument itself. The seller, under a warranty deed, agrees to hold the buyer harmless against any flaws in the title which may subsequently occur, and, in most instances, the seller provides title insurance which compensates the buyer for any damages he may suffer if a title problem arises. This type of deed will be encountered most frequently in appraising residential property.

The next type of deed is known as a *quitclaim deed*. In this type of instrument, the seller transfers only such interest as he may possess in the property without further recourse being available to the buyer. This type of deed is not very desirable from the standpoint of the buyer, since the seller is not warranting a clear title, and the buyer may be faced with all types of future claims against the property. This type of deed is frequently used to transfer property where there is some doubt as to title.

Another type of deed is an *administrator or executor deed,* and this is used in the settlement of an estate or in the sale of certain estate properties. This type of deed is usually satisfactory since the administrator or executor has usually performed all of the functions which would be required of the grantor under a warranty deed situation.

There are occasions in which the administrator or executor requires court action in order to effect the sale and grant a good title to the property.

In some states, such as California, there is a transfer of title known as a *grant deed,* and this type of deed is slightly less binding on the seller than a warranty deed. You will very likely not encounter a grant deed in most parts of the United States.

One type of deed you may encounter is known as a *tax or sheriff's deed.* This is a situation in which there is a forced sale for nonpayment of taxes or some other type of obligation. This type of deed is less binding on the seller than a warranty deed and, in fact, the buyer may be acquiring nothing other than a lot of aggravation. The person whose property has been sold for taxes has the right to redeem the property by paying these back taxes or other claims at any time within a specified period of usually two to three years. Thus, the buyer does not really know if he has title to the property until after this redemption period expires.

In many jurisdictions, the mortgage instrument is simply a deed of trust in which the owner of the property transfers title automatically to the lender, with such transfer being of no consequence or null and void if the loan is satisfied in accordance with the terms of the note. This simply avoids a lengthy foreclosure proceeding in the event that the borrower does not satisfactorily meet the mortgage obligations.

## UNDERSTANDING THE KEY ELEMENTS OF THE DEED

There are certain basic parts of the deed which should always be clearly defined within the instrument. The parties to the transaction should always be clearly identified. The statement as to the amount of the consideration should be shown; however, in most jurisdictions the instrument shows $1.00 and other valuable consideration, or $100.00 and other valuable consideration. You should certainly be aware that, even if the selling price is stated as a certain figure, there may be some non-real estate items involved, so that the consideration as shown in a deed cannot be accepted as a proper sales price for the real estate without taking steps to verify what was included in the sales transaction and also to verify whether or not the amount specified is actually the price paid.

The document should always clearly show the conveyance of title from the grantor to the grantee. The deed should always show a clear legal description of the property being conveyed. The deed must show the interests being conveyed, these usually being fee simple interest subject only to limitations such as easements, leases or unpaid mortgage balances. Deed instruments should be executed and acknowledged by both parties to the transaction with their signatures being witnessed. Any sale is not a completed transaction until the deed is voluntarily delivered by the grantor to the grantee, and the grantee accepts delivery of the deed. In most instances, the deed instrument will specify delivery and acceptance. It has been explained earlier that an owner can transfer only those rights which he possesses. The rights possessed in a property are usually evidenced by some document in writing. This is known as the *title* to a certain piece of property, and it means enforceable ownership claims or rights in the particular property. The title to any property actually passes only after a deed is delivered by the grantor or his agent and accepted by the grantee. Most documents showing transfer of title are recorded, and this is of great importance to the appraiser. Proper methods for acquiring and verifying deeds and other vesting instruments will be explained in subsequent portions of this book.

The types of deeds and property rights transferred have a strong effect on the value of a property. The encumbrances or other restrictions shown on the deed are very important in their effect upon value.

## METHODS OF TRANSFERRING PROPERTY

There are several ways in which title to real property is transferred. The most common way is by private grant such as by deed, dedication to a public use, or a device instrument such as a will. Another method of title transfer is by public grant. This occurs much less frequently now than in earlier years in the United States. An infrequent method of title transfer is by accretion or reliction, which is simply a shifting of the river bed. This would occur when the deed instrument provides that the ownership lines go to the water's edge or to the center of a stream and said water's edge or center of the stream has shifted due to acts of nature. A rather difficult method of transfer is by public policy such as adverse possession or prescription, which is the acquisition of an easement by adverse use.

## IMPORTANCE OF RECORDING REAL ESTATE DOCUMENTS

The preceding paragraphs have discussed the various types of contracts, deeds and other instruments which are involved in real estate. Once these documents are obtained by the person owning the property, it is important that they be recorded. One of the major reasons for recording a deed, lease or other type of instrument is to preserve evidence of any document which might affect title. After these items are recorded, they are public records and are available for examination. It is easy to lose or misplace an important document and, if the instrument has been recorded, it will always be possible to obtain a copy in the event that it is lost or destroyed. Another reason for recording deeds, leases and other claims is to preserve notice of the existence and content of such claims. Most instruments are recorded at the office of the County Records of Deeds, the Town Clerk, Probate Judge or other similar agent. It should be noted that, in most areas, it is not compulsory to record this type of instrument. However, in approximately 20 states, it is necessary that a document be recorded in order for it to establish a priority of claim. In researching the records of the Recorder's Office, County Clerk or Probate Judge's Office, remember that just not being able to locate a recorded instrument does not necessarily mean that the claim does not exist. Diligent research on your part is required to determine the exact ownership rights which are involved with any particular property.

It was mentioned in the preceding paragraph that the importance of recording an instrument is to establish the priority of claims. There is a certain sequence of claims which you should understand. Tax liens, labor liens, mechanics liens and things of this nature have first claim in the order listed. All other claims have priority in chronological order by date of recording. This should clearly explain why it is important to record any items of consequence.

In preparing an abstract of title, a history is prepared on a property based on title research which covers those instruments that are of public record. In some instances, an attorney can prepare an opinion of title, which will list the recorded encumbrances, further illustrating the importance of having these items recorded. To give the buyers some protection regarding the title, the most meaningful method is a title insurance policy which offers both indemnification and defense in the event that a claim arises. An opinion or certificate of title, prepared by an attorney, protects the buyer only to the extent of the attorney's competence and is not as desirable as title insurance.

## UNDERSTANDING THE ECONOMICS OF RESIDENTIAL REAL ESTATE AND THE EFFECT ON VALUE

There are certain economic characteristics of residential real estate which arise from both its physical and legal characteristics. The economic characteristics of real estate must be considered in the context that real estate is immobile, and therefore it must provide services at its present situs, which is a fixed location. Anything, good or bad, which affects the property applies to it in its particular location. Residential real estate cannot be moved to a better market or a better location. It must be used, abused or otherwise analyzed in its particular location.

Another economic characteristic of real estate is that it is highly differentiated. In other words, each parcel of property is unique, if in no other way than by its physical location. Because the property is highly differentiated, it is necessary for you, as the appraiser, to carefully compare and analyze each property and apply sound judgment in arriving at a value estimate. Each valuation problem is a separate research project, requiring detailed analysis and special skills, which should be the unique attributes of the skilled appraiser.

Another economic characteristic of real estate is that it is very much dependent upon its particular environment. It is immobile and is therefore extremely sensitive to the immediate vicinity in which it is located. A good example of this is an attractive residential subdivision immediately prior to the building of a paper mill or a chemical plant, which produce a very obnoxious odor, a short distance upwind from the subdivision. The houses located in this subdivision cannot be moved, and the adverse effect of the unpleasant odor would certainly make a property there less marketable and would adversely affect its value. Anything good, bad or indifferent about a property must be considered as it affects the property in its particular location, since there is no way to relocate the property to get it into a better environment.

Real estate is very durable and is thus a long-term asset. Decisions which are made about real estate involve long-term commitments of resources, and concern in most instances the largest single investment a buyer will ever make.

For a residential property, the amount of rental income which can be realized from renting a middle- to upper-price-range house is very low in comparison with the investment required. The reason is that this class of property is usually sold for the amenity benefits rather than the income which it will produce. A person investing in a residence is looking for a property that will satisfy his needs over a long period of time; thus, a buyer is very much interested in the future prospects of the general area in which a property is located and is particularly concerned with the immediate neighborhood in which it is situated. An investor in a residential property, or for that matter any type of real estate, is usually buying a rather high-priced asset. This requires careful consideration on the part of the buyer before committing his funds, or, if the appraiser is to arrive at a value estimate considering those things which informed buyers and sellers would consider, he must evaluate the property as a high-priced asset and consider those things which the parties to the transaction would consider.

Some type of debt financing is usually involved in most real estate ownership. Most buyers of real estate simply do not have sufficient cash to purchase a property, and this is an important economic consideration. In some instances, even if the buyer had sufficient cash, it would be unwise to pay the full price. For example, if the buyer had $50,000 in cash, on which he could receive 9 to 10 percent interest income, he would be unwise to invest $50,000 cash in a residential property when he could borrow the money on a mortgage at perhaps 8 percent, thus allowing him an advantage by using borrowed money. An additional factor to be considered is that the interest income received on the $50,000 investment would very likely be taxable, while the interest paid on the mortgage would be deductible for income tax purposes. It is almost always desirable to pay part of the purchase price with borrowed funds rather than committing all or most of one's cash resources. It is very important for the appraiser to understand the terms of any real estate purchase which may be used for comparison purposes. Under some circumstances, the purchase price will vary drastically, depending on the type of payment terms.

I am aware of one situation in which the sales price seemed to be totally out of line with other properties in the neighborhood. Investigation revealed that the purchase price was substantially in excess of what would normally have been paid, and also that the seller allowed the buyer to execute a purchase money mortgage at a 3 percent interest rate. This resulted in the seller being able to report as capital gains a substantial sum of money which would otherwise have come to him over the life of the mortgage as interest income. So, as you can see, you should thoroughly understand the purchase terms on any transaction which you are considering for comparison purposes.

Another economic characteristic of real estate is that buyers and sellers normally deal with large sums of money. In appraising residential property, you will very likely be involved in estimating the value for a property which will be the largest single investment the buyer will ever make. You have the responsibility to carefully investigate the market so that the buyer will pay no more for the property than its true market value.

## UNDERSTANDING THE CHARACTERISTICS OF THE REAL ESTATE MARKET

The real estate market is defined as a meeting place for buyers and sellers of real estate of a given type. The characteristics of the real estate market are that it is localized and stratified, which means that properties within a certain type and price range are part of the particular market, that the parties to the transaction are relatively uninformed, that there is an inelastic supply due to the fact that construction of houses or other types of property is time consuming, and there is always a time lag between demand and supply. Another thing which must be understood is that the demand is uneven and stratified, and is affected greatly by both national and local economics. The kinds of real estate market are residential, commercial, industrial, farm, public use and special purpose.

If you have given careful consideration to the items covered in this chapter, you will be ready to move forward into the study of actual appraisal principles. These appraisal principles are the basic foundations for the formation of a successful appraisal practice and will be covered in detail in Chapters 3 and 4. Just as a structure is no better than its foundation, the professional appraiser can be no better at preparing appraisals than his knowledge of basic real estate and/or appraisal principles. The first few chapters of this book are essential ingredients for the solid foundation of a residential appraiser.

# 3

# Key Appraisal Principles and Their Application to Appraising Residential Properties

There are several appraisal principles that are basic to the preparation of any adequately supported appraisal report. Many of the problems an appraiser encounters in the preparation of an appraisal report can be traced directly to a misunderstanding of one or more of these appraisal principles. It has been my experience that the proper application of these principles will inevitably lead you to a well-supported value conclusion and will stand you in good stead if you must appear as a valuation witness in a court case.

This chapter is devoted to a discussion of the most important appraisal principles, except highest and best use. The importance of the principle of highest and best use and the continuous misapplication of this principle warrant coverage in a separate chapter, Chapter 4. Each of the principles will be discussed along with examples of how they apply in appraisal practice, with particular emphasis on the appraisal of residential property.

## VALUE AND ITS CHARACTERISTICS

There are many different types of value which you, as the appraiser, may encounter in dealing with residential properties. Under most circumstances, the purpose of the appraisal is to estimate market value, and most emphasis will be placed on that type of value in this book. However, it is important for you to be aware of some of the other types of value, such as insurable value, book value, rental value, investment value, assessed value and many other less familiar derivatives of value. You could possibly be concerned with an appraisal for insurable value, assessed value and rental value when you are dealing with property such as apartments, hotels or motels which require a projection of income.

Under pure economic analysis, there is no distinction between value and price, whereas these terms are quite different in appraisal practice. Economic analysis assumes that any transaction occurs under perfect market conditions. Appraisal analysis recognizes that the market is imperfect and clearly distinguishes between value and price. Value is the capacity of any economic good to command other goods in exchange. Value for a residential property may be measured in amenities to the owner from the use and enjoyment of the premises. A home has been defined as a machine for living and the buyer is very much interested in the features (amenities) which the particular structure provides as his machine for living. However, for an income-producing property, value may also be considered to be the present worth of the anticipated future benefits, in the form of income, which will be derived from ownership of the property.

Since we are dealing almost exclusively with market value, this term must be clearly defined and discussed. In 1975, the American Institute of Real Estate Appraisers and the Society of Real Estate Appraisers issued a jointly-sponsored publication entitled *Real Estate Appraisal Terminology.* On page 137 of this publication, market value is defined as follows:

> *The highest price in terms of money which a property will bring in a competitive and open market under all conditions requisite to a fair sale, the buyer and seller, each acting prudently, knowledgeably and assuming the price is not affected by undue stimulus.*

This publication further states that there are certain conditions which are implicit in the definition. These conditions are as follows:

1. The buyer and seller are typically motivated.
2. Both parties are well-informed or well-advised, and each is acting in what he considers his own best interest.
3. A reasonable time is allowed for exposure in the open market.
4. Payment is made in cash or its equivalent.

5. Financing, if any, is on terms generally available in the community at a specified date and typical for the property in its locale.
6. The price represents a normal consideration for the property sold unaffected by special financing amounts and/or terms, services, fees, cost or credits incurred in the transaction.

It can be seen from the quoted definition and the conditions which are implicit in it that an estimate of market value requires careful analysis on the part of the appraiser. The absence of one implicit condition can make a sale meaningless for comparison purposes. This matter will be covered in greater detail later in this book.

## PRINCIPLE OF SUPPLY AND DEMAND

Supply and demand is a very important appraisal principle and is a foundation for much of the analysis involved in making an appraisal. Certainly, there can be no market for any good unless there is a demand coupled with the ability to pay. The valuation of single-family residences, apartments or condominiums requires your careful attention to this appraisal principle. You should analyze the supply side of the market by limiting your study to the category of type and class of property under which the subject property falls. If the particular assignment covers a type of property which is in excess supply due to extremely active construction activity within that class of property, or due to a large exodus of occupants from existing structures within that class, then you will find that the market value of the property you are appraising will be adversely affected by this excess supply.

I have known of situations in which large military establishments were closed, eliminating jobs for a substantial number of people. It became necessary for these people to relocate to other cities, thus overloading the market for a substantial length of time. I have also known of circumstances where builders have constructed a large number of properties without a careful feasibility analysis of the demand for this type of property and the period of time over which the supply would be absorbed. Such a situation has a strong adverse effect upon the value of any particular property and you should certainly understand this situation prior to arriving at a value estimate.

On the demand side of the market analysis, there are occasions when a large influx of people arising from the development of a new industry, the expansion of an existing industry or expansion of the number of personnel at some large military or other governmental installation will excessively stimulate demand for housing. Under these circumstances, the buyers will be standing in line to purchase the property and will pay almost any asking price, thus having at least a temporary undue influence on the value of a property. I know of one city where homes were bought before the foundations were poured, and the buyers lived in motels or hotels for months while construction was being completed. Additional factors which can have a very substantial effect upon the supply and/or demand for a particular class of property include the availability of and the interest rates applicable to mortgage money, as well as the effect of inflation upon the cost of new construction.

You should understand that the market value of any particular property is determined to a large extent by the interaction of the forces of supply and demand in the particular market as of the date of the appraisal. To give proper consideration to the principle of supply and demand, it is necessary to have a thorough understanding of the economic outlook for the area in which the appraisal is being made, for the city in which the property is located and, more particularly, for the neighborhood in which the property is situated. You should be aware of the fact that the demand side of the market can change much more quickly than the supply side. Demand can be quite volatile as a result of the influx of new people or the exodus of people creating a low demand. However, the supply side requires a large time lag while new properties are being constructed to meet any change in demand. The analysis involved for each of these factors will be discussed later.

## THE PRINCIPLE OF CHANGE

The principle of change is, fundamentally, the law of cause and effect. This principle holds that economic and social forces are constantly at work and have a direct effect upon the value of real property. The value of any particular property will change as the market conditions change. This is one of the central reasons for making your value estimate as of a given date. The property that was very valuable today may be almost valueless tomorrow due to drastic changes in the economy, particularly as it affects a specific neighborhood in which the subject property is located. Residential properties are especially vulnerable in this respect. There are also acts of nature or catastrophic occurrences which can change the value of a property overnight. Each appraisal report should clearly give an "as of" date. This date is usually the last occasion on which the appraiser viewed the property. It is your function, as the appraiser, to forecast the market conditions and the reaction of typical purchasers to these expected market conditions. This is one of the major reasons for the requirement that you carefully analyze the neighborhood and estimate the stage and life cycle, as well as expected future trends for properties within that neighborhood.

## THE PRINCIPLE OF CONTRIBUTION

The principle of contribution is a very important principle in the appraisal of any property. The underlying concept is that the value of any portion of the property depends on how much it contributes to the value of the whole, or how much the absence of a particular feature detracts from the value of the whole. This principle is applicable to each of the three recognized approaches to estimating value. The actual application of this principle to the three approaches will be covered more fully in the particular chapters which relate to each approach. However, a brief discussion follows here.

## APPLICABILITY OF THE PRINCIPLE OF CONTRIBUTION TO THE COST APPROACH

In applying the cost approach, it is necessary for you to estimate the reproduction cost new of the improvements. Since you are usually dealing with improvements that are not in fact new, it is necessary to estimate and deduct various losses in value from one or more causes, including physical deterioration, functional obsolescence and locational obsolescence. These types of losses in value will be covered in detail later in this book. The principle of contribution applies in estimating accrued depreciation to measure losses in value because of deficiencies within the property or super-adequacies which do not contribute the full cost to the value of the property. It is possible to measure the cost of any particular item versus its value contribution to determine if certain portions of the cost do not actually contribute value equivalent to that cost.

## APPLICABILITY OF THE PRINCIPLE OF CONTRIBUTION TO THE DIRECT SALES COMPARISON APPROACH

The principle of contribution has strong applicability in the direct sales comparison approach. In applying the direct sales comparison approach, it is important to find sales of properties which are similar to the property which you are appraising. Since it is almost never possible to find sales of properties that are identical to the subject, it is necessary to adjust for differences between the properties to allow you to arrive at the amount for which the sale property would have sold had it been identical to the subject. The actual adjustment process will be covered in much detail in the chapter devoted to the direct sales comparison approach. The principle of contribution is used in this approach to measure the differences between the subject property and the comparable properties. For example, it is possible to measure the value contribution of an additional bathroom by finding sales of properties otherwise identical except for one having a single bath and the other having two baths. The net difference in sales price between these two otherwise identical properties is a measure of the contribution of the additional bathroom. This technique can also be followed to measure the value contribution of any particular segment of these structures so that, by sales analysis and the application of the principle of contribution, you can arrive at the indicated value of the subject property by the direct sales comparison approach and feel very confident in the value conclusion thus derived.

## APPLICABILITY OF THE PRINCIPLE OF CONTRIBUTION TO THE INCOME APPROACH

The principle of contribution applies to a substantial degree in the application of the income approach or gross rent multiplier approach. The presence or absence of a particular item for an income-producing property can be measured by the contribution to the amount of income the property will produce. For example, the appraiser can analyze rentals of properties which are almost identical except that one property has two baths and the other has one, or one property is air-conditioned and the other is not, or perhaps one has a garage and the other has none. By measuring the rent contribution of the added feature, it is possible, through the principle of contribution, to arrive at a proper figure for the market rental of the subject property.

It can be seen from the preceding brief discussion that the principle of contribution is indeed very important to the appraiser. It is essential for you to have an understanding of this very important principle and its application. This understanding will place you in a very favorable situation in supporting your value conclusions regardless of the circumstances. It will also be very convincing to the client to see that you have applied this principle in estimating the market value of his property.

## THE PRINCIPLE OF BALANCE OR VARIABLE PROPORTIONS

The principle of balance or variable proportions is misunderstood and misapplied in many residential appraisals. This principle holds that increasing amounts of money spent on improvements continue to yield an equivalent or even an increasing rate of return, up to a point at which expenditures and benefits tend to equalize. Beyond that point, continuing excess spending of dollars yields diminishing returns, thus resulting in the improvements not being in balance with demand within the area. This is an important principle in comparing alternative use patterns and intensities of use for certain types of properties to assist the appraiser in arriving at his opinion of highest and best use. In this particular analysis, the amount of land is usually fixed, since the owner has a specific amount of land to be appraised. The variable in this instance, for residential properties, could be the number of bedrooms, the number of baths, the extent and quality of the built-ins, and other special features which the buyer within that particular area would demand.

A good example of the violation of the principle of balance for residential properties would be the construction of a 3000 square-foot, four-bath house with extremely expensive built-ins in an area where the normal-sized houses would be 1800 square feet with two baths and average quality built-ins. The person who constructs this $80,000 or $90,000 house in an area where the selling price is normally $40,000 to $50,000, will find that he has lost a large amount of his investment, since buyers will tend to heavily discount this excess investment. It is important for you to research the market demand within the area in which you are making the appraisal. You should carefully evaluate the existing structures within the neighborhood and the marketability of the particular structure.

Another example of a violation of the principle of balance is where an owner had a very uniquely designed house constructed in a medium- to high-priced single-family residential neighborhood. This house had tremendous quantities of stone, designed in such a way that the rooms were pie-shaped. The structure, while unique and extremely expensive, was entirely out of keeping with the surrounding properties within the neighborhood. The owner suffered an immediate loss of at least 30 percent of his cost due to the violation of the principle of balance and its effect on the marketability of the particular property.

It should be remembered that properties achieve their maximum value when they are homogeneous with other surrounding properties. This does not mean that the properties within the neighborhood should be so identical that they are like a row of tin soldiers. There should be some variation in design to make the neighborhood attractive. The point here is that the size, quality of construction and general appearance should be homogeneous with other properties in the neighborhood. At the point where the property achieves the best balance with buyer demand, you will also find that it has achieved the maximum productivity, either in amenities of ownership or in income.

In analyzing the productivity of a particular property, remember that there are four agents of production, which are, in order of claim: labor, capital, management and land, which has the residual or last claim on income. Any surplus productivity over and above the return required for the improvements flows to the land, and it should be remembered that if there is an extremely large amount of surplus productivity, it will not endure for long. The statement that "excess profit breeds ruinous competition" is very much applicable to real estate.

## THE PRINCIPLE OF ANTICIPATION

The principle of anticipation holds that value is a function of the anticipated benefits to be derived from ownership of the realty. The chief motivating factors for most real estate transactions are the expectations of buyers or owners about the quantity, quality and duration of benefits that can be derived from the ownership of that particular property. When the property in question is an income-producing property, the anticipation centers around the amount of income that the property will produce in the future, the reliability of this income stream, the duration of the income stream and the risk inherent in the investment. All of this analysis enters into the thinking of a prospective buyer for an income property and is certainly known by the seller. It is an essential part of the bargaining process.

The principle of anticipation, as it applies to residential property, is measured by the amenities which the owner expects to receive from the use and occupancy of the residential structure. Most owners have in mind the particular amenities which are most appealing to them. Some owners place great emphasis on a large family room with a fireplace and special built-in features. This same item might not appeal at all to another owner. A family with children has need for a certain number of bedrooms and baths and requires adequate space to provide the children with an area where they can entertain their friends. Some owners place great emphasis on the availability of outdoor facilities such as covered patios, gas grills or perhaps a swimming pool.

In making an appraisal, you should carefully analyze the needs and desires of the class of owner who is likely to be a buyer of the subject property. By this careful analysis and by giving consideration to the principle of anticipation, you can measure whether or not the subject property would be attractive to the class of buyer who is generally attracted to that particular neighborhood.

## THE PRINCIPLE OF SUBSTITUTION

The principle of substitution holds that the upper limit of value of any particular parcel of real estate tends to be set by the cost of acquiring an equally desirable substitute property, assuming that there are no costly or lengthy delays in making this substitution. This is a very important appraisal principle. It is much used and, unfortunately, quite often abused in making residential appraisals.

In applying the principle of substitution, you must assume that the purchaser will consider the alternatives which are available to him prior to making an acquisition. The very meaning of market value assumes that you are dealing with a knowledgeable buyer and seller. If you should assume that a prospective buyer would overlook the alternatives which are available to him, it would violate the very heart of appraising for market value.

It should be remembered that the acquisition of an equally desirable substitute property does not mean that it must be identical to a particular property, but rather that the substitute property must be one of equal utility. For example, it might not be important to the purchaser whether the substitute property is red or brown brick veneer, or whether it has a black or brown roof covering, as long as the actual space and other amenity features are virtually the same.

There are three alternative means of acquiring a substitute property and these three means also form the bases for the three recognized approaches to estimating market value. Proper application of the principle of substitution will tell the client whether he should buy an existing property, build a new property or acquire a substitute income stream.

## APPLICABILITY OF THE PRINCIPLE OF SUBSTITUTION TO THE DIRECT SALES COMPARISON APPROACH

One alternative which is available to a prospective purchaser is to buy a substitute property similar to the one being appraised. This alternative is usually the one that can be achieved with a minimum of effort and with the least delay. This particular alternative is the basis for the direct sales comparison approach to value estimation. In the application of this alternative, the prospective buyer would very likely try to find a substitute property within the particular neighborhood where the subject is located if he has an attraction to that neighborhood. If he finds no substitute property available within the subject neighborhood, he would then attempt to find an equally desirable neighborhood, and from that point seek to obtain a comparable property available on the market. Consideration of this alternative and the application of the direct sales comparison approach requires you to carefully analyze the subject property so that you are completely familiar with its various amenity features. It is then necessary for you to find sales of properties as near in proximity, sales having occurred most recently, and the sale properties being as nearly similar to the subject property as possible. Once the sales are located and verified, you can then analyze the differences between the features within the subject property and the sale property and adjust for these differences so that you can arrive at the amount for which the sale property would have sold if it had been identical to the subject. This is a reasonable alternative to the prospective purchaser, and it is certainly a reasonable and very strong approach for you to use in arriving at the value estimate for any property which sells with any degree of frequency.

## APPLICABILITY OF THE PRINCIPLE OF SUBSTITUTION TO THE COST APPROACH

A second alternative that is available to a prospective buyer is to build a structure similar to the subject property. This involves constructing a substitute property that would provide the same utility, and does not require that the property be absolutely identical. This alternative is the basis for the cost approach. It is unlikely that an informed buyer would pay more for a property than the cost of building a substitute. One additional factor which the informed buyer would consider is the time requirements for constructing the alternative structure. If there is a long delay in constructing the substitute, and if time is important to the buyer, then it is likely that he would not avail himself of this alternative. Many appraisers tend to fall back on the old clichē that "cost sets the upper limit of value." I am familiar with circumstances in which the buyers were paying $2000 to $3000 more than the cost of purchasing a lot and having a structure built in order to avoid the delay of building a home prior to moving into a prestigious neighborhood. I am also aware of occasions where employees being transferred into a new area needed housing rather quickly and, due to this particular need, they were willing to pay more than the cost of purchasing a lot and building a structure for the advantage of immediate occupancy. The point here is that it is important for you not to get boxed into the use of clichēs which actually are not supported in the real world. It is important to evaluate this alternative and give careful consideration to the reasoning process which would very likely be applied by a knowledgeable buyer in making a decision about the method he would use in solving his need for the particular type of property which is the subject of the appraisal.

## APPLICABILITY OF THE PRINCIPLE OF SUBSTITUTION TO THE INCOME APPROACH

The third and final alternative available to the prospective buyer is to acquire an investment that will produce an income stream of the same size, with the same risk and for the same duration as that involved in the property which is being appraised. This alternative is the basis for the income approach or gross rent multiplier approach to estimating value. If the property being appraised is an income-producing property, then it is reasonable to assume that a prospective buyer who was informed as to his alternatives would not take the position that he must have one particular income-producing property if there were others available which met the same criteria. It is usually true that the investor in an income property is particularly interested in the quantity, quality and duration of the income stream, rather than the bricks and mortar of a particular property. When the appraisal assignment is for a residential property which would very likely be rented, then you can also assume that a buyer of a residential rental property is much more interested in the quantity, quality and duration of income than he is in a particular property in a particular location. You should always be aware of the fact that medium- to high-priced single-family residential properties are seldom rented other than for caretaking purposes for an absentee owner. The properties in the middle to upper price range are generally purchased for amenities only. The informed buyer of a middle- to upper-price-range residential property would evaluate the amenities of one property versus the other so that this third alternative could still be considered by realizing that the amenity features are a direct substitute for the income which would be considered with an income-producing property. The buyer of an amenity property is also looking to thc quantity, quality and duration of the particular amenity features for the subject property, as well as the future prospects of the neighborhood.

## CHAPTER SUMMARY

The preceding pages have discussed at some length the basic appraisal principles. During the process of discussing these appraisal principles, some examples were given to show how these principles apply under certain circumstances. Later chapters will go into more detail concerning how each of these principles apply to the three recognized approaches to estimating market value.

It has been my experience in making appraisals over a substantial number of years that whenever there is a major deviation in the value indicated by one of the three approaches, it is usually due to my failure to properly apply one of the appraisal principles. A review of the steps taken in applying the approaches to value will usually point out to the appraiser the area which he may have overlooked.

The first four chapters are designed to give you an understanding of the basic characteristics of real estate and the appraisal principles which govern the appraiser in arriving at a supportable estimate of value. You most certainly are aware of the fact that the strength of any structure can be no better than the foundation which supports it. The first four chapters of this book are like the foundation for a structure.

# 4

# How to Determine Highest and Best Use for Residential Real Estate

The preceding chapter was devoted to a discussion of the various principles involved in real estate appraising. Because of the extreme importance of the principle of highest and best use, I felt that this subject should be assigned its own chapter. There is no doubt that the principle of highest and best use is the most abused and most misunderstood of all of the appraisal principles. Many of the abuses of this principle occur in appraising residential property; thus, the competent appraiser specializing in residential properties must understand the principle of highest and best use. The following discussion covers the specific steps involved in determining highest and best use. If properly applied, these guidelines will help you avoid the common mistakes that are made in this particular area of appraising. The most common mistakes in determining highest and best use include the failure to understand legal concepts such as zoning, building restrictions, and health department regulations, and overlooking the fact that the site may not be physically adapted to the particular use for which the appraiser is considering it. Another common mistake is the failure to determine the availability of utilities or the approximate cost of making these items available. In many instances, the appraiser fails to do an adequate feasibility analysis to determine whether the proposed use can survive from an economic standpoint.

## DEFINITION OF HIGHEST AND BEST USE

*The Appraisal Terminology and Handbook, Fifth Edition,* published by the American Institute of Real Estate Appraisers, defines highest and best use as follows:

> *The most profitable likely use to which a property can be put. The question of such use may be based on the highest and most profitable continuous use to which the property is adapted and needed or likely to be in demand in the reasonably near future. However, elements affecting value which depend upon events or combinations of occurrences which, while within the realm of possibility, are not fairly shown to be reasonably probable, should be excluded from consideration. Also, if the intended use is dependent on an uncertain act of another person, the intention cannot be considered.* This publication further defines highest and best use as *that use of land which may reasonably be expected to produce the greatest net return to land over a given period of time. That legal use which will yield to land the highest present value. This is sometimes called optimum use.*

## HIGHEST AND BEST USE—AS VACANT LAND OR AS PRESENTLY IMPROVED

If the appraisal assignment involves an unimproved parcel of land, the problem is relatively simple. When appraising an unimproved parcel, you should base your value estimate on the highest and best use of this vacant parcel. You do not have to confront the problem of whether there are improvements which may or may not contribute value to the property as a whole.

When the appraisal assignment involves a property which is presently improved, then the problem is much more difficult. If the appraisal assignment consists of a residential lot which is improved with a residential structure typical of the neighborhood in which it is located, and there is no trend developing toward a change in use, then it is very likely that the highest and best use of the property will be its continued use for residential purposes with a substantial value contribution by the structures located on the site.

The problem becomes much more difficult when the appraisal assignment is of an improved property in an area where there is a definite trend toward a change from residential use to some type of commercial activity. This situation is quite common in the older residential areas of the city, particularly near the central business district or near major intersections. If this change in use is widespread, and if there is a definite demand for similar properties to be converted to a higher use, then you must approach the problem very carefully. Under such circumstances, it is necessary to estimate the highest and best use of the site as if it were vacant and available to be put to some commercial use. If the value of the site when appraised as if vacant is greater than the value of the site as improved with a residential structure, it is obvious that there is no value contribution by the improvements and, therefore, the highest and best use of the site is for a change to some type of commercial activity. There are instances in which the buyers of this type of lot will attribute some interim use value to the improvements for the rent these improvements will produce prior to the time when the site is cleared and developed with some type of commercial structure. There are also some instances in which this type of residential structure is modernized and devoted to commercial use, such as a one-to-four-tenant office building. Under these circumstances, you would conclude that the highest and best use of the property is as presently improved, with a small interim use value attributable to the improvements or, if the structure is in satisfactory condition for rehabilitation and change to office use, then there would be some added value in the improvements.

The key factor in appraising any property is whether the site has greater value as presently improved than it would have if vacant and available to be put to its highest and best use. The value contribution of the improvements does not have to be extremely large to make the highest and best use be the use of the property as presently improved.

## THE FOUR KEY STEPS IN ESTIMATING HIGHEST AND BEST USE

There are four steps which must be considered by any appraiser in estimating the highest and best use of a particular parcel of property. If the appraiser carefully follows these four steps, most of the common errors which occur in making decisions about highest and best use will be eliminated. The four steps are as follows:

1. Determine whether the proposed use is permitted by law.
2. Determine whether the proposed use is physically possible.
3. Determine whether the proposed use is appropriate, specifically regarding the availability of utilities, access, etc.
4. Determine whether the proposed use is feasible from an economic standpoint.

The four steps will be analyzed separately in the following paragraphs, with particular emphasis on their application to the appraisal of residential property. An example of the application of these steps will be given in the summary at the end of this chapter.

## HOW TO DETERMINE WHETHER THE PROPOSED USE IS LEGAL

You may have read an article in the newspaper or heard comments concerning situations in which two appraisers testified at some legal proceedings regarding their value estimate for a particular property. Such newspaper articles or comments very frequently criticize the appraisers for the very large discrepancies in their value estimates. You hear comments such as, "That guy sold out," or, "That guy must have sold his reputation to the highest bidder." Most of these embarrassing variations in value conclusions could have been avoided if one or both of the appraisers had taken the time and trouble to determine whether the proposed use was legally permitted.

You have a moral obligation to become thoroughly familiar with the zoning ordinances in the particular area in which you are making the appraisal. You should also acquaint yourself with building codes, health department regulations and any other legal matters which could affect the use of the subject property. You should carefully study the zoning regulations for the particular property, not only to determine whether the present use is legal, but also whether the proposed highest and best use, if it involves a change in use, is in accordance with local zoning, building code and health department regulations. You should always obtain a copy of the local zoning map and zoning ordinance, a copy of the health department regulations for the particular area and should thoroughly acquaint yourself with the prevailing building codes.

The health department regulations are extremely important in situations where either the water system or the sewerage disposal system must be provided by private means. I know of a situation in which the appraiser assumed that the highest and best use of a particular property was for development into small-acreage home sites. The appraiser failed to check with the health department. If he had, he would have discovered that the regulations specifically prohibited the construction of any structure in an area which had flooded within the past 50 years. He could also have readily found that the soil did not meet the minimum percolation test to allow installation of septic tanks. In this particular instance, even if the zoning regulations had permitted the development into small-acreage home sites, the health department regulations would have entirely prohibited such use. This is a situation in which the appraiser was assuming highest and best use for residential purposes for land that could be used for no purpose other than agricultural activity.

I know of another situation in which the appraiser assumed that the highest and best use of a particular property was for development into a golf course. A simple check of the flooding frequency for this particular property would have shown that it was covered with flood waters several times during any particular year. The site was also zoned "Flood Hazard," which would have automatically eliminated any such use for recreational purposes.

To become a competent professional appraiser, you should not accept an assignment unless you are willing to devote sufficient time to investigate all the legal aspects of a particular property. My years of experience have taught me that it is poor strategy for an appraiser to assume a certain highest and best use for a property without satisfying himself that such a use is legally possible under all of the various use restrictions which may be imposed upon the property. You owe it to your client, as well as to yourself, to thoroughly investigate the legal aspects of any property to determine whether the proposed highest and best use is legally possible.

On occasions, the appraiser will find that the particular lot which he is appraising is too small or has such poor shape that it cannot be separately used. Under these circumstances, the highest and best use of the particular parcel would be the legally permissible use with a further restriction that the site must be combined with an adjoining property. In this event, unless the subject site is a key parcel to the adjoining property owner, it will probably suffer some discount from the amount which could be received for the site if it were of sufficient size and shape to be separately utilized.

## HOW TO HANDLE THE PROBLEM OF A NONCONFORMING USE

There is another legal aspect requiring careful consideration if the appraisal assignment involves a residential property where the structure is located on a 50-foot lot in an area in which the residential zoning requires a minimum of 65 to 75 feet. This situation is known as a nonconforming use. Usually these situations occur when the residential structure precedes the present zoning ordinance. Such a nonconforming use will almost always be allowed to continue for as long as the present structure remains intact. One major problem is that the owner of this structure will very likely encounter difficulty in receiving permission to make any type of addition or improvement of consequence to the existing structure. It is also a virtual certainty that, if the improvements are destroyed, the city will not allow a new residential structure to be erected on the 50-foot lot.

This circumstance requires the appraiser to look carefully at the remaining economic life of the improvements, and he must remember that, if the improvements are destroyed, the highest and best use of this 50-foot lot in a 65-foot or 75-foot minimum-size residential area would be for sale as a remnant parcel to the adjoining property owner. This nonconforming use tends to adversely affect the remaining economic life of the improvements. In estimating the value of the lot, it must be remembered that remnant lots are usually sold to the adjoining property owner and that such an adjoining property owner pays substantially less than the normal price, since he is aware of his unique position as the most likely purchaser.

## WHAT TO DO IF YOUR OPINION OF HIGHEST AND BEST USE CONFLICTS WITH PRESENT ZONING

If your opinion of the highest and best use of a particular property is not in accordance with present zoning for the parcel, then extreme caution is indicated. You should not assume that the change in zoning to the type of use which you consider appropriate can be obtained automatically. In most instances, it is difficult to obtain a change in zoning. Before assuming that the change in zoning can be obtained, you should always contact the local zoning authorities to determine their general attitude toward a change in use to the type of highest and best use which you are anticipating. You should also carefully study recent zoning board actions to see if changes in zoning can be obtained with relative ease. You should always carefully investigate whether there is a current demand in the area for the type of use which you are proposing. A great deal of care is required if you are assuming a use which is not consistent with the current zoning in the area.

## HOW TO DETERMINE WHETHER THE PROPOSED USE IS PHYSICALLY POSSIBLE

You should always carefully inspect the physical characteristics of the appraisal subject site. This inspection should go beyond the surface characteristics and include some knowledge of subsurface soil condition. In many instances, the site will have major drainage problems. If the cost of correcting the drainage problem is high, it is possible that such costs will virtually eliminate the value of the site for the proposed use.

In many areas of the country, the appraiser may find that the soil has a tendency to shrink and expand with the presence or absence of moisture. This type of unstable soil will require substantial additional investment in foundation and, in some cases, this added cost will eliminate the use which might otherwise be feasible. The amount of added cost will certainly be considered by a knowledgeable buyer and may adversely affect the value of the site. There are some lots which have very poor topography. It will frequently be found that the cost of grading or filling a site to make it useable is so high that it will virtually eliminate the value of the site in its present condition.

I know of one situation in which the appraiser assumed that the highest and best use of a particular parcel was for commercial purposes. It was found that the cost to fill this site and place it in a useable condition was approximately $60,000, and that if the site were made useable as to topography, there were competing sites which did not require fill that could be purchased for $50,000. In this particular case, the assumption that the highest and best use of the site was for commercial purposes was entirely in error, and the appraiser had simply not done his homework on the question of whether the proposed use was physically possible. An informed buyer will certainly be aware of the prices of competing lots which do not have topography problems and will reduce his purchase price by a sufficient amount to allow for time and expense of curing the topography problem of the subject site. The shape of a lot may often be such that the required setback and the required side yard and rear yard clearance prohibit the site from adaptation to the proposed use. This problem frequently occurs when the appraiser is estimating the value of a triangular lot.

An item which is frequently overlooked in evaluating the physical characteristics of a site is the problem of adequate drainage. The cost of providing adequate drainage for surface water can be prohibitive, particularly in areas which are extremely flat, providing no runoff, or in areas which have extremely steep topography, which requires terracing or other methods of preventing erosion.

When the appraisal is in an area where it is necessary to provide private wells for water or private septic tanks for sewerage disposal, there are several pitfalls to be on the lookout for. In the area of the availability of water, a large cost item may be extreme depth to which drilling is required before obtaining a water supply. There is also the question of whether the water is sufficiently pure or, as sometimes happens, the water may contain nondesirable mineral elements which must be filtered out before it can be used for household purposes. The question of septic tanks for sewerage disposal requires adequate knowledge of the percolation characteristics of the soil, the size of the household to be accommodated and the local regulations as to the number of feet of field line per gallon of septic tank. Excess cost of obtaining useable water or of installing adequate septic tanks can certainly have an adverse effect upon the value of the site and, in some instances, may eliminate what would otherwise seem to be the logical use.

## HOW TO DETERMINE WHETHER THE PROPOSED USE IS APPROPRIATE

A common error made by appraisers in arriving at an opinion of the highest and best use of a site is to assume that the proposed use is appropriate. There is an unfortunate tendency on the part of uninformed or biased appraisers to automatically assume that every major road intersection is a service station or shopping center site and that every major tract with highway frontage is adaptable to residential development, commercial development or some type of industrial use. Since your goal is always to arrive at a supportable estimate of a market value, you should always make a thorough investigation to determine the appropriateness of the estimated highest and best use.

I know of one situation in which the appraiser said that the highest and best use of a particular parcel was for a single-family residential subdivision. The appraiser failed to investigate the fact that the land had a substantial drop from the nearest sewerage facilities so that it would be necessary to install extremely expensive pumping equipment to provide a sufficient lift back to the sewerage processing plant. The appraiser also overlooked the fact that the cost of running city water lines and sewer lines a great distance from the nearest connection would be extremely expensive, so that the amount that could be realized from lots which would be available for sale on this particular property would be insufficient to attribute any value to the land itself. It is essential for the appraiser to know whether the necessary facilities are available within a reasonable distance of the subject property and, in addition, he should determine the approximate cost of bringing these facilities to the site.

I know of an appraisal in which the appraiser found comparable sales of residential lots similar to those which would be developed on the parcel he was appraising. The error occurred when the appraiser overlooked the cost of installing streets, curbs, gutters, sidewalks, water lines, sewer lines and storm sewers into the subject property. All of these facilities were installed in the subdivision from which the comparable sales were obtained. The appraiser did not allow for time to dispose of the lots or the cost of selling them. This appraisal resulted in a substantial loss to the lender, who was not aware of this major oversight on the part of the appraiser.

If you are asked to appraise a parcel of land which you feel has a highest and best use for development into residential home sites, you should always request a carefully engineered plat for the proposed subdivision. It is also necessary to acquire information about the cost of installing streets, water lines, sewerage lines, storm sewers and other necessary facilities. By careful analysis of the number of lots which can be developed, their probable selling price, the sell-out period, the cost of making the lots ready to sell, selling expenses and other cost elements, it is possible to arrive at the net value of the land as a potential single-family residential subdivision. If the cost involved in developing any subdivision is prohibitive when compared to the potential return, the appraiser should know that the highest and best use of the land may not be for residential subdivision purposes. The test of appropriateness of the proposed use is very important and should not be overlooked.

## HOW TO DETERMINE WHETHER THE PROPOSED USE IS ECONOMICALLY FEASIBLE

Even after the appraiser has carefully applied the first three tests discussed above, he must still apply this very important economic test. Very often, the appraiser may find that the proposed use is legal in every respect, is physically possible, and is appropriate from the standpoint of access and availability of necessary services. Since most real estate transactions have a profit motive, an important question yet to be answered is, "Will it sell?" The proposed use cannot be the highest and best use unless it would provide "the greatest net return."

Many residential subdivisions fail as business endeavors simply because the developer and/or appraiser failed to do the necessary investigation to determine their feasibility. For a residential subdivision to be successful, it must appeal to prospective buyers in several specific aspects. The prospective buyer of a lot in a residential subdivision is concerned with quality and ease of access to educational facilities. The working members of the family are concerned with ease of access to areas of employment. Ease of access, and quality and quantity of religious and recreational facilities are important items. A prospective buyer of a lot in a residential subdivision is very much interested in the availability and cost of municipal services such as refuse pickup. The quality of police and fire protection and other municipal services are very important items to a prospective buyer. A residential subdivision must be located in an area where there is little likelihood of encroachment from inharmonious users. You should also be familiar with the number of people in the typical family, the family income level, the types of buyers who would be attracted to the subdivision and the types of facilities which are in general demand in the area. You should carefully research the market so that you may estimate the normal period needed to develop and dispose of all the lots in the particular subdivision. It is essential that the lot size be typical for the area and that the building restrictions as to size and type of dwelling be compatible with other development in the area. In estimating the value of raw land for a proposed residential subdivision, it is necessary for the appraiser to be aware of whether the typical developer in the area wholesales his lots to other builders or whether such a developer will build and sell a house and lot as a package.

This knowledge is important in estimating the ultimate selling price of the lots to be developed. There is no doubt that a great deal of work is required in determining whether a proposed highest and best use is feasible. You will find that there are no shortcuts in answering this particular question. If you, as an appraiser, are confronted with a client who wants a "quick answer" and is not willing to spend a sufficient amount of money to allow you to carefully research the question of the feasibility of the project, it is almost always a wise move to decline this particular assignment. Accepting an assignment under such circumstances will very likely be the most expensive move you have ever made, even though the fee may appear attractive at that particular time. There are many residential subdivisions, apartment projects and condominium projects in the United States today which would never have been built (and which subsequently have failed miserably) if the appraiser had carefully analyzed the test of whether the use was feasible from an economic standpoint.

## MODEL FOR DETERMINATION OF HIGHEST AND BEST USE

This discussion has covered many of the common mistakes which are made by appraisers in the determination of highest and best use. The discussion also outlined four essential steps to be made in this determination. The following step-by-step example is intended to stress the extreme importance of careful analysis in arriving at a determination of highest and best use.

### MODEL APPRAISAL

Assume that the assignment is to appraise a lot which is improved with a one-story, brick veneer structure, currently in use as a single-family residence. The site is a corner lot which fronts 100 feet on the west side of Main Street, has a depth of 150 feet along the north side of Second Street, and is typical of the area with regard to lot size. The site is located two blocks north of the intersection of Interstate Highway 85 and Main Street. The structure is 30 years old, contains 2000 square feet of living area, and is typical of other single-family residences in the area. The streets are paved with asphalt and have concrete curbs and sidewalks, as well as adequate street lighting. All city utilities are available and all are typically utilized. The entire area within ten blocks in each direction was zoned R-100-S until two years prior to the date of the appraisal. This is single-family residential zoning with a minimum of 100 feet frontage and a minimum of 15,000 square feet of land area. Two years ago, when Interstate Highway 85 was completed, the city zoned the four quadrants at the intersection of I-85 and Main Street, B-3, which is for general business. The remainder of the first block of Main Street on each side of I-85 was immediately zoned O-1, which permits office buildings of not over two stories in height. The four quadrants and the remainder of the first block were acquired and developed for the permitted use within one year of the completion of I-85 and the change in zoning. One year prior to the date of the appraisal, and after lengthy hearings of complaints from residents of the area, the city reluctantly extended the O-1 zoning to the second block on each side of I-85. These two additional blocks have now been sold and the present owners are demolishing the residential structures so that office buildings can be constructed.

The following steps (as a minimum) should be taken in determination of highest and best use of the subject property:

1. Obtain a legal description and, if possible, a plat of the site.
2. Obtain a copy of the zoning ordinances and a zoning map.
3. Visit the subject site and make a very careful inspection of the site to see if it meets minimum zoning standards for R-100-S zoning. In this particular case, the site does meet minimum standards. You should observe the shape, topography, access and availability of necessary utilities and services to see if any problems exist in this area. You find that there are no problems in this respect. You should compare the subject site with others in the neighborhood and, when you do so, you find that it conforms to the typical single-family site.
4. Make a careful inspection of the improvements with respect to age, condition, compliance to existing building codes and conformity to other single-family residences in the area. You find that it is typical of other such structures in the area and that it is well suited to its present use from the standpoint of its utility as a residence.

5. Contact the city zoning officials about their attitude toward extending O-1 zoning into the subject block. Your conversation with these officials and your further study of the extreme reluctance to extend O-1 zoning into the adjacent block one year ago leads you to conclude that no zoning change for the subject property will be likely to occur for many years to come. This conclusion is further enforced by your finding that the demand for two-story office building sites is very slow at the present time. Conversations with investors in interstate-highway-oriented two-story office buildings also indicate their reluctance to build more than two blocks from the point of intersection of the subject street and the interstate.
6. Make a careful analysis of recent sales of properties similar to the subject. This should include sales in the same block as the subject, if this is at all possible. Sales of parcels in the blocks which were changed to O-1 zoning should also be investigated. In order to determine if there are any positive or negative effects on the subject property because of its proximity to the O-1 blocks, it is important to analyze sales of similar single-family houses which are several blocks removed from any interstate or office zoning influence. Your investigation shows that single-family homes very similar to the subject property, except for the fact that they are removed from any interstate or office zoning influence, are selling for from \$35,000 to \$40,000. You also find that a property almost identical to the subject, except for being on the opposite corner, sold a month ago for \$37,500. You find that the properties in the adjacent block, which was zoned O-1 and which is undergoing a change in use to two-story office buildings, sold for \$50,000 to \$60,000 for those nearest I-85, to \$40,000 for the property on the same side of the street but on the opposite corner from the subject in the block zoned O-1. This analysis of sales leads you to conclude that, while there probably is some negative effect on the value of the subject property as a single-family residence because it is adjacent to a block which is being developed for office use, this is offset by the small amount of commercial influence which could be attributed to the subject due to the slight possibility of a future change in zoning.
7. To determine if the highest and best use of the property is as a vacant site or as it is presently improved, you should find out if the improvements contribute any value to the property as a

> whole. Having established by sales comparison that the subject property has a value of approximately $37,500, you should now look at the value of the site as if it were vacant and available to be put to its highest and best use. It has already been established that there is little or no likelihood of a change from the present R-100-S zoning so that the site can only be used for single-family purposes. Sales of vacant lots in areas similar to the subject, and which are zoned R-100-S, show that the typical 100-foot corner lot with a depth of 150 feet sells for $125 per front foot, or a total of $12,500. The total property value of $37,500, less $12,500 for the value of the lot, indicates that the value contribution of the improvements is $25,000. Thus, you can reasonably conclude that the highest and best use of the subject property is to continue its present use as a single-family residence.

It should be noted that each of the four tests for determination of highest and best use were applied to the subject property. If the lot had been substandard in size or if the structure had not been built according to the building code, it would have failed the test for legality of use. If the lot had been of a poor shape, with poor topography or access, it would have failed the test for physical possibility of use. If all city services and utilities were not available, it would have failed the test for appropriateness of use. If there was a strong probability of obtaining a change to O-1 zoning for the subject and if the lot for office use was worth more than the $37,500 for a residence, then the continuation of the present use would fail the test from an economic standpoint. Unless you, as a competent professional appraiser, have applied the four tests and have obtained affirmative answers with each of them, you have not arrived at a proper determination of highest and best use.

Perhaps some clarification should be offered as to why the terms "estimate of highest and best use" and "determination of highest and best use" are used interchangeably in this chapter. The appraiser applies the four tests, which are outlined herein, and it is possible to determine whether a particular property meets the requirements of these tests. Thus, the term "determination of highest and best use" encompasses the items which are determinable by the appraiser. The appraiser can determine the presence or absence of factors in relation to the property so that he may arrive at a supportable "estimate of highest and best use."

# 5

# How to Analyze and Report Factors Which Affect Residential Property Value at All Levels

The first four chapters constitute the foundation for this and all succeeding chapters. The material presented here will follow the steps that are normally taken in making an appraisal. This chapter is devoted to gathering necessary data and to the analysis of the general area in which the property is located, which includes region and city, and then, more specifically, to an analysis of the particular neighborhood in which the property is located. This chapter describes regional and city analysis. Chapter 6 will describe neighborhood analysis.

There are many forces which affect the value of residential real estate. You should have a thorough understanding of these various forces and how they act upon the value of any particular property. You should also understand and apply the appraisal principles as they affect the property within its particular environment. Since real estate is fixed in location, there is no way for the property to be moved into a new environment. It must be analyzed within its own market setting or environment, which identifies the specific forces influencing real estate values. The environment of any particular property includes influences which operate at the international, national, regional and community levels. In analyzing the environmental influences upon value, start at the broadest extreme, which is the international level, and then proceed to the national, regional and community level. This can be pictorially described by looking at the subject property as the center of a bull's eye, with the international forces being the outer extremes of the target, the national forces being next closest, the regional or city forces being nearer to the center, and the community or neighborhood forces being immediately adjacent to the subject property, which is the center of the target. There is no doubt that international and national forces play a very basic role as they affect regional and local or city forces, which in turn have a particular effect upon the immediate neighborhood in which the subject property is located. The following material will be presented beginning with the broadest areas of influence or environment and moving toward those which are more directly involved with the property being appraised.

## HOW TO COLLECT AND ANALYZE DATA RELATING TO INTERNATIONAL AND NATIONAL MARKET AND ENVIRONMENTAL INFLUENCES

There are several factors at the international level which have an influence upon the national environment. The international gold supply or other currency backing, as well as the general monetary supply, has an influence on the balance of payments, which in turn affects imports and exports of manufactured goods. A negative balance of payments can affect the national economy to the extent that we are faced with the devaluation of our currency, either by actual federal action or by the effects of inflation on the economy. Tariff restrictions upon imports or exports can have a great effect on the level of manufacturing within this country. Furthermore, the level of manufacturing can affect employment and the purchasing power of individuals who would be potential purchasers of residential property. The scarcity of crude oil, partially arising from our dependence on imports, has a definite effect upon the cost of motor fuels and, thus, upon the demand for homes in suburban or rural areas.

At the national level, the federal reserve policy, as it affects the monetary supply, will have an effect upon interest rates. The availability and adequacy of mortgage money and the cost of this mortgage money will certainly have an effect on the amount of residential construction and the ease of marketing any type of property which requires a mortgage loan. Any federal action which affects the availability and cost of mortgage money will certainly affect the demand for construction materials and the demand for employees engaged in the manufacture of these construction materials or in the construction of any type of real estate improvement. The Federal Housing

Administration sets construction standards and has a definite influence on the quality and quantity of residential property which is available. Federal laws and regulations affect the inflow to savings institutions and determine the loan policies which these institutions must use in advancing mortgage money. The budgetary policies of the federal government influence the inflationary trend, and this effect is carried through to the employment level in the ability of potential purchasers to buy residential real estate. Taxation policies at the national level affect the purchasing power of individuals to the extent that they may be effectively eliminated from the housing market by the amount of tax extracted by the federal government.

## COLLECTING DATA ABOUT THE REGIONAL MARKET LEVEL AND ENVIRONMENTAL INFLUENCES

The regional area of influence relates to the general area including the city in which the subject property is located. An example of this would be the area identified as the New England section of the United States, the Southeastern section, the Midwestern section or various other regions or areas which are subject to the same general influences. At the present time, the major industrial and residential growth is occurring in the warm-climate areas known as the "Sun Belt." Quite often, you will find that regional influences run counter to the international or national influences. This would be true where a region is blessed with an unusual amount of industrial development, large military installations or any other activities which tend to cause the area to grow faster than it would under normal circumstances. On the other hand, an area may find itself losing a large number of major employers, thus experiencing an adverse effect upon employment and the ability to satisfy desires for real estate. It should be remembered that economic forces and population trends are particularly important at the regional level. Employment and unemployment have a definite effect on the levels of income and the purchasing power of prospective purchasers of residential property. An additional factor which is extremely important at the regional level is the population growth rate and the rate of family formation.

Some areas of the country are experiencing an extremely rapid population growth and, as a result, there is a very good market for residential properties. The attitude of regional residents regarding their inclination to save and/or spend their earnings can affect the availability of mortgage funds from the local savings and loan institutions.

A word of advice here is to simply avoid accepting figures which are gathered by the local Chamber of Commerce or the regional planning agency. It is necessary to analyze the available figures and to give them some consideration; however, you should relate the enormous amount of available statistics to the actual real world influence these statistics may exert upon the demand for and the ability to purchase housing.

At the regional level, it becomes increasingly important for you to specifically identify and acquaint yourself with the market forces in the area, their direction, their strength as they prevail at the current time and their probable future trends within the region. It should be remembered here that you do not have to make a separate analysis for each appraisal on the forces at the international, national and regional levels. The information obtained at this level will continue to be useful until there is a major change at one of these levels which would have some positive or negative effect upon the value of the particular class of property which is the subject of the appraisal. If prior reports are filed systematically by city and/or region for easy reference, you can save much duplication of effort.

## LEVELS OF MARKET AND ENVIRONMENTAL INFLUENCE AT THE LOCAL COMMUNITY OR CITY LEVEL

Many of the economic influences I discussed earlier apply to a more specific extent within the community or city level. These factors include employment, income level, price structure, availability of mortgage money, cost of mortgage money and population growth rates. At the local community or city level, you also become concerned with more specific influences, such as property tax levels and the equality of the tax burden, availability and cost of community services, and quality and stability of the local government. Additional factors specific to the community or city are cultural activities, availability and quality of education, religious facilities and, last but not least, recreational facilities.

One factor that you should never overlook is the general reputation of the community or city. Some cities have acquired bad reputations, and these cities are automatically eliminated from consideration when a person has a choice for establishing his residence. It is recommended that, by interviewing local real estate people, you acquaint yourself with whether there is some merit to this reputation, and you should also investigate the probability that the city can live down this reputation within a reasonable length of time. You should always refrain from letting personal bias enter into your evaluation of any item which might have some influence on the value of a property. You do not make the market; you are simply analyzing the factors which would be considered by a knowledgeable buyer and seller in order to estimate the market value of the subject property. The subject property must be analyzed where it is located, giving a completely objective analysis of all of the factors influencing its value.

## THE PURPOSE OF CITY ANALYSIS

The final environmental influence is found at the local community or city level. As I have previously explained, any parcel of real estate is fixed in its location and must be analyzed in that location. The city in which any property is located provides the setting for that property. Sometimes, an appraisal report will be prepared for a client who has never seen the city in which the subject property is located. Under such circumstances, it is advisable to carefully and thoroughly acquaint the client with that city. This does not mean that you must give a recitation of Chamber of Commerce data, but rather an analysis of the factors which are essential to understanding the environment in which the subject property is located and relating these particular factors to how they specifically affect the value of the type of property being appraised.

I have seen appraisal reports in which the city analysis was simply a recital of a series of statistics, with no meaningful conclusions drawn from these statistics. This type of information is useless to a client and will very likely lead to his eliminating you from the assignment list for future appraisals. A well-prepared city analysis will lay the foundation for subsequent steps in the appraisal process and will give the client an excellent understanding of the environment in which the subject property is located. The length of the data, which are included in this section of the report, is dependent upon whether the appraisal is being made for a local client who is very familiar with the city, or for a client who must be acquainted with the city through the written data furnished in the appraisal report. There is no doubt that you, as the appraiser, should do the necessary research to acquaint yourself with the city as much for a local client as for an out-of-town client; however, it is not necessary to include the volume of data you have gathered within the report itself if it is being prepared for a local client. An example of the format for a city analysis will be found at the end of Chapter 6.

There are four major factors which affect the supply and demand, and the value of residential real estate at the local community or city level. These four factors, each of which is extremely important in city analysis, are:

1. Physical
2. Economic-financial
3. Political-governmental
4. Sociological

## PHYSICAL FACTORS IN CITY ANALYSIS

The physical factors within a city, which influence the market value of property, can be specifically identified. A little time and effort on your part in driving around the city will allow you to become thoroughly acquainted with the physical characteristics of the city and how these physical factors affect the value of the type of property you are appraising.

### Size

The size of a city can be limited by certain natural barriers, such as a body of water, swampy terrain, mountainous terrain or barren areas, in which there is no hope of obtaining water supply. The size of the city can also be limited by governmental action, such as when the surrounding area is owned and utilized for military installations or for some type of park or recreational area. Some cities have adopted a no-growth policy, severely limiting residential growth within that particular city. The City of San Francisco, California is an excellent example of the physical limitations upon the area of a city. The very limited land area there has resulted in extremely small residential lots and in the virtual elimination of any new expansion area. The extreme limitation of available land within an area for any type of additional residential construction will affect the residential market within that city. You can acquaint yourself with any limiting factors regarding the area of the city by driving through the major residential areas.

### Topographical Problems

There are many cities in which the topography is such that the amount of construction area is limited. There is no doubt that extremely steep topography results in added construction costs and may discourage the erection of certain types of structures. There are also areas, such as in New Orleans, Louisiana, where the added cost of pilings due to the extremely shallow water table can have an adverse effect upon building costs and can limit growth severely. Topography problems can have an adverse effect upon the density of development within an area and can have either a positive or negative effect upon the overall attractiveness of the city as a place to live. You should acquaint yourself with the topography and any problems which may arise to limit city growth and/or the marketability of the particular property you are appraising.

### Soil and Subsoil Problems

There are certain cities in which the soil and subsoil conditions pose very serious obstacles to residential construction. In some cities, the rock formation which lies very close to the surface creates very expensive problems in installing building foundations. There are other locales where the soil is extremely elastic, and this requires substantial additional investment in foundations. In many cases, the type of soil will eliminate the possibility of erecting structures with basements. The permafrost in Alaska poses a major problem which is unique to that particular state. You should become generally familiar with the soil and subsoil conditions throughout the entire city and you should certainly be very specific about soil and subsoil conditions within the immediate neighborhood and particularly the subject site. The type of analysis required in the neighborhood will be covered later in this chapter and in Chapter 6.

### Climate Factors

One of the major factors which makes a city attractive or unattractive as a prospective residential area is the climate. If a prospective purchaser has a choice of locating in an area where the temperatures are mild and pleasant, with adequate but not excessive precipitation and little likelihood of tornados and hurricanes, he would certainly choose this area over one in which climatic conditions are poor. There are certain areas of the country, such as Los Angeles, California and Birmingham, Alabama, in which smog caused by automotive and industrial pollution is a major irritant, particularly to persons having some type of respiratory problem. There are certain areas of the country, such as Arizona, in which the low humidity has a tremendous appeal for people with respiratory problems. Certain warm climates, such as in California and Florida, are particularly attractive to people who do not like cold weather and heavy snowfall. On the other hand, some people are attracted to areas where there is adequate snowfall and slopes for skiing. You should always discuss the climate conditions, such as average temperature, average growing season, average annual rainfall and snowfall, only to the extent that these items are positive factors for the city because of their attractiveness or negative factors against the city because of their presence or absence. The point is that climatic factors should be discussed only as they affect the value of the particular property.

## HOW TO HANDLE THE PHYSICAL FACTORS IN CITY ANALYSIS

There is no doubt that certain physical factors which are peculiar to the city in which the property is located do have a definite effect on the market value of the property. You have the responsibility to carefully analyze these physical factors and to report those which are pertinent, so that your client may give these items full consideration in evaluating the attractiveness of the city. The analysis should be objective and factual, avoiding terms which might normally be found in a glowing Chamber of Commerce or industrial development commission report. Any factors you include should be analyzed carefully, and a conclusion should be drawn regarding their effect on the value of the particular property being appraised.

## ECONOMIC-FINANCIAL FACTORS IN CITY ANALYSIS

In analyzing the economic-financial factors which affect the value of a property within a particular city, the most significant factors are those which are called "economic." There is no doubt that economic factors do have an influence on the quantity and the level of housing supply and demand, and they should be given considerable attention in your appraisal report. Care should be taken, however, to consider only the most important economic factors as they relate to the city analysis. It is also essential that the economic factors be analyzed in sufficient detail so that they may be related specifically to the appraisal of the particular property. The city and neighborhood analysis format at the end of Chapter 6 covers these factors.

In order to understand the type and number of housing units which will be required within a given city and the probable rate of absorption for these units, it is necessary to have a thorough understanding of the population characteristics of the city, and this is one of the first items of information included in a city analysis. To estimate market value, you certainly must have an understanding of the marketability for the subject property and, to have that understanding, you must be aware of the demand for and the absorption rate of housing units, particularly within the class of property which is the subject of the appraisal. Some of the most important population characteristics to be considered are:

1. Total present population.
2. The rates of in-migration or out-migration.
3. Historical trend in population growth.
4. The portion of this growth which comes about by natural birth rate versus the net effect of population movement.
5. The sex distribution of the population.
6. The rates of population growth within the various subclassifications.
7. The number and size of household units (present tendency toward singles).
8. The size and distribution of the labor force.

9. The age distribution of the population.
10. The educational or special job skills of the population.

All of this information, relative to past trends in population and to present growth patterns, will enable you to estimate the probable future population trends and their effect on the marketability of your subject property.

**Employment Characteristics**

There is no doubt that the demand for residential property can only become effective demand when it is coupled with the ability to buy. The ability to buy is directly related to the employment level within the city. The availability, types and adequacy of jobs, rates of pay and probable future employment trends are extremely important factors in the decision process for those people who are considering relocating to a particular city. This is a key element in the demand for housing. There are several employment characteristics which are particularly important. Some of these characteristics are:

1. The number of people employed.
2. The percentage of unemployment.
3. The length of time in which this unemployment has existed.
4. The number of job vacancies.
5. How long these vacancies have continued.
6. The skills required to fill these jobs.
7. The types of employers.
8. The number of people employed at present.
9. The growth rate for the employees within that particular employment group.
10. The history of the city for labor relations.

Certain cities have records of continuing labor unrest, and these cities are not attractive either for job seekers or employers. During the course of your research in this area, you will become aware of the stability of employment and the stability and financial strength of the employers within the city, as well as the general attitude of these employers toward the city and their future within the city. In some areas of the country, the cost of doing business has become so high that employers have no option except to close their facilities and relocate in more favorable areas. An essential question to be answered in this analysis is whether or not the employment is likely to remain stable, to grow, or whether the income from this employment will be high enough to permit the prospective demand for housing to become effective demand for housing.

### Income Level

The income levels of the population within any given city are very important factors, because they represent the actual buying power of the residents of the city required for potential demand to become effective demand for housing. The total family income is extremely important, particularly in view of the fact that second and third wage earners' income is now given considerable weight by lending agencies. There is no doubt that the stability of the income level, as well as the trends which are evident from an analysis of the future income prospects within the city, are very important. General income levels, rates of pay, normal work week and the potential for overtime are important, particularly when the prospective buyers of the subject class of residential property are wage earners. If the city is known for providing residences for retired individuals, then it is also important to give consideration to the income, such as retirement plans, social security and other types of income, received by retired people. Much useful information can be obtained by contacting the Chamber of Commerce and the industrial development agencies in the city. Statistics are also maintained by city agencies at the City Hall. You are urged to make a careful analysis of the income within the city so that you may project the ability of the residents to satisfy their desires for housing.

### Economic Base

Information can be obtained about the economic base of the city from the Chamber of Commerce, the industrial development board or the city planning agencies. It is important to know the economic base of the community since it is the sum of all income-producing activities by which a community maintains its economy. You should understand the type of economic base prevalent within the city. Some cities are classified as industrial centers, while others are commercial or trade centers, transportation centers, centers of government employment or educational employment, agricultural centers, or centers for milling, mining or other extractive industries, while some are fortunate enough to have a mixed economic base which tends to eliminate the peaks and valleys of income which are attributed to cities centered around one type of employment. I am familiar with one area in which the only employer is a textile industry. As long as the textile sales are running at a high level, the economy within that city booms; however, during times of low textile business, the city suffers severely. It is suggested that the economic base of a city be analyzed in terms of the strength, growth pattern, stability and its relative position with other cities in the area, as well as the trend toward broadening the economic base, particularly with regard to satellite or supportive activities such as retail and wholesale trade in areas which are otherwise considered to be manufacturing centers. The suggested city and neighborhood analysis format at the end of Chapter 6 will furnish further details about proper handling of this data.

It is also recommended that you acquaint yourself with the spending patterns for families within the city. It is important to know what families do with their disposable income, and particularly their outlook toward either renting or owning residential property. If the appraisal is of a property within a city where there is a rapid turnover of residents, you will find that the trend is more toward rental housing than toward owner-occupancy. This is particularly true in an area where there is a large military center, with a substantial influx of students or trainees who stay for perhaps 11 months and then move out en masse to allow for the influx of an entirely new group. Information regarding the spending habits of the families within a city can be obtained from various city and federal agencies as well as from the local Chamber of Commerce. In addition, the economics departments of major universities can often furnish much worthwhile data.

**Local Tax Climate**

The local tax climate is of extreme importance to prospective purchasers who have the option of moving to one city or some other competing city. Some cities have a local income tax or gross wage tax while others rely heavily on sales tax or some other type of consumer tax. These two items can impose a substantial burden on the income of any family. One of the critical items related to tax burden is the local property tax. In certain areas of the country, the property tax would be one-tenth as great on a property of equal value when compared to certain other cities. Certainly, the local tax rates, levels of assessment and equalization of tax burden are major items to be considered. If a knowledgeable person had the option of locating in City A, where the property tax liability was $20.00 per month, versus locating in City B, where the property tax liability was $150.00 to $200.00 per month, there is little doubt about what his choice would be if other factors are equal. It is extremely important for you to analyze the tax burdens of competing cities within reasonable proximity of the city in which the subject property is located. If you maintain files on all the cities in which you do appraisals, you will soon have this data readily available for easy reference.

**Prevailing Price Levels**

It is important for you to have some knowledge of the general price level within the city. There can be substantial variations in the cost of goods or services in one city as compared with another. The prevailing wage rates, building material costs and profit levels demanded by builders can have a substantial effect on the price of residential property. You should also be aware of comparable prices for other goods and services for the subject city versus other cities within reasonable proximity of the subject.

Since mortgage loans are usually involved in the purchase of any item of real estate, particularly residential property, it is important to know whether there are adequate mortgage funds available and the prevailing interest rate within the city. Lending terms, including length of loans, down payment requirements, and loan-to-value ratios can also be very important factors in the attractiveness of a city. Much valuable data on this subject can be obtained by interviewing local real estate firms and the major residential lenders.

### Competing Properties

There are several items relating specifically to the supply of real estate itself which should be considered. You should be very much aware of the standing stock of housing of various types, and you should know that standing stock is considered to be those residential properties which are currently available and ready for occupancy. You should also be familiar with new construction within the city, the number of conversions from one use to another and the average number of housing units which are absorbed within a given year. Interviews with real estate brokers and lenders, as well as use of data from building permits issued, will aid in solving this problem. Construction costs are certainly an important factor affecting new or renovated structures. The number of vacancies within the city and the rates of turnover for both owner-occupied and rental housing are very important. The percentage of owner-occupied residences within a given city is important, as are any trends away from the status which has existed in the past. The data from Census of Housing will furnish most of this information.

### Fire Protection

The type of fire protection available within the city will have a tremendous influence on the cost of fire insurance. You should determine whether there are unusual factors present in the city as they relate to the cost of fire insurance. If the city is normal for the area as compared with other competing cities, it is not important to dwell too much on this particular item.

### Public Transportation and Ease of Access

One important factor which should be considered is whether or not there are municipal transportation facilities available. If the residents of the city are limited strictly to the use of private automobiles, there is likely to be congestion along the access streets and difficulty in parking at the area of employment. People who are considering locating in a city would require easy access to supporting service facilities such as schools, shopping centers, areas of employment and recreation areas. It is important to know something of the street pattern, the major highway access and any other factors which would be important to the user of a private automobile. It is also important to know the availability and the probable cost to users of city transportation facilities.

## POLITICAL-GOVERNMENTAL FACTORS IN THE CITY ANALYSIS

In preparing a city analysis, it is very important to understand the political and governmental factors which may affect the value of residential real estate. Some political and governmental factors operate at all levels of government, ranging from international, to national, to state, county and city levels. You should always evaluate these political and governmental factors as they relate specifically to the class of property you are appraising.

### International Factors

At the international level, the factors which may have a bearing upon the value of residential property include the prospects of military confrontations which may require an unusually large amount of governmental expenditures to maintain a strong military force. Extremely heavy spending to provide military protection eliminates some funds which might normally flow to the residential housing market. In addition, international trade policies such as tariffs and other trade barriers may adversely affect certain types of materials which are particularly appropriate to residential construction. The high cost and limited availability of imported crude oil adversely affect our balance of payments nationally as well as the value of suburban or rural real estate at the local level.

### Federal and State Factors

The monetary and fiscal policies of the federal and state governments are particularly important to the residential housing market. If the federal government decrees that a tight monetary policy will prevail, there will be a limited amount of loan funds available for residential housing. The federal government also determines the down payment requirements for VA and FHA financing. Federal government also indirectly affects the amount of down payment requirements and the reserve requirements for savings and loan and banking institutions, as well as length of mortgage terms and mortgage payment methods.

**Budgetary Policies**

The budgets for operating the federal and state government are very important considerations. If it is the policy of the federal government to maintain a strong program of social expenditures, such as welfare or federally subsidized housing, the amount of money remaining for loan purposes to non-subsidized housing may be reduced. The placement of federal highways through cities can also have a definite effect on housing for people who are displaced by these highways. The state budgetary policies can also be very important since, in many instances, property taxes will be a major financial factor to support these budgets. If it is the state's policy to have an extremely generous spending outlook, it is likely that the tax burden, which is imposed upon residential real estate, will be rather severe, thus adversely affecting the residential housing market. The budgetary policies at the city level can also have an impact on the value of residential properties. In some cities, the necessary municipal services such as fire protection, police protection, garbage removal and other similar services are paid out of general tax revenues. In other cities, there is a specific charge for some of these services. You should know whether the costs within the specific city in which you are making the appraisal are above average, below average or typical, so that you may determine whether or not this segment of the cost of home ownership is a positive or negative factor.

**Lending Policies**

Since most of the lending institutions who make residential loans are either directly or indirectly controlled by government regulations, it is important to understand these particular policies. You should become familiar with the federal, state and city regulations as they apply to loan policies. The federal government usually establishes the minimum down payment, the interest rate and the amortization period for those loans which it guarantees. There are also certain regulations regarding down payment requirements, interest rates and amortization periods for loans made by banking institutions. Private lending institutions such as insurance companies are usually less restrictive; however, they do not have the ability to lend as large a portion of the total purchase price as the public lending institutions have. This data can be obtained by interviewing brokers as well as the major public and private lenders. In the process of examining the lending policies for those agencies making loans in your city, it is possible that you will find a distinct positive or negative attitude about the city on the part of these agencies, and in that event, it will be necessary for you to determine the effect of this attitude upon the marketability and thus the value of residential real estate in the particular city.

In some cities, you will find that there is a substantial amount of subsidized housing available. The availability of this subsidized housing will tend to eliminate many of the people who might be potential buyers of some of the low-priced homes. This can certainly affect the value of residential real estate and warrants your careful investigation. If your appraisal happens to be in an area where an urban renewal or community development program has been announced, or is in fact underway, you will very likely find that the value of residential real estate within that immediate area has declined substantially. You will usually find that the owners of property within the neighborhood in which an urban renewal or community development program is underway will tend to do little or no maintenance, thus allowing the property to deteriorate rather rapidly. You will also find that, if the homes within the urban renewal area are rental residential properties, there will be substantial vacancy due to the fact that most renters do not wish to go to the trouble of moving into a home which they may have to vacate very quickly to make way for the urban renewal program. There are special allowances to both owners and tenants of properties within an urban renewal area and, in some instances, these special allowances to these displaced families allow them to upgrade their housing to better quality types of homes. You should investigate this possibility and be aware of any potential demand which may be created by this type of program.

**Essential Government Services**

The quantity and quality of government services at all levels within the city are important factors. You will find in some areas that the city government is very unresponsive to the wishes of its citizens and provides only minimum services. In other cities, the reverse will be true, to the extent that outstanding services are provided but at an exorbitant cost to the homeowner. One area which should require your careful attention is the quantity and quality of available fire protection. This will affect the peace of mind of the residents of the city and will certainly have a bearing upon the relative cost of fire insurance. An important service in the minds of any city resident is police protection. If the police department is adequately staffed and responds quickly when a need arises, it certainly makes the city a more attractive place in which to live.

The city street system is another important factor. It is important to have a network of federal and state highways leading into the city, and to have a good street pattern with excellent access to the residential, commercial and industrial sections of the city. You should also know the policy of the city regarding paving assessments in residential neighborhoods.

There may be a substantial variation in the cost of municipal services such as water, gas, telephone and electricity. The cost of utilities is a major concern for any homeowner, and it should be given particular attention in comparing the subject city to any other competing city. Included in the consideration of utilities might also be the policy of the city regarding refuse collection. This service may be provided at a monthly charge, although in some cities, there is no specific charge. The adequacy of refuse collection is equal in importance to the cost of this service, and it should therefore be given careful attention in your investigation.

### Land Use Controls

In Chapter 2, I discussed the fact that police power is one of the restrictions upon the bundle of rights. The adequacy of the city land use controls (which is part of the function of police power) can directly influence the value of residential real estate. I would venture to say that there is no other action which can be taken by city government which would have a more immediate effect upon the value of residential property. The most important function of city government, as it relates to residential property value, is in its zoning policies. In some cities, the zoning is very flexible so that there is no clear protection of land use patterns. In other cities, the zoning is completely inflexible, to the extent that the natural growth of the city may be hampered. The zoning regulations should clearly state the uses to which the land and improvements may be put and the intensity of the particular uses. You should always obtain a copy of the local zoning ordinance and a zoning map, and investigate the policies of the city regarding a change in zoning. You should have some knowledge of the master plan for the city so that you may recognize the direction and type of growth which the city foresees in the future. There should be adequate enforcement of building codes, housing codes, fire codes, electrical codes and plumbing codes. You may find that this enforcement is so lax that many dangerous conditions exist. If your particular appraisal assignment includes a structure which appears to be substandard, particularly with regard to type and quality of construction and electrical wiring, you should check into this very carefully.

### Effect of Rent Controls

Another action of government which may be an extremely negative factor influencing the value of residential real estate is the imposition of rent controls. A good example of this exists in New York City, where the rents have been controlled to the extent that many landlords have simply vacated the premises and turned them over to the city. In areas where rent controls are imposed, you should determine whether the permitted rent is sufficient to allow the property to survive from an economic standpoint. In some instances, the rent controls have resulted in the landlord abandoning the property, the tenants being unable to continue to occupy the property, thus leaving many displaced tenants. Such actions can have a strong effect upon the supply and demand of real estate and should be given your careful attention.

**Educational Facilities**

One of the most important areas of governmental service is the provision of educational facilities. Most potential buyers of residential property are families with children. One of their major concerns is the quality and relative cost of both public and private educational facilities. For a city to be attractive, it should have an excellent choice of educational facilities, and these should be easily accessible by both physical street access and the relative cost of these services. Of all the governmental factors I have discussed, this is probably the most deserving of your concern.

## SOCIOLOGICAL FACTORS IN CITY ANALYSIS

Potential buyers of any residential property are people, and their wishes and attitudes are extremely important. It is your task to identify the attitudes toward the city as they may affect the value of residential property and to be able to ascertain from market behavior the monetary effects of these attitudes.

You will find that people with similar social, educational, occupational and general economic levels tend to want to cluster together in a city. Prospective buyers are interested in the social backgrounds of the area's population and whether or not these people may be sociologically homogeneous with themselves.

The reputation of a particular area may be either positive or negative in the minds of buyers. Many of the negative attitudes which people may hold in regard to a certain city are based upon inaccurate data as reported by the media. Whether or not you agree with the attitudes of these people about the reputation of an area, you must recognize it and treat it in an objective manner in arriving at your value estimate, if such attitudes affect the market value of the property you are appraising.

The people of the United States today are becoming more and more recreation oriented. People who are prospective buyers within a given city will be very interested in access to desirable recreation areas. There is also a tendency for people to pay attention to the availability of cultural facilities within a city. In preparing a city analysis, you should furnish the client with your analysis of the quantity and quality of both recreational and cultural facilities within the city.

In preparing a city analysis, you should report on the relative stability of that city's economic conditions, and its political and social stability. Prospective buyers are not interested in moving into a city which has major problems in these areas. The data you have gathered and analyzed should point to the conclusions shown at the end of your city analysis. The suggested format for city and neighborhood analysis at the end of Chapter 6 will show you how to do this.

# 6

# Methods and Sources of Data for City and Neighborhood Analysis and Suggested Report Format

Chapter 5 was devoted to the factors which affect residential property value and the types of data which should be considered in making a city analysis. This chapter deals with preparing and presenting the data in a meaningful form. You should always remember that the simple listing of a series of charts or data is not sufficient and would serve little purpose as far as your client is concerned. You have gathered all of this information; now, explain to your client what it means.

An analysis of the data should always be pointed toward answering certain questions for the client. He wants to see significant data, reported in an objective manner, and he wants the questions answered about how these data affect the value of residential property within the city. You should always report objectively, regardless of your particular likes or dislikes for the city.

In reporting and analyzing the city data, it is necessary to furnish some information regarding past trends in areas such as population, employment, and availability and cost of city services. However, a simple recitation of past trends does not necessarily provide guidance toward possible future occurrences. It is recommended that you discuss past trends and analyze them to furnish future expectations in each area discussed. A pattern should emerge from an analysis of housing starts as it is related to population growth, employment trends and family formations.

Some of the trends which are essential in evaluating the residential real estate market are economic factors within the city such as:

1. Employment.
2. Wage rates.
3. Average income levels.
4. Cost of living.
5. Price levels.
6. Housing turnover.
7. Vacancies.
8. Mortgage rates.
9. Tax rates.
10. Budgetary policies.
11. Changes in population, such as family size.
12. Composition and age.
13. Mortgage lending policies.
14. Rates of foreclosures.
15. Changes in types of housing which prospective buyers will find desirable.

### Sources of Data

One of the most important sources of data for city analysis will come from your own files after you have accumulated a library of pertinent publications. I have found a very important source of information to be the census data available from the Bureau of Census of the U.S. Department of Commerce. The Department of Commerce also has several other helpful publications, such as a survey of current business, building permits issued, value of construction put in place and statistical abstract of the United States. There is also much helpful information published by other agencies of the federal and state government, as well as Local Chambers of Commerce. Local building departments may be able to provide statistics on the types of residential permits issued, and the public utilities often maintain a great deal of useful information. You may also find it necessary to conduct field interviews to obtain additional data when it is not available from your own files or from the sources I have named here.

After you have gathered all of the data which we have discussed, you should proceed to answer two major questions:

1. First of all, what do the data and the trends revealed in this data mean concerning the supply and demand of the particular type of residential property you are appraising?
2. Secondly, what is the impact of these data and trends toward residential real estate values in the city?

You want to furnish the client with information about the most probable future trends in the area, and all of your analysis should be pointed to this end.

## PURPOSE OF NEIGHBORHOOD ANALYSIS

In Chapter 5, I discussed the factors within a city which have a bearing upon the value of residential real estate. We shall now proceed to discuss the factors within the immediate neighborhood which will affect the value of any residential property. A neighborhood is defined as "that part of an area or community whose physical characteristics are influenced by a similarity of the residents from the standpoint of their economic and social characteristics." The neighborhood in which a property is located is its immediate environment. There is no doubt that anything that occurs in the neighborhood has a direct and immediate effect upon the value of any property within that neighborhood. Thus, we are now proceeding to a more localized analysis which you will find essential in the appraisal of a residential property within any particular neighborhood. In making a neighborhood analysis, remember that "homogeneous neighborhood" does not have an ethnic connotation. The item of primary importance is to look at the characteristics of a neighborhood as these characteristics influence current property values.

For an area to be considered as a neighborhood, it must consist of relatively homogeneous properties, at least in the minds of the residents of that particular neighborhood and in the minds of prospective buyers in that neighborhood. There are several key elements of similarity which merit particular attention. The houses within the neighborhood should be similar with respect to quality, age, size, utility and style. The houses within the neighborhood should also bear some similarity in price range. You will usually find that any house which is overbuilt, and thus overpriced, in the neighborhood will tend to suffer a loss in value, since buyers tend to think more in terms of homes which fall within the prevailing price range in the neighborhood. Furthermore, the neighborhood should be restricted to similar types of land uses with no encroachment of non-homogeneous uses such as would occur when the neighborhood is changing from single-family residential to either multi-family or to some type of commercial use. The residents of the neighborhood should be reasonably compatible regarding the amount of family income and should be of similar educational, cultural and social backgrounds.

You must be able to define the boundaries of the particular neighborhood. There are three types of boundaries which have varying degrees of importance in defining the boundary of a neighborhood:

1. Natural boundaries, such as hills, swamps, lakes, streams, mountains, deserts or oceans.
2. Political boundaries, which are established by agencies of the government, including zoning boundaries, school district boundaries, city limits and police jurisdiction lines.
3. Man-made obstacles, such as streets, highways, railroad lines, utility rights of way, city parks or green belts in which no construction is allowed.

Neighborhood analysis is quite useful to you as well as to your client. Many of the facts which you will uncover in the process of making a neighborhood analysis will assist you in identifying the forces of supply and demand within the neighborhood, in making adjustments in your comparable sales analysis, in identifying and estimating locational obsolescence and in projecting probable changes in price levels within the neighborhood.

Your client will expect you to analyze neighborhood data rather than simply listing it. You are dealing with a property which is completely immobile, and any positive or negative factors within the neighborhood will have an immediate and very definite effect upon the value of every property in that neighborhood. The entire presentation of the neighborhood analysis should be aimed at the wishes and desires of the potential purchaser. The fact that you may not particularly like the neighborhood should in no way affect your objective analysis of this neighborhood, since you are appraising the property for the potential buyer and not for yourself. The analysis of a neighborhood should be a study of the attractions, benefits and advantages of living in a particular location. These items are identified as amenities, and they represent the satisfactions and utility of home ownership, or the wishes and desires of tenants if you are appraising within a rental area, and are very important in a person's final decision about where to establish his home.

There are four major factors to be considered in the neighborhood analysis, just as there were in city analysis. Each of these factors will be discussed separately since each one has a direct influence on the desirability of a neighborhood, and thus on the value of any residential property within that neighborhood. These four factors are:

1. Physical factors
2. Economic factors
3. Legal-governmental factors
4. Sociological factors

## PHYSICAL FACTORS IN NEIGHBORHOOD ANALYSIS: WHAT THEY ARE AND HOW TO ANALYZE THEM

There are a number of physical factors which affect the attractiveness of a neighborhood as a place in which to live. Some of these factors are more important than others; however, all of them warrant your attention.

The physical size of a neighborhood is certainly important, and this can be established only by a physical inspection of the neighborhood. Extremely large neighborhoods, which do not have rigid, protected boundaries, tend to be less desirable than smaller, better protected neighborhoods. Both man-made and natural boundaries, as well as political boundaries, can be very effective protection against the encroachment of non-harmonious uses which would tend to make the neighborhood less desirable.

In some areas, the topography of a neighborhood is extremely rolling and is perhaps even further handicapped by large ravines or gullies. Some areas may be extremely flat, with little runoff of surface water and tending to be undesirable from this standpoint. It will not be difficult for you to determine whether the type of topography within the neighborhood is a plus or a minus factor in rating the desirability of that particular neighborhood.

I know of some cases in which soil and subsoil conditions are major factors in the desirability of a neighborhood. If your particular neighborhood tends to have a very elastic and unstable soil, you will find that the added cost of providing special foundations will be a negative factor. Certain types of soil do not provide nice lawns and are not suitable to typical landscaping. The drainage within a particular neighborhood may be extremely poor, and this can also be a negative factor.

Proximity and ease of access to supporting facilities, such as schools, churches, shopping centers, areas of employment, recreational and cultural facilities, are extremely important. The street pattern within the neighborhood will be a positive or negative factor toward access to these supporting facilities.

There should certainly be conformity of usage of the types of properties within the neighborhood and the area should be very attractive in appearance. It will be readily evident to you whether the residents of the neighborhood have pride of ownership by simply looking at how well the lawns are maintained and at the exterior appearances of the residential structures.

The portion of the neighborhood which is developed and the rate at which this development is occurring will give you some idea about the attractiveness of the neighborhood. There may be nuisances and hazards such as odor, smoke, dust, noise or other negative factors which may hamper the growth of the neighborhood and make it much less desirable and less built up than would normally be the case.

**Climatic Factors**

Climatic factors, such as temperature, precipitation and prevailing winds should be considered. There may be a likelihood of unpleasant odor or dust being blown into the neighborhood by prevailing winds from a certain direction. Furthermore, the amount of precipitation can help or hinder the lawn, landscaping or family vegetable garden.

## ECONOMIC FACTORS IN NEIGHBORHOOD ANALYSIS: WHAT THEY ARE AND HOW TO ANALYZE THEM

The economic factors discussed as they relate to city analysis were much broader in scope than those with which we are concerned here. In neighborhood analysis, you are looking at those economic factors within the immediate neighborhood which would influence the value of residential property.

For a neighborhood to maintain its maximum value, there should be some continuity in its residential development. This does not mean that the development should look like a row of tin soldiers. Each home should have some individual character. The homes should not be monotonous in style.

There should also be comparability in price levels within the neighborhood, in the rent levels for those properties which are rented, and in the pattern of uses within the neighborhood. Usage should be harmonious, and there should be a proper balance between land devoted to single-family housing and land which is available and utilized for intra-neighborhood services, such as schools and churches.

Values within the neighborhood will tend to be most stable when it is in the direction of city growth. If the city tends to be growing away from the neighborhood, supporting services which are essential will also be moving away from the subject neighborhood and into the path of city growth. The direction of city growth can be determined by a study of the most recent residential subdivision plats, the recent areas of activity in building permits issued, and a review of the area of the city in which residential sales are most active.

The amount, source and stability of family income, as well as the type, stability and location of employment for the residents of the neighborhood, are important. The values within a neighborhood can best be maintained when each of these factors are on the positive side. Along the same lines, it should be remembered that the population, household size and age distribution of the residents within the neighborhood are also significant. This is particularly true when you are appraising a property within a neighborhood in which most of the residents are of retirement age and do not need the educational facilities that would be required by a family with small children.

The type of tenancy within the neighborhood, whether the homes are owner-occupied or used by tenants, is important. The turnover within the neighborhood and the number of vacant properties, either for sale or for rent, are good indications of the health and stability of the neighborhood. This can be determined by analyzing the length of time expiring between the date on which a typical residence is listed for sale and the date on which it sells, as well as the discount from listed price.

Lender attitudes about the neighborhood can often be good clues for you. Ratings of lending institutions are usually based on sound reasoning. This can be further substantiated by obtaining information about the foreclosure rate within the neighborhood. Interviews with the major residential lenders will usually yield this data. If the attitude of the person interviewed is negative as a result of personal prejudice or bias, his opinion should be ignored and you should attempt to interview others who are more open-minded.

Several aspects of a neighborhood can be called a part of the cost of home ownership. One of these factors is the assessment level and the amount of ad valorem tax. If this item is unusually burdensome, it can have a very definite negative effect on the value of property within the neighborhood. The adequacy, availability and cost of utilities is extremely important. The fire protection and the insurance rating of the particular neighborhood can affect insurance costs of home ownership.

The development stage of a neighborhood and its probable future trend may be estimated by studying the direction and rate of change. If you are appraising a property in a single-family neighborhood, and you note a tendency toward changing some of the single-family homes to multi-tenant rooming houses, or a tendency toward converting some of the homes to commercial use, then you can certainly conclude that the neighborhood is on the downward trend. For a neighborhood to maintain its maximum value for residential purposes, it should be well protected by physical barriers, by political action such as zoning regulations and by being solidly built up with single-family houses with no tendency toward a change to a more dense residential use or to some type of commercial or industrial activity.

## LEGAL-GOVERNMENTAL FACTORS IN NEIGHBORHOOD ANALYSIS: WHAT THEY ARE AND HOW TO ANALYZE THEM

The actions of government at all levels tend to affect the value of a residential property within a particular neighborhood. The governmental actions which have the most effect are at the local level.

One of the central governmental factors which affect the value of property within the neighborhood is the zoning regulations. A weak zoning board can be a definite threat to the continued existence of what might otherwise be considered an attractive neighborhood. If the zoning can be changed with relative ease by individuals with political influence, a prospective buyer can have little confidence in being able to continue to live in a neighborhood devoted exclusively to residential use.

I know of one case in which a very attractive neighborhood was adversely affected by the construction of a major discount department store. The residents of this neighborhood objected strenuously to a change in zoning to permit the construction; however, they lost the battle and are now faced with the tremendous influx of extra traffic and the noise and other inconveniences that go with the new store.

Enforcement of zoning regulations is of critical importance in estimating the protection which may be provided to residents of the neighborhood. City planning and the enforcement of various types of building codes should also be considered. A plan of development should include the maintenance and protection of the integrity of the subject neighborhood and also provide for anticipated future uses, including necessary services. The building, housing, fire, electrical and plumbing codes will certainly affect the cost of construction and, indeed, the very safety of the residents of the neighborhood. If the city does not impartially enforce these codes, prospective residents of the neighborhood will certainly be adversely affected.

Municipal services, such as fire protection, police protection, recreation, schools and refuse collections, should be relatively inexpensive, of good quality and readily available to the residents of the neighborhood. If there is a specific charge for any of these services, it should be competitive with other neighborhoods.

If the particular neighborhood in which you are making your appraisal shows some evidence of decline, it should not be immediately written off as an irreversible situation. While, in many cases, urban renewal programs can have a negative effect on value, there are also instances in which a properly administered program can have a positive effect. In one such situation, a terribly declining neighborhood was turned around completely and is now an attractive single-family and two-family residential neighborhood in which there is obvious pride of ownership on the part of the residents.

The character of a neighborhood may be well protected by deed or by private covenant. This type of protection is often even better than zoning regulations. The agreements among owners of co-op apartments or condominiums are very important and can have a positive effect on the value of residential real estate. The City of Houston, Texas offers very positive evidence of what can be accomplished by private deed restrictions and the absence of zoning regulations. Houston has no zoning regulations, and yet it is one of the most rapidly growing cities in the United States, and I have found that uses tend to group together so that the neighborhoods are homogeneous and tend to be better than in many cities in which there is a weak zoning ordinance. The important elements relating to cooperative apartment and condominium ownership will be covered in the Appendix section of this book.

## SOCIOLOGICAL FACTORS IN NEIGHBORHOOD ANALYSIS: WHAT THEY ARE AND HOW TO ANALYZE THEM

There can be no market for residential real estate, or for any other economic good, unless there are people who have the desire to acquire the property, coupled with the ability to purchase same. The people within any particular neighborhood must be homogeneous and have a high degree of compatibility in terms of income level, educational level and social level.

The density of the population within a neighborhood is very important. Property values do not necessarily follow the trend toward density within a particular neighborhood.

You will usually find that the higher the proportion of owner-occupancy within the neighborhood, the greater will be the stability of values. This is usually caused by the fact that the owners of a property are likely to be more motivated toward providing excellent maintenance than a tenant would be. The statement that "owners occupy homes—tenants occupy houses," is significant in residential appraising, since this difference in attitudes will usually affect property value.

It will be very obvious to you whether or not there is pride of ownership within the neighborhood. People who have pride of ownership tend to maintain excellent lawns, have excellent landscaping, provide excellent maintenance for the exterior and interior of their structures and evidence a great deal of civic pride by participating in civic and community affairs. I know of one neighborhood in which the homes were rather old, and the area had begun to show a decline in stability. The residents of this neighborhood organized a property owner's group and have now shown such pride in their neighborhood that it has become one of the better residential areas of the city. The effort and civic pride on the part of the residents of this neighborhood have paid them great dividends in terms of the satisfaction derived from living in the neighborhood, as well as monetary gains when and if they find it necessary to sell their property. Prospective buyers will soon become aware of the reputation of such a neighborhood and will be eager to acquire properties within it.

Access to a neighborhood is a significant item. There are certain supporting facilities which should be close enough to be readily acceptable but not so close as to become a nuisance or deterrent. A prime example of this is that schools must be close enough to be readily convenient; however, a school immediately next door can be a negative factor. Easy access to centers of employment, shopping areas, churches, recreational facilities, cultural centers, transportation and government facilities are extremely important. Public transportation can be a vital factor in some neighborhoods.

## METHOD AND SOURCES OF DATA FOR NEIGHBORHOOD ANALYSIS

Earlier in this chapter, I discussed some of the factors which must be considered in a neighborhood analysis. While considering these factors, you will obtain a great deal of data of various types. The simple gathering and recitation of data means nothing unless it is related to the problem at hand and how the particular factors within the neighborhood affect the value of the residential property being appraised. In order to perform appraisals of residential properties in an efficient manner, you must be knowledgeable about the available sources of data.

You will find that your own files are the most important sources of data for a neighborhood analysis. Whenever you are doing an appraisal in a particular neighborhood in which you have not previously worked, I recommend that you gather all of the data for your neighborhood analysis and maintain a file so that the work will not have to be repeated on subsequent assignments. You will very likely do several appraisals within any given neighborhood, and once you have completed and properly filed a neighborhood analysis, a tremendous amount of time will be saved by simply running off a copy of the neighborhood analysis from a previous file. The only necessary alterations would be to reflect changes in trends or any positive or negative factors which had arisen in the neighborhood subsequent to the previous appraisal. I have found that the best method for filing appraisal reports for quick and easy access is alphabetically by street name, in order of street number. This will only require you to know the names of the streets within your neighborhood in order to quickly locate prior appraisals.

There are a number of published studies which you will find helpful in making a neighborhood analysis. The census of population and housing by census tract will furnish statistics which will be very useful. You may also refer to publications by the Federal Housing Administration and the U.S. Department of Commerce. There are several public sources of information, such as deeds and mortgages recorded, foreclosures, building permits, assessment records, zoning, subdivision regulations and restrictions, deed restrictions and the ease with which zoning variances can be obtained in any particular part of the city.

Much information can be obtained from private sources, such as the Chamber of Commerce, utility companies, banks and lending institutions, real estate brokers and appraisers, and studies which are done by the business research centers of certain universities.

You may find it necessary to go into the field and actually interview residents of a particular neighborhood. It is suggested that you inquire about their positive and negative attitudes toward the subject neighborhood as an attractive place in which to live. Quite often, information obtained in these interviews can be coordinated with your own observations and can be tremendously helpful in projecting market trends within the neighborhood.

## HOW TO RECOGNIZE THE CHARACTERISTICS OF A STRONG RESIDENTIAL NEIGHBORHOOD

A strong neighborhood should evidence homogeneity of population, land uses, property types and quality of construction. It should also be stable or growing, and not in the process of stagnation or decline in uses, property values, income levels or population. The neighborhood should be located in the direction of the city's growth. Another evidence of a good neighborhood is the fact that there will be little turnover in home ownership, few vacancies and, when vacancies occur, the property will sell in a short period of time at an excellent sales price. Generally, this sales price should show some evidence of continuing to rise. The neighborhood should also have an excellent rating with a financial institution so that mortgage loans can be readily obtained. The neighborhood should be protected by natural or man-made barriers from intrusion of inharmonious uses. The neighborhood should be conveniently located near both public and private schools of good quality, areas of employment and supporting facilities such as shopping centers. Taxes and assessments within the neighborhood should not be burdensome, and utilities should be readily available at reasonable cost.

In analyzing a neighborhood, you should be particularly aware of the stability in the use patterns within the neighborhood, as well as stability of values. The density of use within the neighborhood should be given your careful attention. If you observe a situation in which the families are doubling up, then the density of use is increasing, and it is very likely that the neighborhood is beginning to decline. You should also consider the character of the residents, either homeowners or renters, to see if there are variations in their social and economic characteristics. The neighborhood should show evidence of civic pride, and the ownership within the neighborhood should be stable. The physical age of the structures is not nearly as important in rating a neighborhood as their economic life and general condition. Some of the clues to a declining neighborhood would be conversions and transitions to new uses, usually to higher density, the presence of older families with no children, the increasing ratio of tenant occupancy to owner occupancy, and movement into the neighborhood of families with lower income and social or educational background. Further clues to a declining neighborhood would be declining sale prices and rentals, and a breakdown in the enforcement of zoning or private covenants regarding the use of property within the neighborhood.

You should be keenly aware of the fact that the future of the neighborhood in which the subject property is located is the key element in the maintenance of the value of the property. You should relate the factors and trends in the neighborhood to their present and probable future effects on the value of the property you are appraising. You should always emphasize the predominant or salient characteristics of the neighborhood and offer a brief summary at the end of the neighborhood analysis, so that the client can see the conclusion you have drawn from the data. The suggested format for the neighborhood analysis, which follows the suggested format for the city analysis, will show you how to do this.

The ultimate goal in writing any appraisal report is to present the data in a manner which can be readily understood by your client and which will ultimately lead him to the same value conclusion. Since the material contained in the city data and the neighborhood analysis will be the first items which the client will see in the body of the report, this segment of the report should certainly receive your special attention. I believe that once you have applied the proper techniques for city analysis and neighborhood analysis, and see how they relate to the value of the particular property you are appraising, you will fully appreciate the importance of this element of the appraisal report.

## SUGGESTED FORMAT FOR CITY ANALYSIS

### CITY OF ANYWHERE, U.S.A.

*LOCATION:* Anywhere is the capital city of the State, the County Seat of Montgomery County, and is the State's third largest city. The city has a population of 129,376, with a metropolitan population of 194,522, according to the latest census. The city is located in the central region of the State. Anywhere is 100 miles south of Steel City, the State's largest city, and it is 190 miles north of Water Town, the State's second largest city.

*GOVERNMENT:* The city government is composed of a Mayor and two Commissioners. The quality of government is above average and efforts are continuously being made to improve the service and public relations. The Police Department is slightly above average and is constantly being upgraded. The Fire Department is well equipped and is classed as one of the best in the South. Generally, taxes are low in comparison with other cities. Assessments on property are generally at 15 to 30 percent of market value. The city has a sales tax but does not impose a gross income tax. The State imposes a 4 percent sales tax in addition to the city sales tax.

*TRADE AREA:* Anywhere's trade area includes at least 13 counties with an aggregate population of approximately 580,000 people. Income from this area is derived from manufacturing, agriculture, retail and wholesale distribution, and extensive State and Federal government activities.

*AGRICULTURE:* The diversification of agriculture is apparent around the city. The city not only serves as a market distribution point for cotton and other crops, but is a livestock

| | |
|---|---|
| | center as well. This city is considered the largest livestock market in the South. The agricultural industry contributes greatly to the economic stability of the city. |
| *MANUFACTURING:* | Anywhere has some 305 manufacturing plants, with approximately 8500 employees and an annual payroll estimated at $45,000,000. The industry is diversified, ranging from glass container plants and meat packing plants, to brick and furniture manufacturing. The industrial growth of Anywhere has been at a steady pace rather than occurring as an industrial boom. It appears that the future industrial growth will follow the same pattern. |
| *GENERAL BUSINESS:* | In addition to the above-mentioned two sources of income, the city is the State Capital and has two permanent Air Force installations. The State Veterans Administration is located in the city, as is a large V.A. Hospital which serves the southern part of the State. Anywhere has approximately 1850 motel rooms and over 500 hotel rooms available. The city, although much smaller in population than Water Town, is next to Steel City in wholesale and retail sales volume. |
| *TRANSPORTATION:* | The transportation system is above average. A modern airport offers connections with all major airlines. The city is served by both major bus lines. Twenty trucking firms offer freight hauling services. Rail transportation is above average. An excellent highway system connects with the Midwest and the East Coast. |
| *PURCHASING POWER:* | It is estimated that the Anywhere trade area has a population of approximately 580,000 people. The population and general business conditions are of a very stable nature, being built on a large number of |

white-collar workers, skilled labor, and an integrated and diversified agricultural industry. The large governmental installations contribute greatly to this stability. The willingness of the residents to apply this purchasing power to the purchase of homes is very evident in the active residential sales market here.

| | |
|---|---|
| *EDUCATION:* | The educational system is above average, with some 40 grade schools, four high schools and four colleges. These schools are, on the whole, staffed by competent teachers of above-average ability. There are several excellent private and parochial schools in addition to the public schools. There are two State-owned trade schools and four privately-owned business schools located in Anywhere. |
| *RECREATION:* | Four social clubs, five golf courses, several city-owned community centers, Y.M.C.A., Y.W.C.A., one baseball stadium, one football stadium, the Garrett Coliseum, the new Civic Center, three beautiful, large, artificial lakes within 35 miles, and many hunting opportunities offer excellent and varied recreational facilities. |
| *CULTURAL:* | There is a very active Little Theatre group in the city. This group offers several stage presentations each year. There is also an excellent dinner theater. There is a county library and a city library. The cultural facilities offered would be considered fair for a city of this size. |
| *CLIMATE:* | The general climate is mild. The normal annual rainfall is 52 inches, with an average temperature of 64 degrees. |

## CONCLUSIONS AND SUMMARY

The steady industrial growth, the trend toward a stable agriculture built around beef and dairy cattle, the large number of Federal and State civilian employees, the two military bases with a large number of military personnel, and the employment in wholesale distribution activities and retail sales indicate a bright economic future for the city.

The city offers opportunities for residents to obtain desired education, to enjoy religious, cultural and social activities, and to own homes and businesses with moderate taxes.

The stable income level, the rapid turnover of military personnel and the steady population growth resulting from industrial expansion combine to create a very active market for residential properties. Sellers should encounter little difficulty in finding a willing buyer for their residential properties, particularly for single-family occupancy.

All factors considered, it appears that the city of Anywhere, U.S.A. has an excellent economic future. The one area of uncertainty is the substantial dependency on income from government installations, which are dependent for their existence on the whims of politicians.

**SUGGESTED FORMAT FOR NEIGHBORHOOD ANALYSIS**

**FOREST HILLS, ANYWHERE, U.S.A.**

| | |
|---|---|
| *LOCATION:* | The Forest Hills neighborhood, in which subject property is located, is a wholly postwar subdivision. This subdivision is a part of the natural eastward expansion of the city. The bounds of the Forest Hills neighborhood are considered to be the Atlanta Highway on the north, Harrison Road on the south, Perry Hill Road on the east, and Three Mile Branch on the west. |
| *TOPOGRAPHY:* | Forest Hills, generally speaking, consists of moderately rolling, well-shaped lots. The shade trees are primarily hardwood, although an occasional pine tree may be seen. The name *Forest Hills* was derived from the fact that the neighborhood consists of moderately sloping hills which were practically covered with natural shade trees. |
| *SOIL:* | The soil is dark red, sandy clay which provides an excellent building foundation and affords a good yard and shrubbery soil. No problems in subsoil are encountered. |
| *UTILITIES:* | The entire neighborhood is completely serviced with city sanitary sewerage, city storm sewers, city water, natural gas, telephone and electricity. All of the streets are paved with 3 inches of sheet asphalt (30 feet wide) and have concrete curbs and gutters. The neighborhood is located inside the City Limits, and is therefore inside both police jurisdiction and the fire protected area. |
| *ZONING:* | Subject property is zoned Residential A-1. This zoning generally restricts to single-family residential uses. The only non-single-family residential use permitted in an A-1 neighborhood would be a church or a school. The City of Anywhere has a very strict City Planning Commission which is in charge of all zoning mat- |

ters. It is considered, based on past experience, that there is no chance of property in Residential A-1 neighborhoods being rezoned for other uses. The tight zoning, of course, is conducive to more stable and higher property values.

*RESTRICTION:* Plat restrictions covering the entire neighborhood are standard. They restrict to single-family dwellings with a minimum area of 1000 square feet, exclusive of porches, stoops, outside storage and carports. Sideline restrictions for each lot are 10 feet from each sideline, and the front building line must be at least 35 feet. The remaining restrictions are typical of those required by FHA.

*DEVELOPMENT:* Development of Forest Hills began in about 1952. The development of the neighborhood was controlled with great care by the developers. This controlled development has been most advantageous to property owners, since the price range and type of homes built have been controlled without allowing any wild speculative pattern to develop. This pattern of controlled development has been followed throughout the entire development period and currently the neighborhood is 95 percent developed.

The type of homes built in Forest Hills are generally in the $35,000 to $45,000 price range. The houses are brick veneer, 3 bedroom, and 1 and 2 bath with living areas ranging from 1050 to 1400 square feet.

Architecturally, the houses are all of the same type, that being the so-called postwar "ranch." There are no extreme contemporary or traditional designs. The homes and yards are well maintained and show an above-average degree of pride of ownership.

This neighborhood is considered to be mature and is therefore stable. The future trend should continue along a relatively level line since, due to the controlled development and the surrounding properties, there exist no circumstances that would tend to downgrade the neighborhood, other than age over a period of years.

It is believed that homeowner demand for homes in this neighborhood will continue to be strong due to the homogeneous nature of the homes, the street system layout, and the convenience of educational, religious and shopping facilities.

*SURROUNDING AREA:*

To the north of Forest Hills is the Wareingwood subdivision. This section is composed of homes in the $39,000 to $44,000 price range.

To the south of Forest Hills is the Harrison Road area. This section is made up of homes in the $38,000 to $44,000 price range.

To the east is located Dalraida, composed of homes in the $45,000 to $60,000 price range.

To the west is the Bradley Heights neighborhood. This section is comprised of homes in the $36,000 to $46,000 price range.

As can be seen from the above, the Forest Hills neighborhood is surrounded by excellent adjoining properties which offer protection against adverse influences due to cheap and nonconforming homes.

*POPULATION:*

Socially and economically, the Forest Hills residents are in the same general class. This class could be considered to be the upper middle income bracket (junior executives, high salaried white-collar workers, some professional men and some commissioned-officer military personnel) with annual incomes ranging from $15,000 to $30,000. Typical family size is four people; that is, husband, wife and two children. The neighborhood is predominately owner-occupied, estimated at 97 percent owners with only 3 percent tenants. This high owner occupancy results from the reluctance of the owners to move and rent their homes.

The military personnel in the neighborhood are primarily commissioned officers. Excellent relations exist between civilian and service personnel. Many of the officers are in Montgomery on a three-year tour of duty and, therefore, choose to buy rather than rent homes.

| | |
|---|---|
| *EDUCATIONAL FACILITIES:* | Two grammar schools, two junior high schools and one high school are in the subject or the immediately adjoining neighborhood. The most distant school is the high school, which is ten blocks from the subject property. There is a kindergarten and a parochial school in the neighborhood. A small college is located approximately 4 miles southwest of the neighborhood. All educational facilities are easily accessible. |
| *RECREATIONAL FACILITIES:* | A new branch of the Y.M.C.A. is located in the Eastbrook Shopping Center. This facility is five blocks from the subject property. Goodwyn Community Center is nine blocks from the subject property. |
| *RELIGIOUS FACILITIES:* | There are numerous churches of all major denominations located in or near the neighborhood. Eastern Hills Baptist Church is two blocks from subject and Dalraida Methodist Church is five blocks from subject. All types of religious facilities are easily accessible. |
| *COMMERCIAL FACILITIES:* | Adjoining the neighborhood is a modern shopping center complex. This complex is composed of the Eastbrook Shopping Center and the Forest Hills Shopping Center which, when combined with the various other stores, branch banks, and doctors' offices located between and adjoining them, offer a complete variety of services to the neighborhood. This shopping center complex serves the entire eastern area of the city, furnishing the usual shopping center goods and services, as well |

as offering doctors' offices, insurance company offices, etc.

The downtown area is located approximately 3 miles to the west. The central business district is easily accessible by private automobile or local city bus.

*TRANSPORTATION FACILITIES:* This neighborhood has easy access to Federal highways. The bus stations and railroad depot are located downtown. The city airport is located on the opposite side of the city, approximately 14 miles from the neighborhood. An excellent four-lane highway connects with the airport; therefore, access is not too difficult. Local city buses run through Forest Hills to the downtown area at 15-minute intervals. The fare is 15 cents and the service is average.

**SUMMARY AND CONCLUSIONS**

A careful study of the subject neighborhood indicates that it is one of the better middle-class residential areas of the city. The homes are brick veneer and are in the $35,000 to $45,000 price range. They are primarily owner-occupied and pride in ownership is very evident in the excellent maintenance of houses, lawns and shrubbery. The future of the neighborhood is considered to be hopeful, since there are no detrimental factors due to inharmonious influences.

The social and economic status of the residents are similar. A comparison of income to home values in the area would indicate that these people are somewhat conservative, which should further strengthen the long-range neighborhood prospects. Homes in the neighborhood are readily marketable.

Subject property is a typical improvement for the neighborhood and no adjustment for economic (locational) obsolescence is indicated.

# 7

# How to Prepare a Site Analysis for Residential Property

The preceding two chapters covered both city analysis and neighborhood analysis. The city analysis can be visualized as the outer portion of a target with neighborhood analysis being the next ring immediately inside. We are now at the center of the target, and that is the subject site. The factors which occur at the international, national, city and neighborhood levels certainly have a bearing upon the value of the particular site which is the subject of the appraisal. Furthermore, there are unique characteristics about the site itself which can affect its value in spite of or in addition to factors at the other levels. This chapter is devoted to an analysis of the site itself, and Chapter 8 will discuss an analysis of the improvements which are located on the subject site.

## PURPOSE OF SITE ANALYSIS

In applying the several approaches to estimating value, the site is always appraised alone, without including the improvements. Since this is so, the pertinent and significant characteristics of the site are identified and analyzed so that it can be properly compared with sales of other sites. The value of any particular site is controlled by its acceptability to the demands of potential buyers for a residential home site which meets their particular needs and desires. Section 1108 of the FHA Underwriting Manual makes the following statement regarding site analysis:

> *Analysis of the site is made for the purpose of establishing the basis of comparison in making the estimate of prevailing market price of site and to determine the degree of suitability for the existing or proposed use.*

## SITE VERSUS LAND DEFINED

There is a general tendency to use the words "land" and "site" interchangeably. In residential appraisals, these terms have different meanings, and it is important that this difference be clearly understood. The 1975 edition of *Real Estate Appraisal Terminology,* which was jointly published by the American Institute of Real Estate Appraisers and the Society of Real Estate Appraisers, defines "land" as follows:

> *In a legal sense, the solid part of the surface of the earth, as distinguished from water; any ground, soil or earth whatsoever, regarded as the subject of ownership, and everything annexed to it, whether by nature, such as trees, and everything in or on it, such as minerals and running water, or annexed to it by man, such as buildings and fences. Thus, land can be further defined as consisting of the surface of the earth, supra-surface air, and sub-surface area.*

The same book defines "site" as follows:

> *A parcel of land which is improved to the extent that it is ready for use for the purpose for which it is intended. This means that the site is cleared, graded, landscaped, and has necessary improvements for drainage, water service, sewer service, electric service, gas service, access by streets and/or alleys and sidewalks when and if appropriate. The residential site is a parcel or lot of land which has the necessary improvements to make it immediately useable for residential purposes in terms of the standard of the market and the neighborhood in which it is located and which is in accordance with the demands of prospective investors.*

## HOW SITE VALUE CHANGES OCCUR

Any man-made improvements which have been erected on a site are subject to depreciation. The site itself is non-depreciable and this is one of the major reasons for requiring a separate analysis in evaluation. This does not mean that a site cannot lose value or increase in value with the passage of time. It does mean that the changes in value are not systematic to the extent that they are measurable as an element of the passage of time, and are not predictable to the extent that the loss in value may be predictable for man-made improvements.

When appraising a residential site, one must realize that the amenities derived from ownership of the property are a substitute for the income stream on an income-producing property. Amenities consist of the satisfactions and attractions associated with the ownership of a residential lot for owner-occupancy purposes. In appraising residential properties, you are dealing with the amenities of ownership rather than a stream of income, and it is therefore essential that you analyze the positive or negative features which would add to or detract from the sum total of the amenities which would be demanded by a potential investor in the site.

You should remember that the site is always valued in terms of its highest and best use; that is to say, it is valued as if it were vacant and available to be put to its highest and best use as of the date of the appraisal. This matter has been discussed at some length in Chapter 4, and will not be repeated in this chapter other than to offer the reminder that the highest and best use of the site is defined as "that reasonable and probable use which is most likely to produce the highest present worth, or will support the highest present value, of the site as of the date of the appraisal."

## REASONS FOR SEPARATE VALUATION OF THE RESIDENTIAL SITE

There are several reasons for separate valuation of the site. In some instances, you are dealing with a vacant site only, and under such circumstances you would be concerned only with the site. In other instances, particularly in applying the cost approach, it is essential to value the site separately so that its value may be added to the value contribution of the improvements to arrive at the total value indication by the cost approach. In appraising income-producing property, it is essential that the site be valued separately so that provision for depreciation or recapture of the investment will only apply to those man-made assets which do depreciate. There are also instances in which it is necessary to separately value the site for adjustment purposes in the sales comparison approach, due to the fact that there may be substantial variation in the value contribution of one site versus another when comparing sales of improved property. In almost every case, the site must be valued separately for ad valorem tax purposes and for income tax purposes if depreciation is involved. The income tax aspects of valuing the site separately become very important when capital gains taxation is involved. In condemnation proceedings, it is usually required by the courts that the land and the improvements which are involved in the condemnation be valued separately. When the improvements are destroyed or partially destroyed by fire or some other catastrophe, it is often necessary to separately value the land so that the value contribution of the remaining improvements can be determined to provide the owner of the insurance policy with proper compensation.

## COLLECTING RESIDENTIAL SITE INFORMATION

You must be able to identify and analyze the operation of the market factors that enter into the determination of the value of any particular site. You must be able to identify the relative importance of the various features of a site and how they apply to value estimation in the particular market in which you are appraising. This requirement should deal within the particular market or sub-market in which your property is located, eliminating the appraiser's alternative of ranging into non-comparable areas of the city in attempting to compare sites by a sales comparison approach. You must be able to understand the importance and pertinence of the various factors which meet the standards of acceptability and desirability on the part of those who are market participants. Your goal must be to identify these standards and relate them to the market as it exists at the time of the appraisal. You will find that it changes substantially with the passage of time. A suggested format for site analysis will be found at the end of this chapter, where the critical features which affect the value of a residential site are discussed at length.

It has been my experience, for example, that the movement away from the long, rambling, ranch-style home to the split-level or multistory residential structure has tended to require lots with less frontage than has been customary in the past. Another major change is that people are no longer willing to pay a premium in most areas for a corner lot. This is because there is no rear yard, less privacy and the owner may be faced with a paving assessment on two streets. An additional problem with a corner lot is that, when automobiles turn the corner at night, their headlights flash across the entire property. An advantage to a corner lot is the ease of automobile access from the side street (which may be less traveled) into a garage or carport located at the rear of the residence. An analysis of sales of corner lots versus sales of interior lots in the subject area will disclose whether the market reflects a premium for corner locations. If analysis shows such a premium, you must, of course, recognize it regardless of your personal likes or dislikes.

## PHYSICAL FACTORS IN RESIDENTIAL SITE ANALYSIS

There are several physical factors about any particular site which will directly affect its value. When you appraise a number of residential properties, you will observe certain physical features which you will make note of on your field forms. Some of the physical features of a site are quantitative in nature and will vary from one site to another, while other characteristics are attributes—that is, advantages or disadvantages from an amenity standpoint—and these are either present or absent and are not quantitative in nature. One physical factor which should be immediately clear to you is that the subject site is immobile and therefore must be analyzed in its fixed location subject to all the positive and negative features which may be present in the area.

## QUANTITATIVE FEATURES OF A RESIDENTIAL SITE

One of the quantitative features of a site is its size, with several interrelated units of measurement, such as front feet, square feet and acres or fractions thereof. In most areas, the zoning ordinance prescribes a minimum number of square feet which a site must possess. These ordinances also specify the minimum frontage, width and setback requirements to the building line. The shape of the lot is also significant because poorly-shaped lots tend to limit the effective area. The effective area is that area within which building construction may take place on any particular lot. You will occasionally encounter a lot with unusual depth or frontage, and then the problem arises as to what value is added by this excess land. You may find that the excess land is of little additional value and may even be a liability because it is a problem to keep properly mowed and landscaped. The point to be remembered here is that no added value is attributed to excess land unless sales of such lots within the area indicate that buyers are willing to pay for this added land area.

## TOPOGRAPHIC FEATURES OF A RESIDENTIAL SITE

Certain topographic features of a lot may be either positive or negative influences on value. Some of these features are discussed in the suggested format for site analysis at the end of this chapter. Poor topographic features can have a definite effect on the cost of making the lot useable for its intended development. In some areas, there is a demand for basement or split-level housing. Under these circumstances, a lot with an adequate but not excess slope is desirable. Whether a slope is desirable or undesirable will depend on the desires of the market participants in your area. Another topographic feature which may be a negative factor is an extremely flat lot which will not provide for adequate drainage. Such lots require substantial filling and possibly the installation of sub-surface drain tile to remove unwanted water accumulation. The opposite extreme of this is an excessively sloping lot where water runoff creates erosion on the site.

## SOIL CHARACTERISTICS OF A RESIDENTIAL SITE

Certain sections of the subject city may be extremely well adapted to landscaping without the necessity of bringing in additional topsoil. Furthermore, the load-bearing capabilities of some soils are much better than those of others. In some cities the soil is extremely elastic, and the added cost of providing exceptionally heavy foundations to prevent cracking of walls and ceilings makes these lots much less desirable. In addition, some areas may have soil with extremely poor water absorption capabilities. This type of soil could make it impossible to install private septic tank systems, thus eliminating the land from the residential use category. Some types of soil are much more difficult to use in constructing a house with a basement. It should be remembered that the soil and subsoil conditions within a particular area can have a very strong effect on the marketability and, thus, the value of any particular lot. Once you have made a number of appraisals within a city, you will become generally familiar with soil and subsoil conditions, and your understanding of this can be further enhanced by conversations with residents of the area and landscaping specialists who work there.

## AVAILABILITY, ADEQUACY AND COST OF UTILITIES

Another feature of a site which certainly demands your careful attention is the availability, relative cost and adequacy of utilities. You should know whether the utilities are public or private and, if private wells or septic tanks are required, you must know something about the cost of making these items available. The availability of services, such as electricity, gas and telephone, is extremely important. The type of sewerage disposal and storm and surface water disposal is very important. I know of one area in which the surface water disposal is so poor that, in periods of heavy rainfall, the residences are subject to possible flooding. This obviously has an adverse effect (25 to 35 percent) on the improved properties within the neighborhood and on the saleability of the undeveloped lots.

## ANALYSIS OF RESIDENTIAL SITE IMPROVEMENTS

If you are appraising an improved property in a developed neighborhood, it is essential that you pay particular attention to the site improvements. These site improvements, such as streets, walks, driveways, walls and fencing, should be in place and in excellent condition. If you are dealing with an improved property, the landscaping, including lawn and shrubbery, should be attractive and well maintained. If you are appraising a site in an area in which additional properties are either under construction or are relatively new, then the criteria which would apply to streets, walks and driveways would be the same as for an established area. The walls, fencing, lawns and landscaping would not yet be completed in such an area, and the criteria here are whether the soil is adaptable to good lawns and landscaping, and whether the topography allows items such as walls and fencing to be readily constructed.

## ANALYSIS OF POSSIBLE HAZARDS AND NUISANCES

The site should be relatively free of hazards and nuisances (such as noise, odor and traffic congestion), favorably positioned with respect to prevailing winds and sun, and the properties should be free from nuisances created by inharmonious uses such as night clubs, garages, service stations and other traffic-generating or noise-creating activities. You should remember that, while proximity to schools is an advantage, there is a definite disadvantage in being immediately adjacent to a school.

## ECONOMIC FACTORS IN RESIDENTIAL SITE ANALYSIS

While there are fewer economic factors specifically related to site analysis, there are some which are significant. Any economic factor which is measurable in dollars and cents, and which exerts either a positive or negative influence on the value of a site, should be given your careful consideration. These economic factors include the prices of competing sites which would tend to set the limit applying to the subject site. Additional economic factors in this category are the tax burden for the subject site as compared to other competing areas, the cost and availability of utilities, the cost and availability of services such as garbage pickup, and the quality of police and fire protection. If there is a specific charge for garbage pickup, this should be noted. If there are unusual charges for sewerage or water connection, these should also be noted, as they could have a definite effect on the value of the subject site when compared with other competing areas.

## UNITS OF COMPARISON IN RESIDENTIAL SITE ANALYSIS

Certain units of comparison apply to site analysis. These are economic factors since they are stated in dollars per front foot, square foot, lot, acre, room or square foot of building area. In appraising residential sites, the most frequently used unit of comparison is price per front foot. Price per square foot is used quite frequently in commercial appraisals and for multi-family sites. Price per lot is used in many areas for residential sites. Price per acre tends to apply to industrial sites, while price per room and price per square foot of building area are used frequently in multi-family analyses. Price per room and price per square foot are based on the number of these units which the land will permit to be constructed under building ordinances or building codes in the area. It is my advice that the units of comparison for land value per room permitted, or land value per square foot of building area permitted, should not be used if the local market conditions will permit comparison using other units.

## LOCATIONAL FACTORS IN RESIDENTIAL SITE ANALYSIS

There is nothing more important to the value of any site than its location. This location should always be analyzed in terms of how it relates to the surrounding sites which would be comparable to it. The size, shape and other physical characteristics of the site should generally conform with the other sites in the area and to the generally prevailing land use patterns. The site should be well located for easy access to desired facilities such as schools, churches, shopping centers, places of employment and recreation facilities. The site should be near enough to all of the desired facilities to permit quick and easy access with little travel cost involved, but it should not be close enough so that these establishments create a nuisance or a hazard. There should be an excellent street pattern to permit easy vehicular access to the subject site. Positioning of the site should be such that owners can make maximum use of morning and afternoon sun, and the site should be properly situated to take advantage of the prevailing winds in the area. These items are discussed at some length in the suggested format for site analysis at the end of this chapter.

## LEGAL-GOVERNMENTAL FACTORS IN RESIDENTIAL SITE ANALYSIS

There are several legal factors which require your attention. Your client should furnish a current legal description of the subject site. This legal description would give you title information, such as the interest held by the current owner, the history of ownership obtained from an abstract, deed restrictions and easements, and any outstanding liens and claims. One factor which can be a surprise to the purchaser of a site is a substantial outstanding claim for a paving assessment. Sometimes certain easements go with the site and are advantageous to it, while in other situations an easement permitting some other party access across the subject site can create a negative factor.

Some of the governmental factors which are always present are items such as zoning, building codes, permitted and prohibited uses under the present zoning, setback requirements, city taxation and assessment policies, available municipal services, and the quantity, quality and reliability of these services. One particular situation which requires your careful attention has to do with whether the present use of the site is nonconforming or whether the site is of such size and shape that the present improvements could not be replaced if they were destroyed. You should be aware of how long the nonconforming use has existed, and the policy of the local government officials regarding continuation of such uses, or policy regarding restoration of the improvements if they are destroyed or in the event that the present use ceases. If it is the policy of the city not to permit replacement of improvements once they are destroyed, then it is possible that your site may become simply a remnant parcel, which may be sold only to the adjoining property owner, and under these circumstances the value of the site will be very low indeed.

## AMENITY FACTORS IN RESIDENTIAL SITE ANALYSIS

In the preceding sections of this chapter, we have discussed some of the various factors which must be considered in site analysis. There is no doubt that all of these factors are important; however, there is one essential ingredient which we have not yet covered. Regardless of how the site may meet all of the previously discussed criteria, the key aspect is that a prospective buyer of a lot seeks to derive personal satisfaction from being in a particular location. The amenities of a site are the benefits and attractive features which accrue to the parcel in its location. The general pride of ownership within the neighborhood, and the ability of the site to provide quiet enjoyment of the satisfactions of home ownership, are very important. A site can be the beneficiary of positive amenity factors or the innocent (but incurable) victim of negative factors.

You must ascertain the desires, tastes and standards of the typical buyers who are participants in the market in the subject area as of the date of the appraisal. The value of a site depends on its ability to provide the required amenities for that type of property.

## ESSENTIAL ELEMENTS TO CONSIDER IN RESIDENTIAL SITE ANALYSIS

The key to any successful appraisal practice is to carefully avoid work habits which waste time. In inspecting a site prior to the preparation of your site analysis, it is suggested that a checklist be used to avoid overlooking some important item. A sample of such a checklist may be found at the end of this chapter, along with the suggested format for site analysis. The checklist should provide for consideration of all essential factors and notation about whether or not certain factors are present. The use of a checklist for inspection purposes will provide you with a list of the things you have observed and will certainly cover all of the things which a typical investor would observe if he were inspecting the site prior to making a decision to purchase.

The suggested checklist provides space for showing square foot area, frontage, width, dimensions and shape of the lot, as well as the portion of the lot which is covered with improvements if you are appraising an improved property. There should certainly be adequate space provided on the checklist for noting the topography, soil and subsoil conditions, site improvements, landscaping and plantings, unusual positive or negative site characteristics, types of streets and whether they are surfaced or not, utilities, essential services such as fire protection, street lighting, waste removal, the type and ease of access, location and setting of the site, its orientation within the neighborhood, and any nuisances or hazards which may be present.

## USES OF RESIDENTIAL SITE ANALYSIS

There are several ways in which a site analysis is utilized in making an appraisal. One of the most important uses for a site analysis is as an aid in estimating the highest and best use of the site. The data gathered in the process of inspecting the site, plus additional off-site data which you will have obtained, will lead you to a conclusion about the highest and best use. If there is any doubt whatever about the highest and best use of the site, or if there is some probability of a change in use to something other than that which is presently prevailing, it will be necessary to investigate further. Under normal circumstances, the data you have gathered during your site inspection will be adequate, when combined with an analysis of the local zoning ordinances and the permitted uses thereunder, to enable you to estimate highest and best use. The analysis for highest and best use purposes should accomplish several goals. These goals include making a determination about the permitted use of the site, its suitability for its present or proposed use, any unusual physical characteristics, any unusual economic characteristics of the site and the market within which it is located, and the type of use which the current buyer in the market would have in mind when submitting a proposal to purchase the site.

An additional use of a good site analysis is to determine whether there is locational obsolescence present. The data gathered here and the comparison with competing sites will enable you to determine if there is something unusual about this location which would have a negative effect on its value.

There is no doubt that a properly prepared site analysis will enable you to determine if the site is readily marketable based on your analysis of the criteria which would be considered by a typical buyer.

It should be obvious that the ultimate purpose for site analysis is to form the basis for the site valuation. After you have gathered all of the necessary data and have carefully analyzed it concerning highest and best use, you should then have the basic data available to use in estimating the value of the site.

## CHAPTER SUMMARY

There are two types of units of comparison which are used in estimating site value. The first type of units of comparison are the physical units, which are actual items of measurement such as square foot, front foot, lot or acre. The other type of units of comparison are called use intensity units or economic units, and these include land value per square foot of building area, land value per room or land value per apartment unit. It is suggested here that, wherever possible, the physical units of comparison be used in estimating site value.

Subsequent chapters will show actual valuation techniques for estimating site value. The data which you have gathered in the process of making the site analysis will allow you to make a well-supported land value estimate.

**SUGGESTED FORMAT FOR SITE ANALYSIS**

| | |
|---|---|
| *LOCATION:* | Subject property is located on the northwest corner of Greenridge Road and Willow Lane Road in the Forest Hills subdivision. |
| *SIZE AND SHAPE:* | This property fronts 101 feet on Greenridge Road and has 150 feet depth on Willow Lane Road. The lot is rectangular in shape and has a total land area of 15,150 square feet. |
| *TOPOGRAPHY:* | Subject site is virtually level, having just enough slope to the rear for drainage. The front of the lot is at street level. Excellent drainage is afforded by the slope of the lot and no drainage problems are incurred. |
| *SOIL AND SUBSOIL:* | The soil is dark red, sandy clay which is excellent for shrubbery, trees, grass and any other type of vegetation. The subsoil is a very hard, red clay which serves as an excellent base for foundations, both poured concrete slab and conventional (poured footings with brick pillars). No soil or subsoil problems are present in the subject site. |
| *UTILITIES:* | City sanitary sewers, city storm sewers, city water, natural gas, electricity and telephone service are available and are fully utilized by subject property. The street is 30 feet wide and has 3 inches of sheet asphalt paving with concrete curb and gutter. There are no sidewalks anywhere in the neighborhood. The lot is located inside the City Limits and is therefore inside police jurisdiction and the fire protected area.<br><br>The site is further serviced by door mail delivery and city garbage collection at no charge. Street lights are furnished and maintained by the City and are spaced at regular intervals along the street. |
| *RESTRICTIONS:* | Restrictions applicable to this site are the same as are found throughout the neighborhood and have been described in the neighborhood analysis. |

| | |
|---|---|
| *ZONING:* | The zoning of this site is Residential A-1, as is the entire neighborhood. The A-1 zone has been described in the neighborhood analysis. |
| *LANDSCAPING:* | The lot is well covered with a good sod of Bermuda grass. There are two large pine trees, three medium-size pine trees, one massive oak tree and one large mimosa tree, providing the lot with excellent shade. There are many smaller trees and shrubs, as well as attractive flowers. The landscaping is slightly above average for the neighborhood. |
| *LOT IN RELATION TO NEIGHBORHOOD:* | The lot conforms to other corner lots in the neighborhood in both size and topography. The typical corner lot is 100 feet by 150 feet. The typical inside lot is 80 feet by 150 feet. This site fits into its surroundings nicely since the area immediately surrounding it conforms both in lot size and type of improvements.<br><br>No particular advantages or detriments were discovered in comparing this lot with others in the neighborhood or with recent lot sales. It can therefore be concluded that this is a typical lot in the Forest Hills area. |
| *HIGHEST AND BEST USE:* | The highest and best use for this site is for a single-family owner-occupied dwelling in the $18,000 to $25,000 price range. The highest and best use would therefore be the present use, which is typical of the neighborhood.<br><br>This conclusion is further supported by the restrictions (single-family homes only) and the Residential A-1 zoning (single-family homes only) of the neighborhood as single-family dwelling in the above-mentioned price range. |

**SITE INSPECTION CHECKLIST**

| | |
|---|---|
| *OWNER OF SITE:* | ____________________ |
| *SITE LOCATION:* | ____________________ |
| *LEGAL DESCRIPTION:* | Block ______ Lot ______ In ______ Subdivision or Brief Legal Description __ ____________________ |
| *LOT SIZE:* | __________ No. Sq. Ft. ______ |
| *SHAPE:* | __________ Problems (If any) Related to Shape __________ |
| *TOPOGRAPHY:* | __________ Problems (If any) Related to Topography __________ |
| *UTILITIES:* | __________ Problems (If any) Related to Utilities __________ |
| *SOIL AND SUBSOIL:* | __________ Problems (If any) Related to Soil and/or Subsoil __________ |
| *LANDSCAPING:* | __________ Comments Related to Landscaping __________ |
| *SITE IMPROVEMENTS:* | (List by Type) __________ Comments Related to Site Improvements __________ |
| *ACCESS:* | __________ Problems Related to Access __________ |
| *STREET:* | __________ Comments Related to Street __________ |
| *CURB AND SIDEWALKS:* | __________ Comments Related to Curb and Sidewalks __________ |
| *STORM SEWERS:* | __________ Comment If Inadequate or Non-Existent ______ |
| *STREET LIGHTING:* | __________ Comment If Inadequate or Non-Existent ______ |
| *CITY SERVICES:* | __________ Comment If All Normal City Services Not Available |
| *ZONING:* | __________ Comment If Nonconforming __________ |

| | |
|---|---|
| *PRESENT SITE USE:* | ______________ Comment if Nonconforming with Zoning or Other Uses in Area ______________ |
| *HIGHEST AND BEST USE:* | ______________ Comment if Different from Present Use and/or with Present Zoning ______________ |
| *DATE INSPECTED:* | ______________ |
| *INSPECTOR'S NAME:* | ______________ |
| *PERSON INTERVIEWED:* | ______________ Comment as to Status of Person, if Not Owner ______________ |

# 8

# How to Prepare an Improvement Analysis for Residential Property

This chapter is devoted to an analysis of man-made improvements which are located on a particular residential site. Every appraisal of an improved parcel must present a thorough and detailed analysis of the structures or other improvements located on the site. This chapter will show you how to prepare such an analysis. These improvements must be accurately identified and all pertinent features of the structure, as well as site improvements, should be carefully analyzed and included in the appraisal report. A properly prepared improvement analysis will identify and analyze the physical attributes of this important segment of the value of any improved residential property.

## PURPOSE OF RESIDENTIAL IMPROVEMENT ANALYSIS AND HOW IT IS UTILIZED

In the appraisal of any improved residential property, the improvement analysis is absolutely essential to the application of all three approaches to value. Since every appraisal requires the consideration of the applicability of each of the three approaches to value, it naturally follows that, if any valuation approach is applicable, the improvement analysis is likewise applicable to the same extent.

In the application of the cost approach, the information obtained while inspecting the improvements and while making the improvement analysis enables you to estimate the reproduction cost of the improvements. If you are not completely familiar with the type, size and quality of the improvements, you will not be able to arrive at a meaningful estimate of their reproduction cost. The improvement analysis is also the basis for estimating accrued depreciation and obsolescence. Factors observed during inspection of the improvements and preparation of the improvement analysis will aid you in determining the amount of physical deterioration which may be present. It will also be possible for you to determine if the structure is functionally adequate, so that you may note the presence or absence of functional obsolescence and the effect that this may have on the value of the structure. One type of obsolescence is locational obsolescence, which is caused by factors outside the property itself. Here, the improvement analysis will be helpful only to the extent that it would measure whether or not the structure is totally out of context with what is expected within that particular area.

One of the most important approaches to estimating the value of residential properties is the direct sales comparison approach. This approach requires you to compare the subject property with sales of similar residential structures. No two structures are identical, so it is necessary to identify, measure, describe and analyze pertinent features of the subject structure, so that it can become the standard of comparison with other properties which have sold. Unless you can identify pertinent features of the subject property and compare it with sale properties which either have these same features or have certain features missing, then you cannot make an adequate estimate of what the sale properties would have sold for if they were identical to the subject. Subsequent chapters will cover the meaningful structural features which should be identified and compared, and will explain how to measure the value contribution of these particular features.

In appraising residential property, the substitute for the normal income approach is called the gross rent multiplier approach. The improvement analysis is an important part of the gross rent multiplier approach in that it identifies specific features of the subject property which make it desirable or, on the other hand, pinpoints areas where the property is lacking in desirability for rental purposes. This analysis can also be applied to comparable rented properties to determine the rent effect which the presence or absence of certain features have on a property, allowing you to estimate the market rental for your property and the proper gross rent multiplier, both of which are essential in this approach to value.

## RESIDENTIAL IMPROVEMENTS DEFINED

The improvements involved in a residential improvement analysis are defined as structures or other man-made improvements which are permanently affixed to a site. In appraising residential property, the improvements include the major residential structure and any attached, semi-attached or detached permanent structures. The non-residential structures include garages or storage buildings if they are permanently attached to the site. Other residential site improvements to be included in the analysis are items such as walks, drives, fences, patios and landscaping. Off-site improvements, such as curbs, gutters, streets, sidewalks and street lighting, are attributes of the site and are not improvements of the type with which we are concerned in improvement analysis.

## UNDERSTANDING THE FUNDAMENTALS OF RESIDENTIAL IMPROVEMENT ANALYSIS

During the inspection of a residential structure, you will observe and note its physical characteristics. A checklist, like the one at the end of this chapter, shows those physical items which will be noted while inspecting the property. There is no doubt that the physical characteristics are very important; however, you should always remember that, regardless of the physical characteristics of a structure, the final determining factor is its acceptability in the market. In dealing with a property where the standards are set by the buyers who are market participants, your particular likes and dislikes are not as important as whether or not the property meets the standards required by the typical buyer. You should ascertain current standards of acceptability which are applicable in the particular area in which you are doing the appraisal. The subject property must be acceptable to the buyers, and to the people who are lending mortgage funds, and it must also meet the local building codes, housing codes and zoning regulations.

## EIGHT KEY FACTORS IN RESIDENTIAL IMPROVEMENT ANALYSIS

The residential structure should be rated with respect to the following eight key factors:

1. Overall structural quality.
2. Resistance to the elements.
3. Overall condition.
4. The suitability, type, age and condition of any built-in or other mechanical equipment.

5. Natural light and ventilation.
6. Overall livability as a residential structure.
7. Visual appeal of the property.
8. Conformity.

The property should conform in all respects to other properties within the neighborhood without giving the appearance of being an identical carbon copy of other structures. It should have some character of its own and yet conform to the generally accepted type, size and quality of structure in its neighborhood.

There are two essential types of residential improvement data which must be gathered and analyzed. The first describes the overall physical condition of the structure. The second type deals with its functional adequacy.

## UNDERSTANDING AND OBTAINING DATA RELATIVE TO PHYSICAL CONDITION OF RESIDENTIAL IMPROVEMENTS

Most of the elements relating to the physical condition of a structure can be determined while making a physical inspection, provided that you follow the items which are shown in the checklist at the end of this chapter. Observations of physical condition include both the structural components and the fixtures and equipment located within the structure. The thing which should be remembered here is that physical condition influences the usefulness of the structure and certainly influences its marketability. When you are appraising a residential structure, you will usually observe certain items which require immediate attention. These items will be observed and classified by the standard of whether the typical purchaser would consider this repair necessary and require it to be done immediately. These items include replacement of broken windows, replacement of screens or other worn-out items which should be immediately replaced to protect, preserve or enhance the marketability of the property. These items form the basis for what is identified as curable physical deterioration, and will be a subject for detailed treatment in Chapter 11.

You will also note certain short-lived items such as water heaters and heating and air-conditioning equipment, which will not last the entire life of the structure and will require replacement within the near future. The age, condition and adequacy of these items will form the basis for an estimate of physical deterioration, which may be either deferred or incurable. This type of depreciation will also be explained in detail in Chapter 11.

Several evidences of physical condition which should be carefully observed are:

1. Settling or cracks in the walls or foundations.
2. Moisture accumulation in the basement or garage.
3. Water damage to ceilings or walls and roof leakage.

This type of physical problem forms the basis for estimating incurable physical deterioration, and this item will be covered in substantial detail in Chapter 11.

One important item is the quality of repairs which may have already been made to the structure, and whether or not these repairs were in keeping with the general quality of the structure itself. I have observed situations in which the owner attempted to perform certain repairs himself, and the net result is that the work was so amateurish that it would have been better if it had never been done. If you observe a situation where the repairs are so poorly done that they are a negative factor, they must be recognized and their correction provided for.

An additional physical feature which should be noted while making the inspection is the type and quality of construction. The quality of the material and the workmanship with which it is applied will be very important in estimating the reproduction cost new of the structure in the cost approach, and in making comparisons in the direct sales comparison approach and the gross rent multiplier approach.

## FUNCTIONAL FEATURES OF A STRUCTURE

The data gathered while inspecting the property will assist you in determining the functional adequacy or inadequacy of a particular structure. The functionally adequate structure will certainly have greater marketability than a structure which lacks certain features. The structure which is functionally inadequate, or which has super-adequacies, will suffer in its marketability. This determination of functional adequacy or super-adequacy will form the basis for estimating functional obsolescence in the cost approach.

## HOW TO IDENTIFY FUNCTIONAL DEFICIENCIES IN A RESIDENTIAL STRUCTURE

Some functional deficiencies which can be readily recognized arise from improper room layout or traffic pattern, inadequate room size, inadequate built-in equipment or inadequate number and type of baths. These items are functional inadequacies and are not as readily recognizable as problems such as insufficient electrical service, heating systems, water supply, insulation, closet space and inadequate air-conditioning in areas in which sufficient cooling capacity is required. Furthermore, the structure which is functionally inadequate fails to provide amenities which are currently in demand in the market, and particularly so in the immediate vicinity. Some examples of this would be houses which do not provide a family recreation room in areas where this is the standard, houses which do not provide central air-conditioning in areas where this is required, and houses which do not provide adequate utility rooms. Another type of functional inadequacy is a structure which is much smaller in size than is typical in the neighborhood. This type of structure will certainly encounter some market resistance and will suffer functional obsolescence. I know of one situation in which an owner had a large custom-designed home built at a cost of $150,000 in an area in which the typical home was built from stock plans and cost about $60,000. The owner was fortunate to eventually sell his $150,000 home for $100,000.

## HOW TO IDENTIFY FUNCTIONAL SUPER-ADEQUACIES IN A RESIDENTIAL STRUCTURE

You will encounter many structures in which there are functional super-adequacies. These are defined as elements which are excessive in quality or capacity for the type of structure when compared with competing properties in the local market. One obvious type of super-adequacy would be a five bedroom house containing over 4000 square feet in an area in which the three bedroom, 2500 square foot house is standard. You will also encounter structures for which the owner has purchased extremely expensive items such as chandeliers and built-in equipment far above the standard required in the neighborhood. Such super-adequacies will not be fully compensated for in the market and must be recognized in the appraisal. You may also encounter situations in which the owner has employed artists to do murals or other types of work to suit his own desires, while the acceptability of this by the general market may be very limited.

For example, one owner had an entire dining room wall covered with a mural of which he was very proud. The owner felt that this mural contributed substantial value to the structure when, in fact, it was so limited in acceptability that it added very little to the value of the structure. To many prospective purchasers, the mural was a negative factor, and their consideration was the cost of hiring a painter and buying a bucket of paint to cover what, to them, was a monstrosity rather than an asset!

Other examples of super-adequacies include items such as expensive gardens or other landscaping features which were designed to suit the whims of a particular owner. While he may feel that this item will add substantial value, it may in fact contribute little or no value. The test here is whether or not this item will be accepted by the market participants, and whether or not they are willing to pay for having this particular item in place. Occasionally, structures will have a solid brick or block wall, or perhaps an extremely heavy foundation or a slate or clay tile roof. While the owner may feel that this adds substantial value, it is usually true that very little added value is involved. This excess investment, which is not recognized by the market participants, is considered to be functional obsolescence caused by super-adequacy in the structure.

## ANALYSIS OF IMPROVEMENT DATA IN RESIDENTIAL APPRAISING

Before proceeding to a discussion of the analysis of improvement data which you may obtain, it is important that three terms be discussed and understood: *economic life, remaining economic life* and *effective age*. Your inspection of the improvements and the subsequent analysis of the data you have obtained will enable you to determine the economic life, remaining economic life and effective age of the improvements.

The *economic life* of an improvement is the period of years over which it may reasonably be expected to provide a competitive net return to the owner. This is further described as the time period over which the structure will provide the services and amenities consistent with competitive costs of other structures. Many well-built and well-maintained residential structures would physically stand for 200 years, but changes in technology and/or buyers' tastes could make the structure totally obsolete, and thus worth less, in 40 years. The economic life of that structure would then be 40 years.

The *remaining economic life* is the number of years during which the structure will most likely continue to provide the services for which it was intended. As of the date of the appraisal, the structure will obviously have a certain remaining time period beyond which it will no longer be economically justified to continue in use. This remaining economic life is the time period over which the improvements will be depreciated in the cost approach as of the date of the appraisal. For example, if the economic life of a residential structure is 40 years and it is 50 percent depreciated as of the appraisal date, then the remaining economic life is 20 years.

The *effective age* of a structure is the difference between the normal economic life and the estimated remaining economic life, based on observed condition and quality as of the date of the appraisal. It should be remembered that effective age may be greater or less than the actual or chronological age. The effective age is always used as the measure of the portion of the structural components which have expired as of the date of the appraisal. You will find quite often that exceptionally good maintenance of a structure will reduce its effective age to much less than the number of actual years which have expired since construction. The effective age of the structure referred to above would be 20 years (40 years economic life minus 20 years remaining economic life).

You should always keep in mind that the economic life, effective age and remaining economic life are to a great extent dependent upon the standards set by the participants in the local market. These items also depend to a lesser extent on the physical condition of the property as observed while inspecting the improvements.

## UNDERSTANDING QUALITY ASPECTS FOR ESTIMATING RESIDENTIAL REPRODUCTION COST

Certain aspects of structural quality will definitely affect the estimate of reproduction cost. The structures should show evidence of good architectural design that creates a pleasing appearance, both externally and internally, and is in keeping with the prevailing architecture within the immediate area. Architectural design should not be identical with that of other structures in the area, but it certainly should not clash with its environment. The key ingredients of good architecture and of the cost elements of a structure include:

1. The proper use of good materials.
2. Good room size and proportions within the structure.
3. Proper provision and placement of windows.
4. Proper arrangement of the plumbing facilities and selection of fixtures of good quality.
5. The selection and proper installation of good quality built-in equipment.

The structure which is designed properly, constructed of good material and evidences good workmanship is definitely of higher quality and, thus, reproduction cost. You will encounter exotic or unusual construction materials which will add a great deal of cost to a structure but will add little to its marketability. After having compared a few of these unusual structures and their sales prices with the selling prices of normal structures, you will be able to readily identify those which will be difficult to sell.

## IDENTIFYING CONDITION ASPECTS OF ESTIMATING PHYSICAL DETERIORATION OF RESIDENTIAL STRUCTURES

There is no doubt that the physical condition of a structure will directly affect its marketability. Some of the aspects of physical condition which you will observe will be cosmetic in nature and readily curable. These are items such as:

1. Painting the exterior trim.
2. Replacing broken glass.
3. Replacing missing screens.
4. Replacing a worn-out roof.
5. Redecoration of the interior of the structure.

This type of repair is usually necessary prior to marketing the property, and it is usually measured by the cost to correct the particular item. You will very likely encounter structures which have had inadequate maintenance, and the effective age of this type of structure will usually be greater than its chronological age. Inadequate maintenance is indicated by rotted wood on the exterior of the structure due to failure to apply paint when needed; rotted window frames, door frames and doors due to failure on the part of the owner to paint or replace these items; roof leaks which have damaged the ceilings, walls and occasionally the floors; and a broken floor due to water seepage or carelessness on the part of the owner. The suggested checklist at the end of this chapter provides space for noting the items which must be given your careful attention in estimating physical deterioration. The proper classification of the various types of physical deterioration and the method of measuring their effect on the value of the structure will be covered in the depreciation section which follows later in this book. I urge you, at this point, to be extremely careful in inspecting both the interior and exterior of any structure you are appraising. In certain cases, it is difficult to obtain admission to the structure to make a thorough interior physical inspection. Make every effort to obtain entry in order to make careful interior inspection, and if you are unable to do so, it should be carefully stated in the appraisal report that the appraisal was made without benefit of an interior inspection and, furthermore, that you do not accept responsibility for items which you were unable to observe in the interior of the structure. If you are uncertain about some important interior features, you may wish to decline the assignment.

While making exterior inspections, you should pay particular attention to whether there is evidence of termite or water damage to the structure, or any broken foundations or wall cracking caused by settlement of the structure.

## OBSERVING AND ANALYZING EFFICIENCY OF DESIGN FOR ESTIMATING FUNCTIONAL OBSOLESCENCE

In appraising residential structures, there often are functional problems which may create market resistance in the sale of a structure. Some very obvious items are architectural matters such as the proper placing of the structure on the site, whether the particular architectural type is in conformity with others in the neighborhood, and whether the structure presents a generally pleasing exterior appearance. There are certain items about the floor plan of a house which are essential to its marketability. The rooms should be adequate in size and properly located within the structure. One of the rooms may be nothing more than a hall for access to the other rooms, leaving little privacy within that particular room. Carports may have been converted into dens or family rooms, usually eliminating the use of one of the walls in the living room and perhaps making the living room nothing more than a hall for access to the den or family room. Occasionally, the traffic pattern of a house will be unusually poor; for example, the main entrance to the house may not have a foyer, and it is necessary to enter directly into the living room before proceeding to the hall or to other rooms in the house. The bathrooms, family room or kitchen may be poorly placed for efficient use of the structure. You should observe whether there are an adequate number of bedrooms and whether these rooms are properly located and of sufficient size to be desirable. The placement of doors and windows is extremely important, particularly as it affects access to the room and placement of furniture within the room. All structures should have adequate closets properly placed for ease of access. Closets should generally be recessed into the walls, rather than projecting out into the room. It is desirable to have walk-in closets with lights inside, rather than small closets which are inadequate even to store the minimum amount of clothing. Check to see if there are sufficient electrical fixtures and whether these are of good quality. It is important to have sufficient wall outlets in order to avoid having to run extension cords along the baseboards or having to put too many appliances on one outlet. An inadequate number of outlets is a frequent problem which may pose a fire hazard. The built-in equipment in the kitchen should be properly placed, of good quality, and in good working order. The placement of the hot water heater is important since hot water heaters placed in a ceiling often rupture and destroy the ceiling in several rooms. Inquire as to whether the heating and air-conditioning equipment is adequate and functional and whether all of the built-in equipment in the kitchen area is in working order. The residence should have adequate kitchen cabinets, properly placed and attractive in appearance.

Occasionally, a residential structure will have very poor cross ventilation and window placement for natural light. There are some residences in which the family room seems to be the only one given major attention. Under these circumstances, the family room will be extremely large and attractive, leaving inadequate space for the remaining rooms and necessitating poor room placement in some situations.

In inspecting a property to determine its efficiency of design, you should be aware of the taste within the particular market and whether or not your property conforms to the prevailing taste. A word of caution here is that you must attempt to analyze what the market desires, without injecting your own particular bias into the situation. If you encounter a three bedroom house with only one bath in an area in which two baths are the standard, you must consider whether the floor plan of the subject structure can be adapted to the installation of an additional bath at a cost which makes sense from an economic standpoint. If you are appraising a property which does not have central heating and air conditioning in an area in which this is the standard, you must determine the cost of curing this problem to see if it makes sense from an economic standpoint. All of the items you will observe while inspecting the property will be essential to your analysis of the marketability of the structure as it is affected by the presence or absence of certain features.

## ESSENTIAL ITEMS TO OBSERVE WHILE INSPECTING RESIDENTIAL STRUCTURES

There is no way to perform an adequate appraisal without making an on-site field inspection. The inspection and rating of the property must be comprehensive and objective. You should always look at the structure through the eyes of the typically informed purchaser, giving consideration to the items which he would deem essential.

Always use a checklist which will allow you to make the essential observations about a property's physical appearance and condition, any recent major repairs, the general deterioration, and any rehabilitation or deferred maintenance which should be required, and which will allow you to estimate the remaining economic life of the replaceable items as well as the basic structure. The form will also allow you to note items which appear to be functionally inadequate or super-adequate and to note the presence or absence of fundamental features in the structure as well as the size, quality and condition of the structure, the fixtures and the equipment. Certain general structural elements which should be examined and noted include the size of the structure, number and type of rooms, age and condition of the structure, quality of construction, functional utility, floor plan, visual appeal and the equipment and features.

While you are on the site, you should note items in need of immediate repair or replacement, the quality and type of repairs previously made, the maintenance and general condition of the structure and its components, and an estimate of cost to repair or replace items in need of immediate repair or replacement. Additional items relating to condition include structural deficiencies such as water damage, leakage, moisture, settling, cracks, peeling paint, cracked windows and worn-out roof. Also note the effective age and the remaining economic life of structural improvements, both long-lived and short-lived.

While inspecting the property, there are certain factors regarding the functional adequacy of the structure which you should note on the inspection form and which will allow you to properly analyze these items. Look at the structure and its adequacy through the eyes of the typically informed purchaser and then answer several questions. Be prepared to answer affirmatively or negatively the question of whether or not there is a sufficient number of rooms and whether they are adequate in size and placement. The same question applies to whether the floor plan is acceptable in the market and whether it has proper traffic pattern. Be prepared to answer the question of whether the structural quality enhances the economic life of the structure. Be able to answer whether there are adequate storage facilities, adequate light and ventilation, and adequate equipment of all types, including kitchen, bath, heating and cooling, electrical service, laundry, water heater, piping and plumbing. You should also be able to answer the question of whether the insulation, window placement, glazing and all elements of heating and cooling are adequate.

Carefully observe certain aspects of the site improvements and make proper notations on your inspection form. The information on the inspection form should be sufficient to enable you to consider the grading of the site and the surface water control, the drains, tiles and other means of water removal. Information should also be shown regarding the water and sewer connections, whether public or private, whether or not there is adequate outdoor lighting, the type and condition of patios, walks, driveways, parking areas, fences and walls. The availability and type of recreational facilities, the type and condition of accessory buildings, such as garages and sheds, and the type, adequacy and appearance of the landscaping, lawns and shade trees should also be observed. The question which must be answered about the site improvements is whether their presence enhances the use and enjoyment of the property and how this would affect the marketability and, thus, the value of the subject property.

## ESSENTIAL ELEMENTS OF A BUILDING INSPECTION CHECKLIST

I have included a checklist at the end of this chapter which I have found to be quite adequate. You may have your own checklist which is equivalent to the one I have suggested. In the event that you wish to design your own checklist, the following are minimum items which should be included:

1. Foundation—type, adequacy, any defects.
2. Sub-flooring—joists, bridging, type of material, adequacy, any defects.
3. Exterior walls—type, condition, quality of workmanship, any defects.
4. Roof—type, style, covering, age, condition, any defects.
5. Windows—type, condition, placement, adequacy, any defects.
6. Exterior doors—type, placement, adequacy, any defects.
7. Insulation—type, where placed, adequacy, any defects.
8. Exterior workmanship—corner joints, overhang, general carpentry, any defects.
9. Wiring—type, adequacy, fixture quality, wall outlets, any defects.
10. Plumbing—types and pipe placements, fixtures, adequacy and quality of baths, any defects.
11. Heating and air-conditioning—type, size, capacity, heat source, adequacy, any defects.
12. Ventilation—type, adequacy, any defects.
13. Floors and floor covering—type, condition, adequacy, probable remaining life of floor covering, any defects.
14. Rooms and room placement—type, placement, traffic pattern, adequacy, any defects.
15. Closets—type, location, size, adequacy, any defects.
16. Overall appearance—visual appeal, placement on lot, marketability, possible market resistance.

17. Built-in features—cabinets, type, adequacy, placement.
18. Kitchen equipment—type, placement, adequacy, probable remaining life, any defects.
19. Shelving—where located, adequacy, type, any defects.
20. Site improvements—type, quality, condition, adequacy, market acceptability, possible market resistance, any defects.

## MEASUREMENT OF STRUCTURES

Several steps in the appraisal process require accurate measurement of the square foot area and/or cubic volume of a structure. This accurate measurement is essential in estimating reproduction cost and accrued depreciation in the cost approach, in making market comparisons in the direct sales comparison approach, and in making rent comparisons to estimate market rental in the gross rent multiplier approach. The structure should be carefully measured and a sketch prepared showing its exterior dimensions.

The most common method of measuring residential structures is to measure the area above the foundation for houses without basements, using the outside dimensions. The usual standard used in estimating reproduction cost is the total number of square feet of living area and the number of square feet of secondary areas such as basements, attic rooms or porches.

## HOW TO DETERMINE THE SQUARE FOOT AREA OF A RESIDENTIAL STRUCTURE

To determine the total living area of a structure, simply measure the outside dimensions, multiplying the length by the width at the foundation, and then multiplying this by the number of stories in the structure. For example, a two-story house with the outside dimensions of 30 feet × 40 feet would have 1200 square feet on the ground floor. Multiplied by two, this would give a total of 2400 square feet of living area in the two-story house. Generally, partial areas, such as basement rooms, are measured by the interior dimensions and are added to the total square feet of living area as calculated for the main body of the structure. An attic room or partially finished upper-floor room is also measured by the interior dimensions and added to the living area. Porches can be handled in two different ways. The square feet of the porch area may be multiplied by the reproduction cost to build a porch, or the total square foot area of the porch may be counted as one-half, or one-third or some other fraction of the cost to build the main structure, resulting in an adjusted square foot area to which the reproduction cost figure is applied. An example of this would be a structure in which the total living area is 2400 square feet, with a porch of 10 feet × 20 feet costing one-half of the amount of the cost to build the main structure. The porch would then be counted at 10 feet × 20 feet, which equals 200 square feet. Multiplied by ½, this equals 100 square feet to be added to 2400 square feet of living area, thus resulting in an adjusted area of 2500 square feet. The same result would be accomplished by simply taking the 200 square feet of porch area multiplied by the reduced cost to construct the porch, and adding this figure to the reproduction cost of the 2400 square feet of main structure calculated at the cost of building such a structure. The method of handling this is optional, but you should always keep in mind that the ultimate goal is to arrive at an estimate of the total reproduction cost of the structure.

## ALTERNATIVE METHOD OF CALCULATING THE AREA OF A RESIDENTIAL STRUCTURE

On rare occasions, the reproduction cost of a structure may be calculated by using the cubic foot content. The standard calculation for cubage is measured by multiplying the length by the width by the height, measured from 6 inches below the basement floor, or the finished surface of the lower finished floor, to the top of the upper ceiling joists. This method of estimating reproduction cost is not recommended for residential structures and is to be applied under limited circumstances even in the appraisal of other types of structures.

## FORMAT FOR PREPARING IMPROVEMENT ANALYSIS OF A RESIDENTIAL PROPERTY

Regardless of the amount of data you have obtained during the inspection of the improvements, that data can only be as effective as your method of presentation to the client. Don't simply recite a series of observed facts, but take time to carefully explain the meaning of these facts as they affect the value of the subject property. The improvement analysis should be separated into key components such as foundation, exterior walls, roof, etc. The following suggested format for improvement analysis is one which I have found to be proper. I recommend that this format be studied and applied in your appraisal practice.

## SUGGESTED FORMAT FOR IMPROVEMENT ANALYSIS

### BRIEF DESCRIPTION OF IMPROVEMENTS

The improvements which are a part of the property herein described and appraised consist of an 11-year-old, 7-room, brick veneer house containing 1090 square feet of floor area, plus 44 square feet of outside storage, a 225-square-foot carport, 240-square-foot patio and 864 square feet of walk, drive and flower box. A sample improvement sketch is included on the last page of this chapter.

### DESCRIPTION OF CONSTRUCTION

| | |
|---|---|
| *AGE:* | Actual age—11 years. Estimated effective age—10 years. Estimated remaining economic life—40 years. |
| *FOUNDATION:* | Steel reinforced poured concrete slab. No basement. |
| *SUBFLOOR:* | 1″×6″ diagonal pine on 2″×4″ screeds. |
| *FLOORS:* | Bath ceramic tile. Kitchen vinyl tile. All other floors select oak. |
| *WALL STUDS:* | 2″×4″ on 16″ centers. |
| *BEAMS:* | One 1″×8″ beam on each side and two 2″×8″ beams down center for support in lieu of ceiling joists. Ceiling follows roof contour. |
| *RAFTERS:* | 2″×6″ on 16″ centers. |
| *SHEATHING DECKING:* | 1″×6″ pine horizontal. |
| *EXTERIOR WALLS:* | Brick veneer. Old brick. Wood trim and metal work is painted. |
| *INTERIOR WALLS:* | Plaster—smooth finish in all rooms except bath. Bath has ceramic tile 4 feet, with plaster above. |
| *CEILING:* | Plaster—smooth finish. Ceiling follows roof line in all rooms except bath and hall. No exposed beams. |
| *DOORS AND JAMBS:* | 3′×6′8″ panel. Jambs steel. |
| *WINDOWS:* | Steel casement. |

| | |
|---|---|
| *ROOF:* | 210″ asphalt shingles, 42″ overhang and ventilated eaves. Gutters and downspouts 26 ga. galvanized iron. |
| *BATH:* | Modern fixtures. Shower and tub combination. Lavatory, commode and built-in medicine cabinet. |
| *KITCHEN:* | Wired for electric stove. Stanthony Corp. range hood. Youngstown double sink. 10½-foot base and 15-foot wall Youngstown metal cabinets. Connection for washing machine (no dryer) in kitchen. |
| *MECHANICAL EQUIPMENT:* | 1. 40 gal., glass-lined, Rheem natural gas water heater.<br>2. Delco natural gas forced air heater. 70,000 BTU input, 56,000 BTU output. Vented to each room.<br>3. 42″ attic fan with metal louvers. Not air-conditioned. |
| *INSULATION:* | Exterior walls and ceilings insulated with fiberglass bats. |
| *CARPORT:* | Poured reinforced concrete floor. Ceiling is painted and stripped plywood, supported by plain 4″ iron columns. Wall of house inside carport is painted and stripped plywood. |
| *STORAGE ROOM:* | Single brick wall, concrete floor, ceiling in plywood, unpainted shelves. |
| *PATIO:* | Poured reinforced concrete. No cover. No grill. |
| *YARD:* | Excellent shrubbery and shade trees. Graded and planted in Bermuda Grass. |
| *WALK AND DRIVEWAY:* | Poured reinforced concrete. |
| *FLOWER BOX:* | Single course of brick on concrete footing. |

## QUALITY OF CONSTRUCTION

Subject property was built approximately 11 years ago by an operative builder, used a short time as a display home, and then offered for sale. A careful examination of the improvements indicates that the construction was of excellent quality and is typical of the area. The property exceeds FHA and VA minimum requirements and is considered to be, on the whole, a well-built house.

## CONDITION OF IMPROVEMENTS

The house was well constructed and has had excellent maintenance. The oak floors show some signs of wear and need sanding and varnishing. Interior walls were recently painted. Exterior trim needs touching up. The roof is in excellent condition and no evidence of leaking was found.

The wiring is adequate except for the fact that no 220-volt connection was provided to accommodate a clothes dryer. The heating system is adequate. The attic fan is adequate for the area served.

The house suffers considerable functional obsolescence. The functional deficiencies are as follows:

1. The main entrance to the house is directly into the dining room rather than into a vestibule.
2. The sloped ceilings limit the potential buyers to those to whom this unusual design appeals. In addition, the sloped ceilings make the house more expensive to heat or cool.
3. The unusual shape of the dining room and hall detracts from full utilization of floor space.
4. No space is available in which an additional bath or half bath could be added. Buyers in the area now require one and one-half to two baths.
5. No space is provided in the heater closet to add a central air-conditioning unit. Buyers in the area now require central air-conditioning.
6. One bedroom is too small for adequate arrangement of furniture.
7. No den or family room is provided, even though this feature is very much in demand by most potential purchasers.

### SUMMARY AND CONCLUSIONS

This property (excluding the sloped ceiling) is a typical improvement for the neighborhood. It is not considered that any economic obsolescence exists due to over- or under-improvement, nor was economic obsolescence found to exist in the neighborhood due to influences from over- or under-building of the neighborhood or from inharmonious influences.

The structure suffers some loss in value from normal physical deterioration, both curable and incurable. There are also items of functional obsolescence, both curable and incurable, which result in a reduction in value from cost if new.

The structure will encounter considerable buyer resistance due to the incurable functional items, particularly the inadequate baths and lack of central air-conditioning. An additional 30 to 60 days over that normally required should be anticipated when offering the property for sale.

**IMPROVEMENT INSPECTION CHECKLIST**

| | |
|---|---|
| *OWNER'S NAME:* | ____________________ |
| *STREET ADDRESS OR LOCATION:* | ____________________ |
| *TYPE OF IMPROVEMENT:* | ____________________ |
| *AGE:* | Year Built ____ Year Remodeled ____<br>Economic Life ____Effective Age ____ |
| *NUMBER EACH TYPE ROOM (LIST):* | ____________________ |
| *FOUNDATION:* | Type ________ Condition ________<br>Adequacy ________ Defects (if any)<br>____________________ |
| *SUBFLOORING:* | Type Material _____ Condition _____<br>Adequacy ________ Defects (if any)<br>____________________ |
| *EXTERIOR WALLS:* | Type ________ Condition ________<br>Workmanship _____ Defects (if any)<br>____________________ |
| *ROOF:* | Type __________ Style __________<br>Covering ___________ Age _______<br>Condition ________ Defects (if any)<br>____________________ |
| *WINDOWS:* | Type ________ Condition ________<br>Placement _____ Adequacy _______<br>Defects (if any) _______________ |
| *EXTERIOR DOORS:* | Type ________ Condition ________<br>Placement _____ Adequacy _______<br>Defects (if any) _______________ |
| *INSULATION:* | Type ________ Adequacy ________<br>Defects (if any) _______________ |
| *EXTERIOR WORKMANSHIP:* | Quality ____________Defects (if any)<br>____________________ |
| *ELECTRICAL:* | Type Wiring _____ Adequacy _____<br>Fixture Quality _______ Wall Outlets<br>_______ Defects (if any) __________ |

| | |
|---|---|
| *PLUMBING:* | Type Pipe _______ Placement _____<br>Type Fixtures _____ Adequacy ___<br>Bath Quality _______ Defects (if any)<br>________________________________ |
| *HEATING AND AIR CONDITIONING:* | Type _________ BTU Capacity _____<br>Heat Source _______ Age of Unit ___<br>Adequacy _________ Defects (if any)<br>________________________________ |
| *VENTILATION:* | Type _______________ Defects (if any)<br>________________________________ |
| *FLOORS AND FLOOR COVERING:* | Type _________ Condition _________<br>Adequacy _____ Age of Floor Cover-ing _____Defects (if any) _________ |
| *ROOM PLACEMENT:* | Adequate Size _____ Traffic Pattern _________ Defects (if any) _________ |
| *CLOSETS:* | Type _________ Location _________<br>Size _________Adequacy _________<br>Defects (if any) __________________ |
| *BUILT-IN FEATURES:* | Cabinet Type _____ Adequacy _____<br>Placement _____________________<br>Other Type _____ Adequacy _______<br>Placement _____________________ |
| *KITCHEN EQUIPMENT:* | Type _______ Placement _________<br>Adequacy _______ Age _____ Probable Remaining Life _______ Defects (if any) _____________________ |
| *UTILITY ROOM & STORAGE:* | Located _____ Adequacy _______<br>Defects (if any) __________________ |
| *SITE IMPROVEMENTS:* | Type _______Overall Quality _______<br>Condition _______Adequacy _____<br>Market Acceptability ____________<br>Defects (if any) __________________ |
| *OVERALL APPEARANCE:* | Visual Appeal ____________________<br>Placement on Lot _________________<br>Marketability ____________________ |

*PERSON INTERVIEWED:* ______________________________

*DATE AND TIME OF INSPECTION:* ______________________________

IMPROVEMENT SKETCH AND
LIST OF IMPROVEMENT TYPES

| | | |
|---|---|---|
| Sing. Res. | Bank | Restaurant |
| Duplex | Market | Fast Food |
| Triplex | Shop Ctr. | Motel |
| Apartment | Factory | Hotel |
| Store | Warehouse | Gar. Apt. |
| Store Loft | Parking Gar. | |
| Store Apt. | Auto Agcy. | |
| Store Ofc. | Theater | Other Comm. |
| Office | Service Sta. | Other Ind. |

SCALE: 1″ = 30′

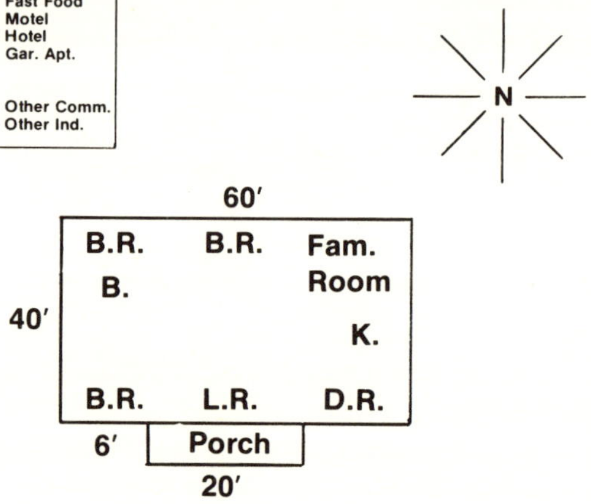


Living Area = 2,400 Sq. Ft.
Porch = 120 Sq. Ft.

# 9

# How to Value the Residential Site

This chapter presents detailed procedures for appraising the site on which the residential improvements are located. There are several practical reasons for arriving at separate value estimates for the site and for the improvements, and these reasons will be explained in detail. A well-supported site valuation is essential to the application of the recognized approaches to estimating the value of a residential property.

## REASONS FOR SEPARATE RESIDENTIAL SITE VALUATION

You will occasionally be called upon to appraise a vacant residential site, and you will find that the data utilized for this type of appraisal is very helpful in making a separate site valuation of an improved residential parcel. Most appraisals for property taxation, as well as for separation of the total purchase price between depreciable and non-depreciable property for income tax purposes, require separate value estimates for site and improvements. Most condemnation appraisals require separate value estimates. Many appraisals of lessor and lessee interest also require separation of value estimates between site and improvements. Such a separation is also required in the event of an insurance claim.

The most important reason for arriving at separate value estimates for the site and its improvements is that such separations are essential to the proper application of the three approaches to estimating value. In the application of the cost approach, the site must be valued separately so that the value contribution of the improvements may be estimated with reasonable accuracy. The sum of the site valued separately and the depreciated reproduction cost new of the improvements cannot exceed the combined value of the entire improved property under normal market constraints. In the application of the gross rent multiplier approach, the value contribution of the site may be a factor in estimating the market value of the subject property in comparison with similar residential properties which are currently rented. The proper application of the direct sales comparison approach requires that the site be separately appraised, since adjustments are essential to reflect differences in site value.

## DETERMINING WHAT IS TO BE VALUED

In residential appraising, you are valuing the site. This means that the land has been improved by grading, providing street access and providing essential utilities, in addition to any other necessary site preparations which ready it for residential use. If you are appraising a vacant piece of land where none of the above-listed items have been accomplished, I would advise you to proceed with extreme caution. Under such circumstances, you should probably obtain some engineering assistance in estimating the cost of converting the vacant land into a satisfactory residential site. The task of the appraiser is much simpler in an established residential area where an established market exists for residential sites.

## ESTIMATING HIGHEST AND BEST USE OF THE RESIDENTIAL SITE

The residential site is always appraised as if it were vacant and available to be utilized for its highest and best use. As has been previously explained, the contemplated highest and best use must be a legal use, it must be feasible in terms of market acceptance and it must provide the greatest benefits from ownership and/or use of the site. There is usually little doubt as to the highest and best use of most residential sites, since most such appraisals are of residential properties within well-established residential areas with no trend toward a change in use. In areas where changes in use patterns are occurring, the appraisal of the site based on its highest and best use as though currently available for such use will indicate whether there is any value contribution made by the improvements. For example, if a site is worth $50,000 for use as an office site and if the site plus residential improvements is worth $40,000 for such residential use, it becomes obvious that the residential improvements have reached the end of their economic life. When the site is valued at its highest and best use, all forms of depreciation and obsolescence are charged to the improvements. The only instance in which the site value is reduced would be for the cost of clearing the site if such cost exceeds salvage value of the improvements. Be sure that your estimate of highest and best use meets all essential criteria, including the requirements that it reflect current market conditions and can be demonstrated by market demand.

## DETERMINING MARKET ENVIRONMENT OF SUBJECT RESIDENTIAL PROPERTY

Any estimate of market value must consider the reactions of the typical purchaser, who is assumed to be informed as to his alternatives within the particular market in which the property is located as of the date of the appraisal. Implicit in the assumption of the informed purchaser is that he will know the approximate current cost of acquiring a site of the same size and with similar location and amenities as the subject property. The appraiser must likewise use the most current market data available to him. The comparable sales must be as nearly like the subject site as possible, in size, shape, access and neighborhood environment, if the appraiser is to arrive at a well-supported value estimate.

## UNDERSTANDING THE VARIOUS METHODS OF RESIDENTIAL SITE VALUATION

There are four methods of site valuation. By far the most meaningful method is the use of *direct sales comparison.* This method is applied by finding recent sales of sites most similar to the subject site, adjusting these sales for differences, and arriving at an amount for which these sites would have sold if they had been identical to the subject property. The direct sales comparison method should be used in all appraisals if adequate sales data are available. Another method of site valuation is the *land residual technique,* which is secondary in usefulness to the direct sales comparison method. In this method, the value contribution of the improvements is deducted from total sales price of comparables with the residual value being the site. This seldom applies to residential appraisals and is almost meaningless unless the improvements are new and have suffered no loss in value. The third method is to value the site by *abstraction* from total sales price by a ratio such as site value to total property value or site value to construction cost. This method is generally not very useful and should be applied only when there is no other logical solution. The fourth method is the *cost of development* or *site production,* which is generally used to determine the amount which a developer would be justified in paying for raw acreage which he could ultimately develop into residential sites. This method has very limited applicability in normal residential appraising.

## DIRECT SALES COMPARISON—SITE CHARACTERISTICS

Since most lenders (both public and private) and most courts in condemnation cases look almost exclusively to the direct sales comparison method of site valuation, there is no logical reason to apply any other method of site valuation if comparable sales are available. In applying the direct sales comparison method of site valuation, there are physical characteristics which can be reduced to units of comparison, such as front feet, width, depth, shape and lot line dimensions. Other physical elements are drainage, topography, soil and subsoil, access, availability of utilities, and adequacy and cost of municipal services. Other areas of comparison include location, zoning, date of sale, and terms and conditions of sale, particularly if not typical of the current market.

In selecting the comparable sales to be used in the direct sales comparison method, it is recommended that a minimum of three sales be used, but preferably five or six. The sales should be as nearly identical to the subject as possible and should be as nearly current as possible. Sales prices must be verified with at least one of the parties to the transaction and each sale should be carefully inspected by the appraiser. *Only* those items which are meaningful, and which affect the sales price of lots in the area under current market conditions, should be considered as elements of comparability. The use of excessive elements of comparison can cause the appraisal to be too difficult to understand.

## SOURCES OF COMPARABLE RESIDENTIAL SITE SALES

There are several useful sources of sales data. The source used most frequently is recorded deeds, with data taken from the recorded document regarding deed book and page, grantor, grantee, date of sale, stated consideration, size and location of site, with brief legal description, and any encumbrances and/or deed restrictions. Another source which is usually helpful are the assessor's records, including property cards and maps. Zoning maps and building permit records are also useful. Other appraisers and/or real estate brokers may also help, particularly if you are ready to reciprocate. You might also watch for newspaper advertisements of lots for sale or signs placed on lots by owners or brokers. Avoid the use of listings if completed sales transactions are available.

## COMPARISON OF RESIDENTIAL SITE SALES

In comparing site sales with the subject property, the appraiser seeks to determine what the sale property would have sold for if it had been identical to the subject site in every important aspect which would be recognized by the informed buyer. The physical units of comparison are front foot, square foot, per lot or per acre. Most residential lots are compared on a per-front-foot basis. However, the buyer is usually interested in acquiring a lot that will provide an adequate residential building site and may be thinking of a price per lot with no further refinements. In some cases, excess frontage and/or depth can be a liability rather than an asset. Adjustments should reflect the market reaction to the presence or absence of a particular attribute, with the cost of the particular item being almost meaningless. The amount of the adjustment can be obtained by comparing sales with a particular characteristic with other sales of sites otherwise identical except for the absence of this particular item. For example, the cost of a paving assessment may or may not measure the difference between a lot on a paved street and one on an unpaved street. The only way to determine market treatment of this or any other item of comparison is to go directly to the market.

The comparable site should always be adjusted to the subject property. This is logical since the goal of the adjustment is to arrive at the price for which the comparable site would have sold if it had been identical to the subject.

## METHODS OF ADJUSTING COMPARABLE RESIDENTIAL SITE SALES

There are three generally recognized methods of adjusting comparable sales. The method most frequently used is to adjust the sale property to the subject on the basis of *plus or minus dollar adjustments.* For example, if the comparable site sold for \$20,000 and was \$3000 better than the subject in terms of location and \$2000 poorer than the subject in terms of topography, the indicated value of the subject site would be \$19,000 (\$20,000 − \$3000 + \$2000). Another method of adjusting comparable sales is by *plus or minus percentage adjustments.* If the comparable site sold for \$20,000 and was 15 percent better than the subject in terms of location and 10 percent poorer than the subject in terms of topography, the indicated value of the subject site would be \$19,000 (\$20,000 × 15% = −\$3000, and \$20,000 × 10% = +\$2000). I prefer lump-sum dollar adjustments over percentage adjustments, but either method is satisfactory because each element of comparability is considered separately and each adjustment, whether lump-sum dollar or percentage, can be proved from the market. The third method is the *cumulative percent-*

*age adjustment*. This method is much less satisfactory since the adjustments are interrelated instead of being considered separately on their own merit. For example, the cumulative percentage adjustment for the sale previously given would be .935 (.85 × 1.10), thus indicating the value of the subject site to be $18,700 ($20,000 × .935) rather than $19,000, as is indicated when each difference is considered separately on its own merit. I do not recommend the cumulative percentage method of adjusting comparable sales due to the problems involved with use and explanation, and the fact that the order in which the adjustments are made can also affect the final result.

## CORRELATING COMPARABLE RESIDENTIAL SITE SALES WITH VALUE OF SUBJECT RESIDENTIAL SITE

After you have analyzed the market in the area in which the subject site is located, you will have selected from three to six sales which are most recent and most similar to the site you are appraising. Ideally, the sale properties would be identical to the subject in every respect, thereby eliminating the need to make adjustments. Since this situation almost never occurs, you will have the sales you have selected arrayed on a comparison grid similar to the example at the end of this chapter. Each sale will have been adjusted in order for you to arrive at an estimate of what it would have sold for if it had been identical to the subject property. These indicated values based on the adjusted sales will show a value range which should be reasonably close if you have carefully applied your adjustments. I recommend that you never average the indicated values and that you also avoid using weighted averages. The appropriate method is to give most weight to the most recent sales which are most similar to the subject site, thus requiring the least adjustments both in number and dollar amount. I also recommend that the value estimate for the subject site be in even-dollar amounts rather than some odd-dollar figure such as $24,991, when most sales are in even dollars such as $24,500, $25,000 or $25,500. Your final value estimate should reflect normal market behavior.

## HOW SEPARATE SITE VALUE IS USED IN RESIDENTIAL APPRAISING

Having arrived at a separate value estimate for the subject site, you will find that it is utilized in each of the three recognized approaches to value in the manner illustrated in the following simplified illustrations.

A. *COST APPROACH:*

| | |
|---|---|
| Reproduction Cost New of Major Improvements | $50,000 |
| Subtract: Depreciation and Obsolescence | $10,000 |
| Indicated Value of Major Improvements | $40,000 |
| Add: Value Contribution of Site Improvements | $ 5,500 |
| Total Value of All Improvements | $45,500 |
| Add: Site Value as Indicated by Sales Comparison | $25,000 |
| Value as Indicated by Cost Approach | $70,500 |

B. *GROSS RENT MULTIPLIER:*

| | Rent Comp. No. 1 | Rent Comp. No. 2 | Rent Comp. No. 3 |
|---|---|---|---|
| Sales Price | $60,000 | $65,000 | $70,000 |
| Monthly Rent | $ 300 | $ 325 | $ 350 |
| Built-ins | +$ 25 | same | same |
| Lot Value | +$ 15 | +$ 15 | −$ 5 |
| Indicated Monthly Rent for Subject | $ 340 | $ 340 | $ 345 |
| Monthly Market Rent for Subject | | | $ 345 |
| Indicated Gross Monthly Rent Multiplier | | | 200 |
| Indicated Value of Subject Property as Indicated by Gross Rent Multiplier Approach ($350 × 200) | | | $69,000 |

C. *DIRECT SALES COMPARISON:*

| | Sale No. 1 | Sale No. 2 | Sale No. 3 |
|---|---|---|---|
| Months Expired Since Sale | 6 | 3 | 1 |
| Sales Price | $65,000 | $75,000 | $70,000 |
| Time of Sale | +$ 1,625 | +$ 950 | +$ 350 |
| Age and Condition | +$ 5,000 | −$ 7,500 | −$ 100 |
| Size | +$ 3,250 | −$ 3,750 | +$ 4,750 |
| Lot Value | −$ 5,000 | +$ 5,000 | −$ 5,000 |
| Indicated Value of Subject | $69,875 | $69,700 | $70,100 |

| | |
|---|---|
| Indicated Value of Subject Property (Giving Most Weight to Sale No. 3) by Direct Sales Comparison Approach | $70,000 |

With the value indicators shown in the preceding examples, it is likely that the final value estimate would be $70,000. Most weight is usually given to the value indicated by the direct sales comparison approach if adequate sales are available.

**SUGGESTED FORMAT FOR SALES ADJUSTMENT GRID FOR RESIDENTIAL LOT SALES**

| | *Sale No. 1* | *Sale No. 2* | *Sale No. 3* |
|---|---|---|---|
| Months Since Sold | *6* | *3* | *1* |
| Lot Size | 90′ × 160′ | 100′ × 160′ | 100′ × 150′ |
| Sales Price | $17,500 | $19,000 | $20,000 |
| Sales Price per Front Foot | $ 195 | $ 190 | $ 200 |
| Location | + $ 10 | + $ 10 | same |
| Trees | − $ 5 | same | same |
| Depth | − $ 5 | − $ 5 | same |
| Topography | + $ 5 | + $ 5 | − $ 2 |
| Time of Sale | + $ 5 | + $ 3 | + $ 1 |
| Indicated Value per Front Foot for Subject | $ 205 | $ 203 | $ 199 |
| Subject Lot Size | | | 100′ × 150′ |
| Indicated Value per Front Foot | | | $ 200 |
| Indicated Value of Subject Site (100 × $200) | | | $20,000 |

*NOTE:* Sale No. 3 was most recent transaction and required the least adjustments, thus is given most weight in arriving at the final value estimate. All adjustments are supported by comparison of market transactions.

# 10

# How to Estimate Reproduction Cost of Residential Improvements

This chapter deals with the first step in applying the cost approach to estimating the value contribution of improvements located on a residential site. One alternative available to a potential buyer is to construct a substitute property which would provide the same utility in the form of amenities as would the property being appraised.

Having already arrived at a value estimate of the residential site based upon its highest and best use, the next step is to estimate the reproduction cost new of the improvements. The step after that is to estimate all types of accrued depreciation which are present within the subject property as of the date of the appraisal. Methods of estimating accrued depreciation will be discussed in detail in Chapter 11. The fourth step is to subtract the estimated accrued depreciation from reproduction cost new in order to arrive at the value as indicated by the cost approach for the major improvements. In the fifth step, the estimated present value of the site improvements is added to the estimated present value of the major improvements, with the resulting figure being the estimated value contribution of all improvements as indicated by the cost approach. The final step is to add the site value as previously estimated to the indicated value of all the improvements, with the resulting figure being your value estimate as indicated by applying the cost approach.

## APPRAISAL PRINCIPLES APPLICABLE TO THE COST APPROACH

The *principle of highest and best use* is applied in appraising the site as if it were vacant and ready to be utilized for the most productive permitted use. The *principle of substitution* applies since you, as the appraiser, assume that the typical informed purchaser will normally pay no more for a property than the cost he would encounter in producing a substitute property which would provide the same amenities as the subject property. The appraiser usually assumes the cost of producing an exact replica of the subject property, beginning with an estimate of reproduction cost. The *principle of contribution* applies, since the value of the improvements is based on their contribution to the value of the entire property when the site is appraised as if vacant and available to be utilized for its highest and best use. The *principle of balance* applies in determining if the improvements located on the site are proper and in accordance with market demand. Over-improvement or under-improvement of a site can affect value. Maximum value can be realized when the principle of balance shows that the subject improvements are proper.

## REPRODUCTION COST NEW VS. REPLACEMENT COST NEW

Most appraisals of residential property will start with *reproduction cost new* in applying the cost approach. Reproduction cost new requires an estimate of the cost of producing an exact replica of the subject property with all of its inherent features, whether positive or negative. The appraiser can then work with the subject property as it exists to measure all types of accrued depreciation which may be present. For example, if the subject property has 12-foot ceilings, the reproduction cost estimate would assume a structure with 12-foot ceilings. Under this circumstance, the appraiser would measure and deduct the value effect of having the added space to heat and cool; thus, this added height would have a negative value. When appraising an extremely old residence or a unique residential structure with a great deal of ornamental trim which probably couldn't be duplicated currently, it will probably be necessary to arrive at an estimate of replacement cost if you apply the cost approach at all.

*Replacement cost new* assumes an estimate of the cost, in current dollars, of producing a structure which provides the same utility or amenities as the subject property. This method is not often used in the appraisal of residential property. This method does not require an estimate of the cost of producing an exact replica as does reproduction cost new. For example, the estimated replacement cost new of the house with 12-foot ceilings would actually account for the cost of building equivalent space to provide the same utility, but with normal ceiling height instead of 12 feet. The replacement cost new estimate eliminates the necessity of estimating and deducting functional obsolescence as a part of accrued depreciation.

## WHY REPRODUCTION COST SHOULD BE USED IN APPRAISING RESIDENTIAL PROPERTY

The major reason to use reproduction cost new rather than replacement cost new is that you can be more convincing in your appraisal report if you have given careful consideration to all of the positive and/or negative features of the subject property as these particular features may affect value. An item of functional obsolescence which is obviously present in the subject property should be given proper treatment, rather than simply being ignored by the selection of what might be an easier method of cost estimation.

## UNDERSTANDING WHAT COST MEANS AS AN INDICATOR OF RESIDENTIAL PROPERTY VALUE

One factor of extreme importance is that cost—whether we are speaking of original cost, reproduction cost or replacement cost—is seldom the same thing as value. Cost does not create value; it is simply the amount of dollars expended. Market value is the economic worth of the property; therefore, any type of cost is not indicative of value until all types of accrued depreciation have been carefully estimated by analysis of market reaction and deducted from cost to arrive at the value contribution of the improvements.

## ESTIMATING REPRODUCTION COST OF RESIDENTIAL IMPROVEMENTS

There are several methods available to the appraiser for estimating reproduction cost. The best method is to develop current unit costs from recently constructed residential properties of various types within your local area. This type of cost can be secured by working with builders on unit costs of residential structures currently under construction or costs of recently completed structures. This does not mean the actual direct and indirect construction cost to the builder. The unit cost should be the cost to the buyer after the builder has added his overhead and profit. The cost which should be utilized is the same as would result from the builder entering into a lock-and-key job with the purchaser to turn over to him a residential structure complete in every way and ready for immediate occupancy. This method of cost estimation is time consuming and would not be feasible unless a large volume of residential appraisals are made or unless several appraisers share in the cost. Many real estate brokers also build residential structures, so that much of the data you need may be obtained from your own company. I suggest that you obtain construction cost data from other builders also.

The most frequently used method in estimating reproduction cost new is a cost manual which can be purchased from several different firms. This method is sufficiently accurate for most residential appraisals if the costs are adjusted to fit local conditions and if the cost factors are carefully applied.

The most complicated appraisal assignments may require you to employ a cost estimator. The expense involved with this type of assistance is quite high and is usually not justified. Some larger real estate firms who also build will themselves employ cost estimators.

A very useful source of cost data is your own files, particularly where you have appraised new properties which are subsequently sold. The cost data you use should be kept current due to rapidly changing construction costs.

## METHODS OF ESTIMATING RESIDENTIAL CONSTRUCTION COST

There are four generally recognized methods of cost estimation. Each of these methods is useful, but the one you should use depends to a large extent on the complexity of the particular appraisal problem. Each method will be discussed separately and in order of the frequency of its use in residential appraising.

1. *Comparative unit cost method:* This method is used extensively and almost exclusively in appraising a normal residential property. This method requires the combining of all costs to the buyer into cost per unit, with cost per square foot of building area being the cost unit most frequently used. Cost per cubic foot of building area is occasionally used as a unit of measurement. A further refinement is to break the total building cost down into cost per unit for main structure with separate unit costs for areas such as porches, garages, carports or basements. This approach may be simplified by arriving at the effective area of the structure through assigning percentages of main area construction cost to each of the less costly areas such as those listed above. For example, if you found that carports cost half as much per square foot to build as the main living area of a residence which has 2400 square feet of living area and a 400-square-foot car-

port, the effective area would be 2600 square feet (2400 + 50% of 400). An alternative would be to price each area separately at its respective unit construction costs and add the two figures to arrive at the estimate of reproduction cost new. The source of unit cost most frequently used is a cost manual published by a reliable firm. When you use a cost manual, you should be certain to follow instructions including an adjustment to local construction costs. Most cost manuals provide a factor to adjust the unit cost shown to the construction cost level in a particular area. A cost manual, when used carefully, is accurate enough for most residential appraisal assignments. If you maintain a file of recent construction costs in your area, you can convert this data to unit costs and perhaps achieve some additional degree of accuracy, although at somewhat more time and expense on your part.

2. *Trade breakdown or builder's method:* This method is used for appraising a more complex or unique property. This method estimates the installed cost per unit (including builder's cost, overhead and profit) of the major functional portions of the structure. For example, cost per square foot for major components, such as excavation, foundation, framing, exterior walls, roof, interior walls, floors, plumbing, heating and electrical, is developed by using either cost services or local construction costs multiplied by the number of units for each component to arrive at reproduction cost new of that particular component. The total of all these component costs results in an estimate of reproduction cost new for the subject property. The resulting cost figure should be cost to the buyer and not actual cost to the builder, since the builder could not survive economically unless he also recovered his overhead plus a reasonable profit. If you work for a firm that also builds residential structures, you probably have a great deal of this data available in the files of the construction department. I recommend that you obtain data from other builders as well, without relying exclusively on data from within your own construction department.

3. *Unit-in-place method:* This method is somewhat similar to the trade breakdown or builder's method. This method is more detailed in that it utilizes unit costs of many separate components of the structure, rather than looking at major functional areas. This method is used only in appraisals of complicated or unique structures. While it may be possible for the average appraiser to use this method by careful study and application of a cost manual, or a detailed breakdown of costs on recently constructed properties, and arrive at an acceptable estimate of reproduction cost new, it is unlikely that the additional accuracy which might result from its use would justify the ad-

ditional time and expense involved. It is more likely that the services of a qualified cost estimator would be required and, in most instances, the nature of the problem would not justify the added cost to the client. If you are going to employ a cost estimator, it is suggested that he be instructed to arrive at an even more detailed cost estimate, which would be required to apply the quantity survey method discussed below. Look carefully at the complexity of the problem to see if the added cost is justified even if your firm has a construction department with an estimator on salary.

4. *Quantity survey method:* This method is very expensive to apply and is rarely used in appraising residential property. The only occasion where its use might be justified in appraising residential property would be when the assignment is to appraise a mansion, castle or other residential property so unique that there is little or no sales or income data available, thus making the cost approach the only available approach to estimating value. This method requires the services of a qualified cost estimator who follows the same procedures which a knowledgeable builder would follow in preparing a bid to construct the subject property. It is necessary to make detailed estimates of quantity required and cost of every item going into the structure, as well as detailed estimates of cost of labor and amount of overhead and profit added by the builder. The resulting estimate would be the figure utilized in the cost approach as the reproduction cost new of the subject property. I recommend using this method only with extremely complicated appraisals in which you have an almost unlimited fee.

## METHODS OF ESTIMATING COST OF RESIDENTIAL SITE IMPROVEMENTS

There are two generally accepted methods of estimating the cost and/or value of site improvements such as walks, drives and landscaping. Each method will be discussed separately in order of its frequency of use.

1. *Depreciated cost basis:* Since the residential site improvements are usually a minor part of the total property cost or value, it is proper to add the value of these items to the reproduction cost new minus accrued depreciation of the structures. The value contribution of the site improvements can be determined by a comparison of the installed cost new of these items with properties sold with or without the particular item. This indicated value contribution can be estimated, although with somewhat less accuracy, by a careful inspection of the site improvements, allowing you to arrive at a percentage

good as applied to current installed cost by using the observed condition method of estimating depreciation.

2. *Cost new installed basis:* This cost can be estimated by using a cost manual adjusted to local conditions, by obtaining local costs yourself, or by employing a cost estimator. The method of cost estimating used would very likely be determined by the complexity of the problem. The resulting cost figure would be the reproduction cost new of the site improvements and would be added to the reproduction cost new of the structures to arrive at the total estimated reproduction cost new for the subject improvements. This method also requires you to consider accrued depreciation for the site improvements in arriving at the value estimate indicated by the cost approach. If your firm also builds residential structures, you may have ready access to installed cost of various site improvements.

## SUMMARY

The necessity for using the cost approach as an indicator of value in appraising a residential property is determined to a large extent by the type of improvements involved in the appraisal and the complexity of the assignment. The applicability of each of the three recognized approaches to estimating value should be analyzed and all approaches used for which adequate data are available. If you determine that the cost approach is applicable, then it logically follows that you should estimate the reproduction cost new and not replacement cost new of the improvements. The estimation of reproduction cost new is one of the most important steps in the cost approach and requires careful attention. The various techniques (with examples of their application) for estimating reproduction cost new has been discussed earlier in this chapter. The techniques of estimating reproduction cost new were discussed in order of preference.

Many of the users of this book will very likely be employed by large firms which engage in many areas of the real estate business. I recommend that those who have the responsibility of making appraisals take full advantage of both in-house data and in-house specialists as sources of cost data.

# 11

# Cost Approach—How to Estimate Accrued Depreciation—Summary and Value Conclusion from this Approach

The preceding chapter presented data regarding the proper methods for estimating reproduction cost new of residential improvements. If the appraisal assignment involved new improvements which represented the highest and best use of the site (thereby eliminating the necessity of estimating accrued depreciation), the appraiser would simply add his site value estimate to the estimated reproduction cost new of the improvements, and the cost approach would be complete. However, the appraisal assignments which you receive will almost always be of properties for which the type and dollar amount of accrued depreciation present in the subject improvements must be identified so that it can be deducted from reproduction cost new to arrive at the value contribution (economic worth) of the improvements. This chapter presents the proper methods for identifying, classifying and estimating the dollar amount of the various types of accrued depreciation in appraising a residential property. The procedures outlined here apply even for estimating the probable selling price when obtaining a sales listing where no formal written appraisal is required.

## WHAT IS ACCRUED DEPRECIATION?

One definition of *accrued depreciation* is that it is the amount of loss in value arising from all causes as measured against reproduction cost new. Accrued depreciation may be further defined as the difference between reproduction cost new of the improvements, and their present value or economic worth as of the date of the appraisal. The total amount of accrued depreciation may consist of several different types and may be caused by a variety of factors, both within the property and extraneous to it. Another name for accrued depreciation is *diminished utility*. The difference between the utility of the subject property when new and the utility present in the property as of the date of appraisal is measurable in dollars and is called either accrued depreciation or diminished utility. The term used most often, and the one I prefer, is accrued depreciation.

It should be clearly understood that accrued depreciation applies to the loss in value of man-made improvements and not of land. While it is true that the value of land may change, such change does not occur in any systematic manner as would generally be true of man-made improvements. While accrued depreciation may occur with passage of time, there is no direct proportionate relationship, and the use of age-life tables is almost meaningless in this context.

## WHY ESTIMATE ACCRUED DEPRECIATION OF RESIDENTIAL IMPROVEMENTS?

The residential site should always be valued as though it were vacant and available to be devoted to its highest and best use. The site value is estimated by an analysis of market data. If the site as presently improved is worth more than the site alone, then the highest and best use of the property is as presently improved. One very important procedure for arriving at an estimate of the value contribution of the improvements is to start with reproduction cost new, and deduct accrued depreciation, to arrive at an estimate of present value. The estimate of the various types of accrued depreciation, and the dollar amount of each type of loss in value, are very helpful in making the necessary adjustments in the direct sales comparison approach and in gross rent multiplier analysis. It is also necessary to separate land and improvement value for both income tax and property tax, as well as for condemnation proceedings and insurance purposes. The amount of accrued depreciation is estimated by analyzing market reaction to the presence or absence of certain features of the subject property. Since all three approaches to value rely on market data, the analysis necessary to arrive at an estimate of accrued depreciation is helpful in the proper application of the other two approaches.

## HOW TO DETERMINE THE LIFE OF RESIDENTIAL IMPROVEMENTS

You probably know of some residential structures that were built over 100 years ago, many of which are currently being used for residential purposes. At the other extreme are residential structures which are demolished after only a few years of residential use. This illustrates the fact that there are several different lives involved with residential improvements. Some important terms which you should understand before you begin to estimate accrued depreciation are as follows:

1. *Physical life* of an improvement is the number of years it is expected to remain standing in sufficient condition to permit its use for the purpose intended. Most residential improvements are torn down long before the physical life is exhausted due to changes in technology or changes in use brought about by economic conditions.

2. *Economic life* is the number of years over which the improvements are expected to provide a net return which is competitive in the market. The point in time at which the improvements on the site cease to add value to the site when it is appraised as though vacant and available to be put to its highest and best use is the end of their economic life. Many residential improvements reach the end of their economic life long before they physically wear out. For example, if residential structures in your area tend to be demolished when they are about 50 years old—due to changes in technology, changes in land use patterns or changes in purchaser demands—then the economic life of such a structure when new is 50 years.

3. *Effective age* of the improvements is the number of years of economic life which have elapsed as of the date of the appraisal. Effective age may have little relationship to actual years elapsed since the property was constructed. The quality of construction, the type and quality of maintenance and changes in technology, buyer demand and economic conditions, can alter the effective age of a structure. For this reason, an age-life table is too rigid to be useful in estimating effective age. If the structures you are appraising had an economic life when new of 50 years and an effective age of 10 years as of the date of the appraisal, the accrued depreciation would be 20 percent ($100 \div 50 = 2\%$, $2\%$ per yr. $\times$ 10 yrs. $= 20\%$). The 20 percent total accrued depreciation may consist of several different types. Procedures for classifying the different types of accrued depreciation of residential improvements and assigning dollar amounts to each, will be developed later in this chapter.

4. *Remaining economic life* of the improvements is the remaining number of years from the date of the appraisal over which they are expected to provide a competitive net return. For example, if the economic life of the residential improvements when new was 50 years and the effective age as of the date of the appraisal was 10 years, then the remaining economic life would be 40 years (50 yrs. − 10 yrs.). If a purchaser was willing to receive a return of his investment on a straight-line basis over the remaining economic life of the improvements, he would require 2.5 percent (100 ÷ 40 yrs.) of his investment back each year for the next 40 years.

## RELIABILITY OF ESTIMATE OF ACCRUED DEPRECIATION OF RESIDENTIAL IMPROVEMENTS

A number of factors may affect the reliability of your estimate of accrued depreciation and the amount of weight given to the cost approach in arriving at a final value estimate for a particular property. First of all, if the improvements are old and/or unique, the validity of the estimate of reproduction cost new may be doubtful. Furthermore, it follows that for older and/or more unique properties, there would logically be large amounts of accrued depreciation which would be more difficult to estimate. The care given to area and neighborhood analysis can directly affect the reliability of your estimate of accrued depreciation. The care you exercise during your field inspection will have a direct effect on how accurately you can estimate accrued depreciation. Since much of the information you need to measure the impact in dollars of the various types of accrued depreciation comes from market analysis, the reliability of your estimate is greatly dependent on the care you apply to this analysis. As with most things in life, you can get no better result than that warranted by the effort you put into achieving it.

## TYPES AND CAUSES OF ACCRUED DEPRECIATION OF RESIDENTIAL IMPROVEMENTS

There are three major types of accrued depreciation, with the first two types having several sub-classifications. These three major types are physical, functional and locational accrued depreciation. Each type will be discussed separately, with information about definition, causes and methods of measuring the dollar effect of each major type and each sub-classification within its particular area.

1. *Physical deterioration* is the loss in value from cost new caused by the normal aging process. As a man-made improvement ages chronologically, there is a loss in utility brought about by wear

and tear and the stress of heat, cold, moisture, wind or other forces of nature. The rapidity of this physical deterioration can be affected by the original construction quality, the quality and efficiency of maintenance, and the type of climate in which the property is located. Physical deterioration is divided into three sub-classifications as follows:

A. *Physical curable deterioration* consists of those items which require immediate attention in order to protect, preserve or enhance the appearance and/or desirability of the property. These items include painting and replacing broken glass, missing screens, rotted wood, and torn or soiled wallpaper. This item is measured by the cost to cure or correct the problem. For example, if the house you are appraising needs the exterior trim painted at a cost of $300, broken glass and missing screens replaced at a cost of $200, rotted wood replaced at a cost of $250, and torn or soiled wallpaper replaced at a cost of $250, then the total physical curable deterioration is $1000. When you estimate reproduction cost new, the resulting figure assumes that you have a replica of the subject property as though new measured in current dollars; therefore, the cost of renewing these worn items must be deducted from reproduction cost new, and $1000 of the total reproduction cost new has been separately handled here for estimating accrued depreciation.

B. *Physical curable deterioration deferred* consists of certain short-lived components of the structure which will require replacement before the building reaches the end of its economic life, but which are only partially worn-out as of the date of the appraisal. These short-lived items include roof, heating and cooling system, floor covering such as tile and carpet, built-in appliances and hot water heater. Some authorities insist that these items are "incurable," since their immediate replacement is not required as of the date of the appraisal. It is my position that a component which can be replaced is a "curable" item, but its time of cure is merely deferred until replacement is required. Whether this loss in value is called "physical curable deterioration deferred" or "physical incurable short-lived items," the method of measurement is the same. If the roof had an economic life when new of 20 years, an effective age of 10 years and reproduction cost new of $1000, the accrued depreciation is 50 percent of $1000, or $500. If the heating system had an economic life when new of 20 years, an effective age of 5 years and reproduction cost new of $2000, the accrued depreciation is 25 percent, or $500. The total physical curable deterioration deferred for the two items is $1000 and the portion of the total reproduction cost new which has been separately handled here for estimating accrued depreciation is $3000.

C. *Physical incurable deterioration* is the loss in value from cost new of those components of the structure which will likely survive for the full economic life of the man-made improvements and therefore will not require replacement. This category consists of items such as foundation, framing, wiring and plumbing. The dollar effect of the physical deterioration of this portion of the reproduction cost new is measured by the percentage of the economic life of the structure when new which has expired as of the date of the appraisal. For example, if the economic life of the residential structure when new was 50 years and the effective age at date of appraisal is 10 years, then the percentage of the economic life which has expired at that time is 20 percent (100 ÷ 50 = 2%, 2% per yr. × 10 yrs. = 20%). If the total reproduction cost new of the building was $44,000, and you have already separately depreciated $1000 of the reproduction cost new in estimating physical curable deterioration and $3000 of reproduction cost new in estimating physical curable deterioration deferred, the remaining reproduction cost new which is subject to physical incurable deterioration is $40,000. Thus, the total remaining reproduction cost new of $40,000, when depreciated at 20 percent, results in an estimate of $8000 ($40,000 × 20%) for physical incurable deterioration.

From the preceding examples, the total physical deterioration for the subject structure would be:

| | |
|---|---|
| Physical Curable Deterioration | $ 1,000 |
| Physical Curable Deterioration (Deferred) | $ 1,000 |
| Physical Incurable Deterioration | $ 8,000 |
| Total Physical Deterioration | $10,000 |

2. *Functional obsolescence* is the loss in value from either deficiencies or super-adequacies which exist within the structure. As changes in technology and/or changes in purchaser demands occur, the residential structure will cease to provide some of the utility for which it was intended. For example, the residence with only one bath meets substantial buyer resistance, as does the home with no central heating and cooling system in most areas of the country. Most buyers today want a den or family room and those residential structures which do not offer this feature will usually meet buyer resistance. Residential structures with excessive ceiling height usually meet with buyer resistance due to the added cost of heating or cooling this ex-

cess space, which really adds little or nothing to the utility of the house. Functional obsolescence is divided into four sub-classifications as follows:

A. *Functional obsolescence curable (structural deficiency)* arises when the structure as it presently exists is lacking in some items but the design is such that the problem can be cured or corrected by adding the missing element. The construction, when the structural design permits it, of an additional bath, additional closet space, additional kitchen cabinets or a modern heating and cooling system, when required by purchaser demands, are examples of functional obsolescence curable (structural deficiency). The principle of contribution applies here since an informed person would only correct the deficiency if the cost of curing the deficiency added at least the dollar amount of the cost to the value of the property. If you find that the cost of correcting the deficiency is justified by the value increase after the correction, then the only charge against the reproduction cost new of the subject property as it presently exists is the additional cost in current dollars of making the addition or correction over what it would have cost in current dollars if the deficiency had been eliminated when the property was originally constructed. This is due to the fact that the reproduction cost new of the structure as it presently exists does not include any amount for reproduction cost new of the item not presently in the structure. The only charge against reproduction cost new of the present structure is the penalty for inefficient original design. If you find that installation of an additional bath will return at least its cost in value increase, you will know it is curable. If you find that the second bath could have been added when the structure was built at a cost of $1800 in current dollars, and that it will cost $2300 to add it now due to the added time and expense required to rearrange some of the space, then the charge against reproduction cost new of the structure as it presently exists would be $500 ($2300 − $1800) for functional obsolescence curable (structural deficiency).

B. *Functional obsolescence curable (structural super-adequacy)* arises when the structure contains certain items which are excessive as measured by current market standards. For example, a residence with three heat pumps when one central unit with slightly larger capacity than any of the three separate units would be adequate, is considered to have functional obsolescence (structural super-adequacy). Whether the super-adequacy is curable depends on whether the cost of substituting the one heat pump unit for the three which presently exist would be justified either by an equivalent increase in value or sufficient reduction in utility cost to recover the investment over the economic life of the new system. If the replacement cannot be economically justified, then the item is considered to be incurable. The reproduction cost new of the present structure would include reproduction cost new of the item which was super-adequate. If the condition is found to be curable, the reproduction cost new of the structure as it presently exists would be reduced by the excess reproduction cost new of the super-adequate item over the present dollar cost of the replacement plus a design penalty if there is cost of removing the old systems and correcting ducts, vents, etc., in excess of the resale value of the items removed. For example, if the reproduction cost new of the three separate systems was $4000, and the cost new of the replacement system was $3000, and the cost of removing the old systems and correcting ducts and vents exceeded the resale value of the units by $500, the total functional obsolescence curable (structural super-adequacy) charged against reproduction cost new of the present structure would be $1500 ($4000 − $3000 = $1000, $1000 + $500 = $1500).

C. *Functional obsolescence incurable (structural deficiency)* arises when certain items are entirely missing or are deficient within the structure as it presently exists and the cost of correction exceeds the value which would be added by making the correction. The principle of contribution applies here since it assumes that a prudent person would not spend a dollar to cure a deficiency unless he can expect at least an equivalent increase in value. Some examples of this type of deficiency include inadequate heating or cooling systems which were either not physically possible to replace due to structural design and/or for which it would not be economically feasible to do so if the cost of installation exceeded the value added. Other items which would fit into this category are inadequate wiring, plumbing, closets, kitchen cabinets or poor traffic pattern and room layout due to poor design. The most frequently used method of measuring this type of obsolescence is to determine the loss in rental value to the subject structure arising from the particular deficiency by comparing rent differences between residences with and without the particular item. Once the rent loss is determined, it is multiplied by the gross monthly rent multiplier applicable to the subject property to estimate the functional obsolescence incurable (structural deficiency). If the subject property lacks an additional bath and you find a rent loss of $15 per month and a gross monthly rent multiplier of 150, the indicated functional obsolescence incurable (structural deficiency) would be $2250 ($15 × 150). If you can find no rental data for the property you are appraising, the alternative method is to find sales of homes which are very similar, with the exception of the presence of the particular deficiency you are trying to estimate, and this comparison will tell you the value attributed by the market to the presence or absence of the particular item. If your subject property lacks an additional bath, you can make market comparisons which might show a range of from $2100 to $2300 added value for an extra bath, and from this data you could feel relatively confident in charging $2200 as functional obsolescence incurable (structural deficiency).

D. *Functional obsolescence incurable (structural super-adequacy)* arises from the inclusion of components within the structure which add to the reproduction cost new but do not add proportionately to the utility of the building nor to its present value. Some examples are excessive ornamental trim, excessive ceiling height, excessive foundation or extremely ornate and/or expensive fixtures, which might be a personal whim of the owner but which would not have particular appeal to a prospective buyer. The super-adequate item may be physically impossible to cure because of structural design or it might not be economically feasible to cure it under the principle of contribution if the costs involved do not result in at least the equivalent increase in value. The method usually applied in estimating functional obsolescence incurable (structural super-adequacy) is to deduct the excess reproduction cost new of the super-adequate item over reproduction cost new in current dollars if the structure did not have the super-adequate item. In addition, the remaining reproduction cost new would be penalized by multiplying the excess cost (if any) involved in utilizing the super-adequate item by the gross monthly rent multiplier applicable to the subject property. For example, if the structure had 12-foot instead of 8-foot ceilings, the added cost of wall framing and wall covering in current dollars might be $1500, which would be part of the reproduction cost new of the present structure, but which would contribute no value. The average monthly cost to heat and cool the extra room height might be $10, thereby reducing the rent proportionately, and the appropriate gross monthly rent multiplier is 150, thus indicating additional functional obsolescence incurable (structural super-adequacy) of $1500 ($10 × 150). In this example, the total functional obsolescence incurable (structural super-adequacy) would be $3000. An alternate method of estimating functional obsolescence incurable (structural super-adequacy) is to compare sales of properties which are very similar, while lacking the super-adequate item or having it. This method is particularly applicable when little or no rental data are available. For example, if you found that houses otherwise very similar sold for $2900 to $3100 more with 8-foot ceilings than those with 12-foot ceilings, you could be relatively confident in charging $3000 against reproduction cost new of the present structure for functional obsolescence incurable (structural super-adequacy).

3. *Locational (or economic) obsolescence* is the loss in value arising from factors outside the property itself. Due to the fact that real estate is fixed in location, it cannot be moved away from any extraneous factors which may have a negative impact on its value. The value loss is measured in economic terms (dollar amount), but the property being fixed in location can be said to be suffering locational obsolescence. While the term "locational obsolescence" is preferable, the alternate term, "economic obsolescence," is used quite frequently and has the same meaning.

Some of the factors which cause locational (or economic) obsolescence are noise, dust, smoke or odor-producing activities nearby which would negatively affect the property. Other factors are excessive traffic flow in front of the property, changes in zoning or building codes which would allow undesirable uses to encroach on the area, or other government actions would have a negative impact on the property.

When you appraise the site at its highest and best use with comparable sales and/or other market data, you have already accounted for any locational obsolescence which may be present in the site. It is essential to charge only the portion of the locational obsolescence which is attributable to the improvements against the reproduction cost new of the improvements. I recommend that the prevailing ratio of improvement value to total property value within the subject area be utilized to allocate total locational obsolescence to the improvements. For example, if the prevailing ratio of improvement value to total property value within the subject area is 3 to 1, then the portion of total locational obsolescence to charge against the reproduction cost new of the improvements would be 75 percent ($3 + 1 = 4$ parts, $100 \div 4 = 25$, $25\% \times 3 = 75\%$).

The usual method of measuring the value impact arising from locational obsolescence is to multiply the rent loss by the gross monthly rent multiplier. It is also possible to measure the impact by direct sales comparison by comparing sales otherwise similar except that some are located within the affected (subject) area and the others are outside the area. Remember that when you measure locational obsolescence by direct sales comparison of total property values, you still need to separate the value effect between site and improvements for most appraisal assignments.

If you are appraising a residence located near a chemical plant which produces an extremely offensive odor, and you find that it rents for $20 per month less than almost identical residences outside the area, it is reasonable to assume a monthly rent loss of $20 arising from locational obsolescence. If your investigation shows that the applicable gross monthly rent multiplier for the subject property is 150, then the total dollar amount of locational obsolescence is $3000 ($20 × 150). If the prevailing ratio of improvement value to total property value within the subject area is 3 to 1, then 75 percent of $3000, or $2250, is the amount of locational obsolescence which should be charged against the reproduction cost new of the improvements. I would offer a word of caution regarding locational obsolescence, and that is to be certain that the particular factor which you feel is offensive is recognized by the market participants within the area in which the subject property is located. Factors which may have a substantial negative value impact in one area or with one particular class of market participant may have little or no impact in another area or with another group of potential buyers. It is market reaction which counts, rather than your own personal likes or dislikes. It is important for appraisers to mirror the market and measure the actions of those buyers and sellers within the particular market segment in which the subject property is located.

## A SIMPLIFIED METHOD OF MEASURING ACCRUED DEPRECIATION OF RESIDENTIAL IMPROVEMENTS

So far, this chapter has furnished detailed description of the various types of depreciation and how to identify and measure the impact of each type. You will find that most appraisals won't require a detailed breakdown of each type of depreciation. For most appraisals, it will be sufficient to identify those items which require prompt correction and to simply calculate the remaining depreciation on an age-life basis based on observed condition. I am not advocating the rigid use of an age-life table. When you have done a number of appraisals in your area, including the necessary sales comparison, you will get a feel for the total economic life, effective age, and remaining economic life of the typical residential structure. This can be tested by deducting the value contribution of the improvements from the reproduction cost new of the improvements for some of the properties which have sold to determine the amount of depreciation as measured by the market.

If you find that the economic life of the type of residential structure you are appraising is 50 years and that, by your observation, it has an effective age of 10 years, then the total accrued depreciation is 20 percent ($100 \div 50 = 2, 2 \times 10 = 20$). This result can be tested by comparing value conclusion by the cost approach (using the observed condition method of estimating depreciation) to sales prices of similar homes within the subject area. The final result of any value conclusion must meet the test of reasonableness. The best technique to use for estimating depreciation is the least complicated method available, provided it arrives at a value result which reflects the market within the area. Those of you who work for large firms with construction departments, performing both new residential building and residential renovation or remodeling, will have a great deal of very useful information available to you. Many appraisers who concentrate exclusively on residential appraising can also build files of valuable data about market measurement of accrued depreciation.

## SUMMARY AND VALUE CONCLUSION OF RESIDENTIAL PROPERTY FROM THE COST APPROACH

Chapter 9 furnished data about the proper procedure to be utilized in appraising the residential site, which is the first step in applying the cost approach in appraising a residential property. Chapter 10 discussed the correct method for estimating reproduction cost new for the residential structure, as well as other man-made improvements which may be a part of the property being appraised. The estimate of reproduction cost new is the second step in applying the cost approach in appraising a residential property. The earlier portion of this chapter defined the various types of accrued depreciation and furnished data about the proper procedures for estimating the dollar amount of the depreciation as it relates to reproduction cost new. The estimate of accrued depreciation is the third and perhaps the most important step in applying the cost approach in appraising residential property. The final portion of this chapter brings the preceding data into summary form for ease of application to residential appraising.

## APPLICABLE APPRAISAL PRINCIPLES

The major appraisal principle involved in applying the cost approach is the principle of substitution. This principle operates on the logical assumption that the informed and rational buyer will pay no more than the cost to him of producing a substitute property which provides the same utility as the subject property. This principle should be used to test the value indicated by the cost approach. If your final value estimate is noticeably higher or lower than the prevailing market for similar properties within the area, then you should review all the data utilized in the cost approach to determine in what respect the principle of substitution has been violated in your appraisal.

The principle of contribution is also of significance in applying the cost approach to the appraisal of residential property. This principle simply holds that a dollar spent on a property should return at least a dollar in value, otherwise the expenditure is not economically justified. This principle is primarily applicable in determining the highest and best use of a property. When you find that the improvements presently on the site add little or nothing to the value of the site when appraised as if vacant, then a change in use is indicated. This principle also applies in estimating accrued depreciation. The value effect of the presence of any particular feature is measured by application of the principle of contribution. The appraiser uses his judgment in estimating the dollar amount of adjustments in determining all forms of accrued depreciation.

One item of primary importance for you to understand is that cost is not value; the number of dollars spent do not necessarily indicate value. You will find situations in which owners have spent many dollars on particular items within a residential structure, or perhaps on the entire structure, which are not acceptable to the buyers within the particular market segment in which the subject property is located. When this occurs, look to market response and not to dollars expended, regardless of how much the owner may stress cost.

## RELATION OF COST APPROACH TO OTHER INDICATORS OF VALUE

When you begin to apply the actual mechanical steps necessary to the cost approach, you will find that it is related in some aspects to both the direct sales comparison approach and the gross rent multiplier approach. You will also find that the data utilized in the three approaches is market-oriented. In estimating site value for use in the cost approach, for sales adjustments in the direct sales comparison approach, and for rent differential adjustments in the gross rent multiplier approach, you usually rely on data from recent market transactions. The cost factors used in estimating reproduction cost in the cost approach are derived and/or verified from current market data. This cost data may also be utilized, provided great care is exercised, in making adjustments in the other two approaches. The estimates of accrued depreciation for individual items within the structure, as well as for the whole structure, are derived to a large extent from market analysis. The data derived from market analysis for estimating accrued depreciation in the cost approach may also be used for sales or rental adjustments in the other two approaches. The valuation of other improvements for use in the cost approach is usually market-derived and may be used as sales or rental adjustments in the other two approaches.

The value as indicated by the cost approach must be within a reasonable range of the value indicated by the direct sales comparison approach and the gross rent multiplier approach. This is logical since all three approaches are interrelated and all are market-oriented. If there is substantial deviation (10 to 15 percent is within reason) in value indicated by any of the three approaches, you should carefully review each approach and the underlying data to find the cause and correct it.

## USES AND LIMITATIONS OF THE COST APPROACH IN APPRAISING RESIDENTIAL PROPERTY

You will occasionally be called upon to appraise a special purpose property such as a church, school, fire station or other limited use structure. You may also be called upon to appraise a uniquely designed residential structure or one which is extremely luxurious. The key element in such special purpose structures is that there are no sales or rentals of this type of property, thus eliminating the application of either the direct sales comparison approach or the gross rent multiplier approach. Under such circumstances, the cost approach is uniquely applicable, thus necessitating extreme care.

The cost approach is often the most meaningful approach when appraising a new structure or proposed construction from plans and specifications. If the new or proposed construction is economically feasible, the necessity of estimating accrued depreciation is eliminated, leaving the appraiser primarily concerned with the accuracy of site value and cost estimate for the improvements.

The cost approach may also be used to project various hypothetical structures upon a site in order to arrive at the optimum level of development to yield maximum return. This approach can also be used to project proposed additions to existing improvements so that maximum return can be achieved for dollars spent.

The cost approach is almost exclusively used in estimating the quantity of insurance which should be carried on a particular structure. This approach is also used in estimating the amount of insurance compensation which should be paid when the property is either damaged or destroyed.

The major limitation on the use of the cost approach is when the subject property has suffered a large amount of accrued depreciation. Such depreciation is very difficult to estimate and the reliability of the cost approach decreases almost in direct proportion to the increase in the age of the structure or other factors which cause accrued depreciation to increase. The cost approach also becomes less reliable when the improvements have been poorly maintained and/or are not the most profitable use of the site.

It will often be very difficult and probably excessively expensive to estimate the reproduction cost new of the improvements. It may be necessary to employ cost estimators to estimate costs and engineers to assist in estimating accrued depreciation. Only the most complicated appraisals with an almost unlimited fee would justify the use of the cost approach under such circumstances.

## SUMMARY AND FORMAT FOR COST APPROACH

Just as with any tool at our disposal, the cost approach is useful in most appraisals and should not be easily discarded. It is also important to understand the limitations of the cost approach. You will probably hear people say (some being appraisers who should know better), "The cost approach sets the upper limit of value." The cost approach value indication *may not,* and in fact *need not* be the highest value shown by any of the three approaches. The fact is that reproduction cost new with no depreciation deducted would *usually* set the upper limit to the amount which an informed buyer would pay for the property. This is consistent with the principle of substitution, which says that an informed buyer would pay no more for a given property than the cost of producing a substitute property provided he were free to produce such substitute and could do so without encountering excessive or expensive delay. As appraisers, we should avoid the trap of making statements which are based upon inaccurate clichés.

The suggested format for the cost approach in a simple narrative appraisal report of the typical residential property is as follows:

**SUGGESTED FORMAT FOR COST APPROACH IN A SIMPLE NARRATIVE APPRAISAL REPORT OF THE TYPICAL RESIDENTIAL PROPERTY**

| | | | |
|---|---|---|---|
| Living Area | | 2200 Sq. Ft. | |
| Porch | ( 200 Sq. Ft. @ 50%) | 100 Sq. Ft. | |
| Carport | ( 400 Sq. Ft. @ 50%) | 200 Sq. Ft. | |
| Patio | (1200 Sq. Ft. @ 25%) | 300 Sq. Ft. | |
| Effective Area | | | 2,800 Sq. Ft. |
| Reproduction Cost per Sq. Ft. | | | $ 25.00 |
| Reproduction Cost New | | | $70,000.00 |
| Less: Physical Curable Depr.: | | | |
| | Paint Exterior Trim | $ 500 | |
| | Replace Roof | $2500 | |
| | Replace Rotted Wood | $ 500 | |
| | Replace Carpet | $1500 | |
| Total Physical Curable | | | $ 5,000.00 |
| Amount R.C.N. Not Previously Depreciated | | | $65,000.00 |
| Economic Life When New | | 50 Yrs. | |
| Remaining Economic Life | | 40 Yrs. | |
| Effective Age | | 10 Yrs. | |
| % Accrued Depr. (100 ÷ 50 = 2% × 10 Yrs.) | | | 20 % |
| Amount of Depreciation ($65,000 × 20%) | | | $13,000.00 |
| Indicated Value of Major Improvements | | | $52,000.00 |
| Add: Present Value of Site Improvements | | | $ 3,000.00 |
| Add: Lot Value (by Sales Comparison) | | | $20,000.00 |
| VALUE AS INDICATED BY COST APPROACH | | | $75,000.00 |

# 12

# How to Apply the Direct Sales Comparison Approach in Appraising Residential Property

Most appraisal assignments you receive will require an estimate of market value. In most areas of the United States, you will find that there is an active enough market for residential property to enable the appraiser to find a sufficient quantity of recent comparable sales. Under such circumstances, you will find that the direct sales comparison approach is the most meaningful approach to value in appraising residential property, whether you are appraising single-family, multi-family or condominium property.

## ELEMENTS OF MARKET VALUE

In using the direct sales comparison approach for appraising residential property, it is essential that all sales used for comparison purposes be recent sales of properties similar to the subject, and such sales must be normal market transactions. In our earlier discussion of the definition and meaning of market value, I suggested some of the essential ingredients which must be present if the sale is to be considered as a normal market transaction.

In applying the direct sales comparison approach, all of the comparable sales should be carefully analyzed and you should not use a sale for comparison purposes unless certain elements of market value are present. Of primary importance is that the sale should be an arm's-length transaction with no unusual pressure on either the buyer or the seller. This condition would rule out sales to settle domestic squabbles, sales to obtain cash to pay for hospital charges or other health care, sales which are caused by employment pressures requiring hurried moves, and sales to obtain immediate cash to avoid a serious financial problem. Another important element is that the sale property should have been exposed to the market for a sufficient time to allow a number of potential buyers to become aware of it. This condition eliminates the use of rash, spur of the moment sales which might not be representative of the current market.

It is also important for the element of the informed buyer and seller to be present in the sales transaction. This condition eliminates sales which are not reflective of the rational and prudent behavior which one would expect of buyers and sellers who had adequate market information available to them. Another very important element which should receive your attention is that the payment involved should be under terms and conditions typical within the particular market. This condition eliminates the use of sales in which the sales price is overstated and an abnormally low interest rate is applied to the financed portion, in an attempt to convert substantial sums of money to capital gains rates of taxation rather than being taxed at normal rates as interest income.

You will also find sales prices inflated enough so that the buyer can borrow all of the true selling price, thus making this sale meaningless for comparison purposes. Sales which are not consistent with terms and conditions typical of the current market will usually clash with those which are typical, and this will help you to identify and discard such sales when applying the direct sales comparison approach.

## APPLICABLE APPRAISAL PRINCIPLE

The major appraisal principle involved in the direct sales comparison approach is the principle of substitution. This principle, as it applies in residential appraising, says that an informed buyer will pay no more for a given residential property than the cost to him of acquiring an equally desirable substitute property. In applying the direct sales comparison approach, the appraiser finds recent sales of similar competitive properties and applies the principle of substitution in adjusting these sales for differences to arrive at a value indication for the subject property. This process simply formalizes the steps which an informed buyer would logically follow.

## MARKET STANDARDS FOR SALES SELECTION

In appraising a residential property by application of the direct sales comparison approach, you are really analyzing the market behavior of purchasers. Since one or two sales transactions may not accurately reflect typical purchaser behavior, it is necessary to have a sufficient number of verified sales. I recommend that at least four sales be analyzed, with as many as ten sales not considered to be excessive. You should avoid using too many sales, since this can not only overburden the appraisal report but can also be confusing to your client. The sales should be as current as possible, should be local sales within the same neighborhood if possible, should reflect the actions of the typically informed purchaser, and should have been purchased for a continuation of the present use, unless your subject property is also ready for change to a different use under the criteria of highest and best use.

## USES AND ADVANTAGES OF DIRECT SALES COMPARISON APPROACH IN APPRAISING RESIDENTIAL PROPERTY

The direct sales comparison approach is particularly well suited to the appraisal of residential property. Where there is an active market with a substantial volume of sales (as is usually true with residential property), this approach comes nearest to reflecting the attitudes of market participants. The direct sales comparison approach should be given major weight in reaching a final value conclusion when adequate market data are available.

The direct sales comparison approach is preferred by the courts in making value decisions. One word of caution to the appraiser is that extreme care is necessary in gathering, verifying and analyzing comparable sales which will be used in a court case. The courts have little or no patience with sloppy work in applying the direct sales comparison approach. The opposing attorney can easily discredit and embarrass the appraiser under such circumstances.

The data obtained for use in making adjustments in the direct sales comparison approach are also used in estimating accrued depreciation in the cost approach and in making rent adjustments in the gross rent multiplier approach.

## LIMITATIONS OF DIRECT SALES COMPARISON APPROACH IN APPRAISING RESIDENTIAL PROPERTY

One major limitation on the use of the direct sales comparison approach is the lack of adequate comparable sales data in many instances. This would be true in cases of residential appraising in which the subject is either unique in design, age, type and condition, or is an extremely expensive luxury home. These types of residential properties seldom sell in sufficient quantities to provide adequate data. You may also have problems finding adequate recent sales transactions in small towns or rural communities.

Another limitation on the use of the direct sales comparison approach is that the comparable sales reflect historical data, while we are attempting to estimate current market value. The fact that a sale has occurred recently at a certain price can be used as a guide in estimating current value. The key word here is *recent,* and the further removed from the current date, the less meaningful the sale may be. It is essential that your sales files be kept very current. You should be aware of and adjust for any unusual events which may have occurred to affect the values within the area between the date of the sale and the date of the appraisal.

Another problem, but not necessarily a limitation, in using the direct sales comparison approach is the difficulty involved in identifying and measuring the dollar effect of differences between the sale property and the subject property. It is only those differences which the typical buyer considers, and not the appraiser's own likes and dislikes, which should be considered as adjustments. The only logical method of measuring the dollar effect on sales price of the presence or absence of a particular feature is to compare sales of otherwise identical properties to arrive at the buyer's reaction to the particular item. The validity of the value indicated by the direct sales comparison approach is in direct proportion to the effort put into deriving it.

## SOURCES OF COMPARABLE RESIDENTIAL SALES DATA

I stressed in the earlier part of this chapter that the appraiser must have an adequate number of verified sales transactions if he is to arrive at a meaningful value estimate by use of the direct sales comparison approach. There are several useful sources which the appraiser may use in obtaining such sales data. These sources may be divided into two types, which are public and private, as follows:

### PUBLIC SOURCES OF SALES DATA

1. *Deed and mortgage recordings* are found in the county and/or city recording clerk's office. The offices where these documents are recorded may have different names in various areas, but their function is the same: to keep a continuing record of all real property and many personal property transactions. You can check the records yourself, and obtain copies of the individual documents you select, by paying a modest copying fee or, if you live in a city of

substantial size, you can subscribe to a service which will give you data on every recorded document. In many instances, the cost is well justified by the time saved. If you are part of a large real estate firm, you may have clerical personnel who can obtain this data for you on a regularly scheduled basis.

2. *Tax assessment records* are helpful in many areas. While the values shown on such records may be meaningless as a current indication of value, you can usually find data about recent transfers within the immediate area of the subject property so that you can follow up on the transactions which appear to be comparable. You can also obtain data about lot size, age, size and condition of improvements, plot plans and sometimes even aerial photographs from the assessor's files.

3. *The city or county planning commission or zoning board* may have maps, building permits or construction data which you may use for follow-up to obtain sales data.

4. *FHA or VA sales reports* can be used as a source of sales which can be further verified for use as comparable sales. These sales require close follow-up before they can be used with any degree of confidence.

## PRIVATE SOURCES OF SALES DATA

1. *Multiple Listing Services* are excellent sources of comparable sales data if they are available in your area. In many instances, the card or fact sheet about a property will give much needed construction data, site data, availability and cost of financing, as well as a description of non-real-estate items. Many such services will show the date on which a property was listed, the asking price, the date of sale and the sales price. This is very helpful in analyzing the general market activity in the area and may indicate if the property met with abnormal market resistance. Most real estate firms are members of Multiple Listing. The data provided by this service has many other uses, besides providing common listings, to which real estate salesmen have access.

2. *Market data subscription services* are available in many areas. If such a service is available at a reasonable price, this may be your best source. Be sure that the data is both current and accurate before subscribing to a market data reporting service.

3. *Title and/or abstract companies* will research sales in a particular area for you for a fee (which may be excessive for your appraisal assignment). Here again, you should have confidence in the company selected.

4. *Other appraisers* will usually share comparable sales data with you at little or no cost, provided you are ready to reciprocate. Don't expect them to analyze the sale for you.

5. *Brokers, lenders, builders and regular investors in real estate* will cooperate with you in finding comparable sales data if you approach them correctly. Remember, you are asking them to do you a favor and they deserve the most courteous attention.

6. *For sale (or sold) signs* in the area are excellent leads to be followed in securing comparable sales data. Keep in mind that offered prices are what the seller would like to receive, and may be well above the market.

7. *Newspaper articles and classified advertisements* are useful as leads in seeking comparable sales.

8. *Your own files* are the most important source of comparable sales data. You should keep a current file of verified sales which you may have secured from any or all of the previously listed public and private sources. An additional source of comparable sales data comes from properties you appraised which have subsequently sold. You have all the necessary information available on such sales except verification of sales price. I have found that the most efficient method of filing comparable sales is alphabetically by street name, from the lowest to the highest street address number. This type of sales filing system tends to group the sales which are most similar and also allows you to quickly find sales data nearest in location to the subject property. If you are part of a medium-to-large-sized real estate firm, it will very likely be advantageous to have one person assigned to maintaining a file of verified sales.

## SOURCES OF SALES VERIFICATION

The most important source of sales verification is either the buyer or the seller. If the data obtained from one of the actual participants are sketchy or seem to be out of line with normal market reaction, it may be necessary to contact the other party. Every effort should be made to obtain verification from one of the principals before turning to the other potential sources, such as the broker, lender or closing attorney. I suggest that you obtain as much data about the sale as possible before approaching anyone to verify the sale. Most people will assist you if you approach them courteously, particularly if they see that you have already done some work and are not taking the easy way out by simply "fishing around" blindly for sales information. Remember that all sales must be verified before you use them. Many of you will have a large number of verified sales from various departments within your own real estate firm.

## DATA WHICH SHOULD BE OBTAINED ON COMPARABLE SALES

There are several essential items of data which should be obtained for each comparable sale. These items include date of sale, volume and page where recorded, parties to transaction, type of deed, legal description, stated consideration and/or transaction stamps, verified sales price including when and with whom verified, unusual motivating factors, financing terms, easements or other restrictions, and details about any personal property which may have been included in the sale.

The appraiser should also obtain information about property type, size, area, number and type of rooms, with notations about unusual or inefficient floor plan. It is essential to know the age and condition as well as the effective age of the principal structure. The type, age, condition and probable remaining economic life of built-ins or other special features should also be noted. Data about site and placement of improvements on the site should be included as should type, size, age and condition of accessory structures. Zoning, deed restrictions, assessments and tax burden should be noted, and notation should be made of any functional or locational problems which may be present, and the overall appearance and market appeal (or lack of same).

## UNDERSTANDING THE VARIOUS ELEMENTS OF COMPARISON FOR RESIDENTIAL COMPARABLE SALES

It is almost always necessary to adjust comparable sales for differences between the sale property and the subject property. Sales which require no adjustment are almost never encountered. In making adjustments, you should be certain that the items you consider significant enough to require adjustment are clearly recognized by market participants. Only pertinent adjustments should be made without attempting to make a great number of adjustments, some of which may be meaningless in reaching a final value conclusion. The sale property should always be adjusted to the subject property. The goal of the adjustment process in the direct sales comparison approach is to arrive at the price the sale property *would have sold for* if it had been identical to the subject.

## PHYSICAL ELEMENTS OF COMPARISON FOR RESIDENTIAL COMPARABLE SALES

There are certain physical elements of comparison which can be considered on a unit basis, such as square foot, cubic foot or number of rooms. There are certain physical elements, such as the presence or absence of particular attributes and/or functional inadequacies or super-adequacies.

Some physical elements of comparison are architectural conformity, size, number of rooms, age, condition, structural type and quality, special features, functional adequacy, accessory buildings, site and site improvements. It isn't necessary to make a separate adjustment for each of these physical elements. For example, size and number of rooms may be combined, as may age and condition. It would also be possible to combine architectural conformity with structural type and quality, and to combine accessory buildings with site improvements.

## LOCATIONAL ELEMENTS OF COMPARISON FOR RESIDENTIAL COMPARABLE SALES

There are certain locational elements of comparison which should be considered. This can be made as a single adjustment item, but should consider conformity with age, condition, size, type and price range of houses in the neighborhood. Also to be considered are the amenities and facilities in the neighborhood, as well as conformity with zoning or other use restrictions.

## OTHER ELEMENTS OF COMPARISON FOR RESIDENTIAL COMPARABLE SALES

The date of sale is a very important item to consider for sales adjustment purposes. Since you are attempting to estimate current value, it is necessary to adjust the sales price to what it would sell for if the only change since the date of the sale had been caused by passage of time. The best method of estimating the proper time adjustment is to have a sale and a current resale of the same property. You can also look at the change in sales price as time passes for similar new homes in currently developing subdivisions. You should avoid using cost of living index or similar types of general purpose indices to arrive at time adjustments.

Conditions of sale is a possible adjustment item. This would reflect unusual conditions which would make the sale something less than a normal arm's-length transaction. I suggest discarding a sale which requires this adjustment if you have a sufficient quantity of sales without it.

## UNITS OF COMPARISON FOR RESIDENTIAL COMPARABLE SALES

If the appraiser can reduce property differences to meaningful units of comparison, he can prepare an appraisal report which can be more easily understood. The units of comparison utilized must reflect the thinking of current market participants.

The most common units of comparison for reasonably similar residential property, listed in order of frequency of use, are as follows:

1. Sales price per square foot of living area.
2. Sales price per square foot of foundation area.
3. Sales price per room.
4. Sales price per cubic foot of building area.

## THE COMPARABLE SALES ADJUSTMENT PROCESS FOR RESIDENTIAL PROPERTY

The appraiser must adjust each comparable sale to the subject for meaningful differences. The validity and amount of any adjustment should be clearly supported by market analysis so that the appraiser can explain and defend it. The subject property is always the standard by which the comparable sale is measured.

There are three methods of making adjustments, as follows:

1. *Plus and minus dollar adjustments* are the most commonly used and are the easiest method to explain. This type of adjustment looks at the value effect in dollars of the presence or absence of certain features. For example, if the subject property had an extra half-bath that contributed $1000 in the market, the comparable sales price would be adjusted upward by $1000. This same procedure, utilizing either plus or minus lump-sum dollar adjustments, would be applied for each difference.

2. *Plus and minus percentage adjustments* are frequently used, and differ from plus and minus dollar adjustments only in that the dollar differences have been converted to percentage differences. This method adds nothing to the accuracy of the final value indicator and is more difficult to explain and defend than plus and minus dollar adjustments.

3. *Cumulative percentage adjustments* are a very poor alternative to the other two types of adjustment and I strongly advise you not to use this method at all. This method of adjustment requires a chain calculation to arrive at a cumulative percentage, thus making the adjustments interdependent rather than independent. For example, if the subject property is 10 percent better in terms of location, 5 percent better in condition and 10 percent poorer in terms of built-ins, the cumulative percentage adjustment to apply to comparable

sales price would be 1.0395 percent (1.10 × 1.05 × .90). This method is extremely difficult to explain and defend.

## CORRELATION OF ADJUSTED RESIDENTIAL COMPARABLE SALES

After several sales are adjusted, you will have as many different indicators of value for the subject property as there are comparable sales. However, if you have done your analysis carefully enough, the range of value indicators should be relatively narrow. You should never average these indicators or even use a weighted average to arrive at a final value estimate by the direct sales comparison approach. The proper technique is to examine each comparable sale and give the most weight to the value indicated by those sales which were most recent and/or most like the subject property, thus requiring the least adjustment.

## SUMMARY

The direct sales comparison approach is the most meaningful approach for appraising residential property, and it warrants your best effort. The best method for displaying comparable sales is to use a sales grid with an accompanying explanation for each adjustment. The schedule which follows offers a suggested format. I recommend that your residential comparable sales be arrayed in such a grid format even if they are not to be part of the report you furnish the client. You should also have supporting data and an adequate explanation for each of the adjustments made to the comparable sale. Even if the appraisal is for in-house use by your employer, or for your own use, you will find it quite helpful at a later date to have documentation for what you did through this very important approach to value.

**DIRECT SALES COMPARISON APPROACH**

**SUGGESTED GRID FORMAT FOR SCHEDULE OF ADJUSTMENTS**

| *ITEMS OF COMPARISON* | *SUBJECT PROPERTY* | *COMPARABLE #1* | | *COMPARABLE #2* | | *COMPARABLE #3* | |
|---|---|---|---|---|---|---|---|
| Date of Sale | Date of Appraisal | 3-8-79 | | 4-14-79 | | 5-9-79 | |
| Age | 11 years | 11 years | | 11 years | | 11 years | |
| Condition: | | | | | | | |
| Interior | Good—needs floors refin. | Better | –$100 | Better | –$175 | Comparable | |
| Exterior | Good—needs touch-up | Comparable | | Better | –$ 75 | Poorer | +$ 100 |
| Number of Rooms | 6 rooms, 1 bath | 6 rooms, 1 bath | | 6 rooms, 1 bath | | 6 rooms, 1 bath | |
| Functional Design | Sloped ceiling | Better | –$500 | Better | –$500 | Better | –$500 |
| Area—sq. ft. | | | | | | | |
| Living area | 1090 | 1080 | +$100 | 1100 | –$100 | 1080 | +$ 100 |
| Carport | 225 | 225 | | 225 | | None (225 × $4.25) | +$ 950 |
| Garage | None | None | | None | | 250 (× $8. s.f.) | –$2000 |
| Storage room | 44 | 45 | | 45 | | 50 (6 × $4.50) | –$ 27 |
| Patio | 240 | 200 (40 × $.75) | +$ 30 | 280 (40 × $.75) | –$ 30 | 260 (20 × $.75) | –$ 15 |
| Landscaping | Excellent | Comparable | | Comparable | | Comparable | |
| Walks and Drive | Good | Comparable | | Comparable | | Comparable | |
| Construction Quality | Good | Comparable | | Comparable | | Comparable | |
| Equipment | Good | Better eq. & central air-cond. | –$950 | Comparable | | Comparable | |
| Lot Value | $3500 | Inside lot | +$200 | Inside lot | +$200 | Corner-comp. | |
| Conditions of Sale | | | | | | | |
| Sale Price | | $15,000 | | $14,600 | | $15,100 | |
| Net Adjustment | | –$ 1,220 | | –$ 680 | | –$ 1,392 | |
| Sales Price Adj. to Subj. | | $13,780 | | $13,920 | | $13,708 | |
| Rounded off to | | $13,800 | | $13,900 | | $13,700 | |

*VALUE CONCLUSION—MARKET DATA APPROACH— $13,800*

**SUGGESTED FORMAT FOR NARRATIVE APPRAISAL REPORT EXPLANATION OF ADJUSTMENTS—DIRECT SALES COMPARISON APPROACH TO VALUE**

On the preceding page, the direct sales comparison approach to value was set forth in detail. This approach to value compared three homes with the subject property. In comparing these homes, certain adjustments had to be made and a plus or minus amount applied to the sales price of each comparable. A discussion of each of the adjustments is set out below.

*DATE OF SALE:* The sales all were in 1979 and no change in the single-family home market has occurred since the date of the sale. No adjustments for time were considered necessary.

*AGE:* The homes were all built in the same year as subject. All have the same physical age and the same effective age. No adjustments for age were considered necessary.

*INTERIOR CONDITION:* The interior condition of comparable no. 3 was the same as subject. Comparable no. 1 needed some interior painting and floor finishing, but was in better condition than subject, needing only approximately $75 worth of interior painting and floor finishing, as compared with $175 for subject. Comparable no. 2 needed no interior painting or floor finishing, compared with $175 for subject property.

*EXTERIOR CONDITION:* The exterior condition of comparable no. 1 was the same as subject. Comparable no. 2 needed no exterior painting, compared with $75 needed for subject property. Comparable no. 3 was in poorer exterior condition than subject and required $175 of exterior painting and caulking, as compared with $75 touch-up for subject property.

| | |
|---|---|
| *NUMBER OF ROOMS:* | All of the comparables, as well as the subject property, have six rooms and one bath. No adjustments for number of rooms was necessary. |
| *FUNCTIONAL DESIGN:* | Comparables 1, 2 and 3 suffer the same functional deficiencies in floor plan as subject property. After careful analysis, it is this Appraiser's opinion that all of the comparables and subject are equivalent in functional design and that all of the comparables are better than subject property for one reason only. This reason is the unusual sloped ceiling of subject property. The ceiling follows the roof line and thus makes the house more difficult to heat or cool. An analysis of the cost of fuel to heat the additional space in the winter and of electricity to operate the attic fan for cooling the additional space in the summer indicated an average cost of $2.50 per month over that required for the standard design. Further analysis of the market indicates that the number of potential buyers will be somewhat reduced due to the unusual ceiling design. In view of the above facts, an adjustment of $500 was made to each comparable to compensate for additional utility cost and for reduction in number of potential buyers. |
| *AREA—SQ. FT.* | Comparables nos. 1 and 3 contained slightly less living area than subject. Comparable no. 2 had slightly more living area than subject. Comparable nos. 1 and 2 had carports of the same size as the subject. Comparable no. 3 had no carport but instead had a single-car, finished garage. Comparables nos. 1 and 2 had storage rooms only 1 sq. ft. larger than subject. Comparable no. 3 had more storage than subject. Each of |

| | |
|---|---|
| | the comparables, as well as the subject, had a plain, reinforced concrete patio. Comparable no. 1 had a smaller patio than subject while comparables nos. 2 and 3 had larger patios than subject. The adjustment for square foot differences have been based on the approximate building costs. It was found after careful analysis that in homes of this type and age the purchaser will generally pay approximate building costs for extra square feet of area. |
| *LANDSCAPING:* | The landscaping of subject and all of the comparables was excellent and no adjustments were considered necessary. |
| *WALKS AND DRIVE:* | The walks and drive of subject and all of the comparables were of reinforced concrete, all were in good condition and no adjustments were considered necessary. |
| *CONSTRUCTION QUALITY:* | Construction quality of subject and all of the comparables were equal and no adjustments were considered necessary. |
| *EQUIPMENT:* | Comparables nos. 2 and 3 had the same equipment as subject and were equal in age and condition. Comparable no. 1 had a larger water heater, a better range hood, and a better heating system than subject. Comparable no. 1 also was centrally air-conditioned with a 3-ton G.E. unit. An analysis of the single-family residence market indicates that the typical buyer will pay from $700 to $850 more for a centrally air-conditioned house. The other items of equipment would demand approximately $200 additional over that in subject. Therefore, an adjustment of $750 for central air-conditioning and |

| | |
|---|---|
| | $200 for other equipment was made to sales price of comparable no. 1. |
| *LOT VALUE:* | Comparable no. 3 is a corner lot, as is subject, and is considered equal to subject. Comparables nos. 1 and 2 are 80′ × 150′ inside lots. Generally, 80′ × 150′ lots in the neighborhood sell for approximately $40 per front foot or $3200. The lots of comparables nos. 1 and 2 are above-average in topography and landscaping and are estimated to have a market value of $3300. Therefore, an adjustment of $200 was made for lot value on comparables nos. 1 and 2. |
| *CONDITIONS OF SALE:* | No unusual conditions were found which would require adjustment to the sales price of either of the comparables. |

**SUMMARY AND CONCLUSIONS**

Each of the three comparables sold at a price higher than the value conclusion for the subject property. However, the properties are highly comparable in age, size, location and construction quality. All of the comparables fit well within the range of prices for the neighborhood as does the subject property. The adjustments are 7.5 percent for comparable no. 1, 4.5 percent for comparable no. 2, and 9 percent for comparable no. 3. It is the opinion of this Appraiser that the adjustments required are within reason and that the data presented lends itself to a supportable value conclusion as stated in earlier portions of this book. I recommend that a minimum of four sales and a maximum of ten sales be used for comparison purposes. Three sales were used here for ease of listing since the same format applies under all circumstances.

**SUGGESTED FORMAT WHEN FORMAL NARRATIVE APPRAISAL REPORT IS NOT REQUIRED**

The grid format should be used even if kept in your files in handwritten form. When comparable sales are arrayed in grid form, with the major elements of comparison listed for the subject property and for each sale, the possibility of omitting important items is substantially reduced. You will find that the time required to prepare such a sales comparison grid is not too burdensome. I would recommend that a grid form be pre-printed, listing those items which warrant recognition and adjustment as determined by your analysis of the local market. If a particular appraisal assignment does not require some of the types of adjustments which you have pre-printed on the form, you can simply show "NA" for "not applicable."

The explanation of adjustments on the preceding pages in the format for a narrative appraisal report would apply here but in much simpler form. I strongly recommend that you write a brief explanation for each adjustment rather than relying on your memory. This applies even if the explanations are kept in handwritten form in your files. Make the explanation long enough so that you can use it to jog your memory.

# 13

# How to Apply the Gross Rent Multiplier Approach in Appraising Residential Property

In preceding chapters, I have discussed and illustrated the proper application of the cost approach and the direct sales comparison approach to appraising residential property. For most residential appraisals, these two approaches are more important than the one covered in this chapter, which is the gross rent multiplier approach. Under normal conditions, the direct sales comparison approach is most meaningful, the cost approach is of secondary importance and the gross rent multiplier approach is the least meaningful in appraising a residential property. However, the appraiser who wishes to do as well-supported an appraisal as he possibly can will use all of the tools at his disposal, and these will include the gross rent multiplier approach if it is at all applicable. The purpose of this chapter is to present the rationale for the gross rent multiplier approach, its proper application, and its limitations.

## RATIONALE OF THE GROSS RENT MULTIPLIER APPROACH

In appraising an income-producing property, the appraiser converts an estimated stream of future net income into an indication of present value by applying an appropriate discounting factor known as a capitalization rate. Most residential properties are not purchased for their ability to produce a stream of net income. Most such properties are purchased for the amenities they offer, such as the ability of the residential structure to provide those features and services expected by an owner-occupant. Because of this unique feature of residential property, the normal income approach is not applicable. The gross rent multiplier approach is the closest thing to the income approach available for use in appraising residential property. The multi-family apartment building is considered to be an income-producing property, requiring the normal income approach in which net income is capitalized. This is illustrated in the Appendix on multi-family apartments.

A gross rent multiplier is nothing more than a number which describes the sales price of a residential structure as a multiple of its monthly unfurnished rental at date of sale. This requires relating actual rental at date of sale to actual sales price on the same date. If you attempt to adjust the rental at date of sale to conform to your idea of what that rent should have been, you are no longer analyzing market reaction and instead are making up your own data to suit your whims and/or prejudices. You have every right to discard a sale which appears to be severely distorted, but not to re-work it so that it fits your idea of what the pattern should be.

You will usually find that sales prices and gross monthly unfurnished rentals of similar residential properties are subject to the same market influences and thus tend to move in the same direction. The gross rent multiplier approach is very simple to apply and this simplicity can lead to a great deal of abuse in its application.

The mechanics of applying the gross rent multiplier approach involve finding a number of sales of residential properties which were rented at time of sale, and dividing the sales price by their monthly unfurnished rentals at date of sale to obtain a multiplier or ratio. For example, if a home sold for $50,000 and was rented for $250 per month, the multiplier or ratio would be 200. If you analyzed several such sales of similar rented properties, you might have multipliers ranging from 195 to 215, and might conclude that your subject property should sell for 200 times its gross monthly unfurnished market rental. You would next estimate the market rental of the subject property by comparing it with similar rented properties and adjusting for differences, and you might conclude that the monthly unfurnished market rental for the subject property would be $275. The value thus indicated for the subject property by the gross rent multiplier approach would be $55,000 (200 × $275). It is very important to stay within the subject's class of property when applying the steps outlined above. If you are employed by a real estate firm which both sells residential property and manages residential rental property for itself and/or others, you have a distinct advantage in that much useful information is available in-house from company records.

## APPLICABLE VALUATION PRINCIPLES

There are three major valuation principles which are applicable to the gross rent multiplier approach. These principles, in order of importance, are substitution, contribution and anticipation:

1. *The principle of substitution* is equally applicable to all of the approaches to value. As it applies to the gross rent multiplier approach, the principle simply states that no informed buyer who is free to act will pay more for a residential property than the cost to him of acquiring a substitute residential property which will produce an equivalent rental stream with the same risk and of the same duration. This assumes that the informed buyer will be aware of the alternatives available to him and will act accordingly.

2. *The principle of contribution* is also applicable to all of the approaches to value. This principle applies to the gross rent multiplier approach in two different aspects. First of all, the presence or absence of certain features in a residential structure will affect the amount of monthly rental income it will produce, and the owner's ability to keep it fully rented. The principle of contribution applies here in measuring the dollar impact on monthly rental. For example, you may find by comparison that the absence of a second bath might reduce the monthly rental by $10 per month, and this rate could be used to arrive at the monthly market rental of the subject property. Secondly, you will find that the amount and duration of the income stream which a given residential structure will produce will affect its value. The principle of contribution states here that the dollar amount of monthly unfurnished rental income does affect value.

3. *The principle of anticipation* applies to the income approach for income-producing properties since the informed buyer bases his decision to purchase a given property on the quantity, quality and duration of the stream of net income which he *anticipates* the property will produce. This principle applies to the gross rent multiplier approach since the informed purchaser of a residential property would buy in *anticipation* of the quantity, quality and duration of the monthly unfurnished rental which the property will produce. This is true even if the purchase is for immediate owner-occupancy, since circumstances could change and make it necessary to rent the property. The informed buyer is paying the present worth of the future income stream.

## DATA REQUIREMENTS AND SOURCES FOR APPRAISING RESIDENTIAL PROPERTY

It should be obvious from my earlier explanation of the mechanics of applying the gross rent multiplier approach that we are dealing with market data and its analysis. For proper application of this approach, it is essential that you have several (at least four and preferably six to ten) recent sales of properties similar to your subject property, which were rented at date of sale. Conclusions drawn from your opinion of what the property *would* have rented for if it *were* rented are meaningless. Sales price and the amount of monthly unfurnished rent should be verified with at least one of the parties to the transaction. If there are furnishings of consequence involved in the sales price and/or the monthly rental, the best move is to discard it for analysis purposes unless you can be very confident that you can adjust the sale and rental accurately enough to properly eliminate the effect of the furnishings. The data required on each sale should be as complete as you would need for the direct sales comparison approach. This quality and quantity of data will allow you to arrive at an appropriate multiplier and a supportable monthly unfurnished market rental estimate for the subject property. If sufficient data are not available to allow you to arrive at a well-supported multiplier and an equally well-supported market rental figure, the gross rent multiplier approach is simply not applicable and you should so state in your report. Unsupported figures can mislead your client and cause you substantial embarrassment.

There are several sources of information to use in applying the gross rent multiplier approach. The sources are primarily from public records and private individuals and organizations. The data sources are primarily the same as those available for use in the direct sales comparison approach. These sources were discussed in detail in Chapter 12, and so will not be repeated here. One additional source of data, which is particularly applicable to the gross rent multiplier approach, is to contact brokers who specialize in managing residential property. If they are approached courteously, these people can supply you with sales of rented properties, comparable rentals and the impact on monthly rent of the presence or absence of a particular feature.

In securing comparable rental data in making adjustments to arrive at an estimate of monthly market rental, you should only consider and adjust for items which would be important to a tenant. Amenities which may be very important to an owner who occupies a *home* may be given minimal consideration by a tenant who occupies a *house*. Keeping these factors in mind will avoid waste of time and effort in gathering and analyzing data which are more complex than that required for the particular appraisal assignment.

## PROCEDURES FOR APPLYING THE GROSS RENT MULTIPLIER APPROACH

The procedures for application of the gross rent multiplier approach are relatively simple and were discussed earlier as the mechanics of the approach. An example of the proper procedure for applying the gross rent multiplier approach is given at the end of this chapter.

## FINAL VALUE INDICATORS BY GROSS SALES COMPARISON APPROACH

If you are appraising a residential property which is rented or in a class of property where an active rental market exists, and you have an active sales market for this class of rented property, then you can arrive at a meaningful value estimate from the gross rent multiplier approach. Another advantage to the approach is that it is a simple, direct and easily understood method of estimating the value of currently rented or normally rented residential property. The adjustments to sales price of comparable sales and to monthly unfurnished rentals of property rented at time of sale are not necessary or warranted, thus simplifying the approach. The only adjustments required are in adjusting comparable monthly unfurnished rentals to arrive at the market rental of the subject property. The required rental adjustments are kept to a minimum to reflect only the major amenity differences which would be important to a tenant.

## LIMITATIONS OF THE GROSS RENT MULTIPLIER APPROACH

One important limitation of the gross rent multiplier approach is that it has little meaning when you are appraising a residential property for owner-occupancy, particularly when it is of the property class not normally rented. Gross rent multipliers and/or rental data obtained from sales of properties which were rented when sold probably do not adequately reflect the amenities of owner-occupancy. This is particularly true for middle-to-upper-price-range residences. Even when the appraisal is of a property which is normally rented, you may find it difficult, if not impossible, to find adequate sales and/or rental data. You will also find it difficult to apply the gross rent multiplier approach to a residential neighborhood which is undergoing a change in character or in use, since the tenant can react quickly to adverse conditions and can move away from a problem much more quickly than the owner can dispose of a property. Major deterioration of a structure is usually reflected more in sales price than in rentals. Rent controls or excessive tax burden can distort normal ratios. The relationship between sales price and rentals may not apply equally in different neighborhoods and for different classes of property. A major limitation is that the simplicity of the approach tends to lead to abuse in many instances. The gross rent multiplier approach does not apply at all to multi-family housing of more than two units. For most multi-family housing, the normal income approach is applicable.

## FINAL VALUE INDICATOR BY GROSS SALES COMPARISON APPROACH

After you have analyzed several sales of properties which were rented at date of sale, you will have as many rent multipliers as you have comparable sales. There is no adjustment to be made to either sales price or gross monthly unfurnished rental of these comparable sales. The multipliers thus obtained should fall within a reasonable range of each other (usually not over 15 percent apart) if you have selected similar comparables which are subject to the same market influences. For example, if your rent multipliers for five sales were 190, 196, 200, 205 and 210, you would consider these to be within a reasonable range. Never average these multipliers or use a weighted average. Analyze the sales and select those two or three which are most like the subject property to narrow down the range considerably, and then you can estimate the rent multiplier for the subject property from within the narrower range. If one of the sale properties is almost identical to the subject, you may want to place sole reliance on the multiplier indicated by that sale. Just be sure that there is support for the multiplier you select. For illustration purposes here, I will select comparable no. 3, which shows a multiplier of 200 and is well-bracketed by comparables 2 and 4.

The monthly unfurnished market rental analysis will also give you a range of rentals for the subject property. If you have been careful in your selection of rent comparables and in your adjustment process, the range of indicated rentals should be relatively narrow (not over 5 to 10 percent). Here again, as in the case of the rent multiplier, don't average the indicated rentals or even use a weighted average. Follow the same procedure outlined for selection of a rent multiplier. For purposes of illustration here, we will assume that the monthly unfurnished market rental of the subject property is estimated to be $300.

Given these facts, the value indicated for the subject property by the gross rent multiplier approach would be $60,000 (200 × $300).

## SUGGESTED FORMAT FOR APPLICATION OF GROSS RENT MULTIPLIER APPROACH IN PREPARING A NARRATIVE APPRAISAL OF A RESIDENTIAL PROPERTY

The usual income approach in which a net income stream is capitalized into an indication of value is usually not applicable to single-family residences. As a substitute for the usual income approach, a multiple known as a gross monthly rent multiplier is generally used. A monthly multiplier is used in lieu of the gross annual rent multiplier. A gross monthly rent multiplier is developed by dividing the purchase price of properties similar to the subject property by the current actual unfurnished rental value of said properties. These multipliers are then analyzed and correlated to form an opinion of a proper gross monthly rent multiplier for the subject property. The purchase prices must be adjusted for change in the market since date of purchase and for any subsequent improvements made to the properties.

While the vast majority of homes in the neighborhood were owner-occupied, there were a few rentals from which a reliable gross monthly rent multiplier could be developed. One factor supporting the rental market in Anywhere, U.S.A., is the large number of military personnel spending short tours of duty at the Air University, the Air War College, and the Air Force base.

The following sales of rental houses similar to subject property were located:

| Address | Date of Sale | Sales Price | Monthly Rental | Gross Monthly Rent Multiplier |
|---|---|---|---|---|
| 3234 Willow Lane Rd. | 1-30-79 | $13,000 | $100 | 130 |
| 3360 Willow Lane Rd. | 1- 9-79 | $13,200 | $100 | 132 |
| 111 East Haven Rd. | 2-19-79 | $15,900 | $110 | 145 |
| 3716 Willow Lane Rd. | 3-30-79 | $14,500 | $110 | 132 |

All of the above properties are recent sales and no time adjustment is required. No improvements have been made since date of sale. The sales prices and monthly rentals were verified. The properties are all located in same neighborhood as subject.

The gross monthly rent multipliers range from 130 to 145. The Appraiser is of the opinion that the gross monthly rent multiplier applicable to the subject property is 132. This opinion was formed after a thorough analysis of the properties listed above, with particular emphasis on sales from $13,000 to $14,500 as being most comparable to the subject property.

The market rental value of the subject property has been established at $105 per month. This opinion was formed after analysis of the monthly rental of similar properties. The indicated market value as developed by the income approach is:

$105 × 132 = $13,860, rounded off to $13,850

ESTIMATE OF VALUE BY THE GROSS RENT MULTIPLIER APPROACH:
$13,850

**SUGGESTED FORMAT FOR ADJUSTMENT GRID IN PREPARING A NARRATIVE APPRAISAL OF A RESIDENTIAL PROPERTY**

| | Subject Property | Rent Comp. #1 | Rent Comp. #2 | Rent Comp. #3 |
|---|---|---|---|---|
| Monthly Unfurnished Rental | NA | $120 | $115 | $125 |
| Rooms | 5 | 6-$10 | 5-same | 6-$10 |
| Baths | 1½ | 2-$5 | 2-$5 | 2-$5 |
| Built-ins | Std. | Std.-same | Good-$5 | Std.-same |
| Location | Avg. | Good-$5 | Avg.-same | Avg.-same |
| Indicated Market Rental for Subject | see below | $100 | $105 | $110 |

Rent comparable no. 2 required the least adjustment and should be given the most weight in arriving at an estimate of the market rental for the subject property. Comparables nos. 1 and 3 required more adjustment, but they both clearly bracket the market rental indicated by rent comparable no. 2.

Based on my analysis of the various rent comparables, it is my conclusion that the monthly unfurnished market rental of the subject property is $105.00.

NOTE 1: Three rent comparables are shown above for ease of listing, but I would suggest that a minimum of four to as high as ten be used in actual practice.

NOTE 2: When no formal narrative report is required, I recommend that the above steps be taken in work sheet form and retained in your file.

# 14

# Guidelines for Correlation (Reconciliation) and Final Value Estimate in Appraisals of Residential Property

After careful application of the three recognized approaches to value (cost approach, direct sales comparison approach and gross rent multiplier approach), you will have three different indications of market value for the subject property. If you have used sound logic in applying the three approaches, the three indicated values should be within a reasonable range of each other. If the value indicators are more than 15 percent apart from highest to lowest, it is logical to assume that some basic appraisal principle has been either overlooked or misapplied, indicating the need to review the data gathered and how it was utilized in each approach to value.

Since the ultimate goal in almost all appraisal assignments is to arrive at a single value estimate rather than a range of values, it is necessary for the appraiser to carefully review the steps taken in applying the three approaches to value and resolve this mass of data into his final opinion of value. This review process has been historically called *correlation,* and this term is still most commonly used. Another term which is gaining in popularity and which means the same thing is *reconciliation.* The care with which you conduct this review process is of the utmost importance in every appraisal you make. The purpose of this chapter is to furnish some guidelines for you to follow when you appraise residential properties.

## HOW CORRELATION (RECONCILIATION) APPLIES TO THE THREE APPROACHES TO APPRAISING RESIDENTIAL PROPERTY

As you apply each of the three approaches to value throughout the entire appraisal, you will already have done a certain amount of correlation or reconciliation in arriving at your three indicators of value. In applying the cost approach, you have arrived at a site value estimate after analyzing several sales of vacant residential lots, adjusting the sales for differences to arrive at a number of indicated site values for the subject site, and correlating or reconciling these indicated site values into a final value estimate for the subject site. You also have to analyze a number of reproduction cost figures for the subject structure and correlate or reconcile these to the proper reproduction cost figure used in the cost approach. The correlation or reconciliation process will very likely be required in analyzing various sales for estimating accrued depreciation in the cost approach.

In the direct sales comparison approach, you will find it necessary to correlate or reconcile value differences indicated by a number of sales to account for the presence or absence of certain features, so that a proper adjustment can be made for comparing sales with the subject property. After each sale has been adjusted to the subject property, you will have as many different indicated values for the subject as there are sales. It is necessary to correlate or reconcile these indicators into a single value estimate for the subject property as indicated by the direct sales comparison approach. You will generally find that most weight should be given to those sales which require the least adjustment.

In applying the gross rent multiplier approach, you will analyze several sales of residential property rented at the time of sale, and from this analysis you will derive as many gross rent multipliers as there are sales. It will be necessary to correlate or reconcile these multipliers into one which is applicable to the subject property. It has been my experience that the most recent sale of a residential property which is most similar to the subject property should be given major weight in arriving at a gross rent multiplier. You will also have to analyze a number of rents and adjust for differences to arrive at a well-supported estimate of the market rental for the subject property. The correlation or reconciliation process applies in analyzing rent comparables to arrive at the proper adjustment for the presence or absence of certain features. After you have analyzed several rent comparables and applied adjustments, you will have several different figures, although usually within a narrow range, for the indicated market rental for the subject property. The correlation or reconciliation process applies here in arriving at a single figure as the proper market rental for the subject property. I usually find that most weight should be given to those rentals which are of properties most similar to the subject and which require the least adjustments.

## HOW CORRELATION (RECONCILIATION) APPLIES IN REACHING A FINAL VALUE ESTIMATE IN APPRAISING RESIDENTIAL PROPERTY

The last point at which the correlation or reconciliation process applies is in arriving at a final value estimate. After the value indicators from each of the three approaches are listed, you can readily determine if they are within a reasonable range of each other. If the range is too wide (over 15 percent), I recommend a thorough review of each approach in order to determine where corrections may be required. Most major variations are caused by unintentional violation of some basic appraisal principle, and your review of the steps in each approach should make the error reasonably easy to locate and correct. If the three value indicators are within reasonable range, your task is much simpler and you will arrive at a final value estimate in which you can have a great deal of confidence.

## HOW TO CORRELATE (RECONCILE) VALUE INDICATORS TO A FINAL VALUE ESTIMATE

After all of the applicable approaches to value have been completed, it is recommended that the value indicated by each approach be listed on a summary sheet. After the indicators are listed, you should immediately check to see if they are within a reasonable range of each other. If there is a variation of more than 15 percent between the highest and the lowest indicator, a careful review of each step in each approach and a correction of any errors which you may find are in order. If, after review and correction, the value is still out of line, I recommend that you consider whether one or more of the approaches might not apply to the particular appraisal assignment and therefore should be eliminated or at least given minimum weight.

For example, if you are appraising a very luxurious home or a home with a unique design, there may be inadequate sales data for a meaningful direct sales comparison approach. Very luxurious homes, uniquely designed homes, or even relatively high-priced homes are seldom rented, so that the gross rent multiplier approach would most likely have little or no meaning. When you are appraising a very old residential structure which is extremely ornate in design or which suffers a large amount of functional and/or economic obsolescence, the value estimate by the cost approach would very likely be suspect and should be given minimum weight. Some appraisal assignments in areas where there is little or no sales activity will require you to range outside the subject neighborhood for comparable sales if any can be found at all. If this situation occurs, my advice is to accord less weight to the direct sales comparison approach if you use it at all.

## TECHNIQUE FOR ARRIVING AT A FINAL VALUE ESTIMATE AFTER REVIEWING AND MAKING NECESSARY CORRECTIONS

After you have resolved the problem of having your applicable value indicators within an acceptable range of each other, the next step is to correlate or reconcile these figures into a final estimate of value. The experience and sound judgment of the appraiser is put to the supreme test at this point. *Never* average, or even use a weighted average, of the value indicators to arrive at a final estimate of value. Such a practice will cause you to be open game for a cross-examining attorney in court, and can also lead your client to wonder whether he employed an appraiser with sound appraisal judgment or someone who is simply capable of a junior high school math exercise! You should review the basic strength and/or weakness of the underlying data used in each approach. After such a review, you should have a good idea as to which of the value indicators has most merit. For a residential property where there is an active current market, the value indicated by the direct sales comparison approach will usually be most meaningful and should be given the most weight. If the structure is not extremely old and does not suffer extensive obsolescence, you will usually find that the cost approach is secondary in importance to the direct sales comparison approach. In most instances, the value indicated by the gross rent multiplier approach will be least meaningful. Occasionally, an appraisal assignment on a special purpose property where you have no sales or rental data will leave you with a carefully applied cost approach as the only alternative. When appraising multi-family property of more than two units, the income approach, where net income is capitalized, will be most meaningful.

You should round off your final value estimate to an amount which is typical of the market in your area for that particular class of property. For example, if property in the class to which your subject property belongs usually sells in $500 increments, then you should round off your final value estimate to a figure such as $40,500, $41,000 or $41,500, rather than something like $40,489, $41,011, or

$41,472. As an appraiser, your goal is to render a supportable estimate of value, and you are never accurate enough to deal in exact odd-dollar figures, particularly when the very market you are seeking to interpret does not do this.

## WHY CORRELATION (RECONCILIATION) SHOULD BE IN WRITTEN FORM FOR ALL RESIDENTIAL APPRAISALS

Most appraisals of residential property will be form reports rather than narrative reports. The form report is usually brief and does not provide space for discussion of your rationale in applying the correlation or reconciliation process. I recommend that you summarize your reasoning and conclusions on some type of simple, handwritten sheet, which you can retain in the file along with your copy of the form report. This additional documentation may be of great assistance to you at a later date when you will not want to entirely trust your memory. If your appraisal assignment requires a narrative report, you should discuss each of the three approaches separately. If one or more of the recognized approaches does not apply to the particular property you are appraising, you should state this fact and furnish valid reasons for excluding the approach. Your discussion of each approach should weigh the merits of the underlying data and the strength and/or weakness of each approach. Your discussion should lead the reader of the appraisal report through your reasoning process, and should clearly lead him to the same final value estimate as the one you reached. The sample correlation (reconciliation) and final value estimate which follows illustrates the proper method to be applied in a narrative appraisal report.

If you are an employee of a medium to large brokerage firm or lending institution, the natural tendency is to do the minimum amount of documentation, since the appraisals are for in-house use. I strongly recommend that you take the small amount of additional time to write a simple correlation (reconciliation) to document what you did, rather than relying on your memory.

**SUGGESTED FORMAT FOR CORRELATION (RECONCILIATION) AND FINAL VALUE ESTIMATE TO BE USED IN NARRATIVE APPRAISALS OF RESIDENTIAL PROPERTY**

In the preceding portions of this report, the value of the subject property has been estimated by the three approaches to value as follows:

| | |
|---|---|
| *COST APPROACH* | $44,000 |
| *DIRECT SALES COMPARISON APPROACH* | $43,800 |
| *GROSS RENT MULTIPLIER APPROACH* | $43,900 |

The typical purchaser of a residential property buys it for its use rather than for income purposes, and for this reason the gross rent multiplier approach for single-family dwellings is normally weak. Most single-family residences purchased for rental purposes offer considerably less amenities than the subject property and consequently would be lower priced. In view of the above facts, it is the opinion of the Appraiser that the value indicated by the gross rent multiplier approach should be given least weight.

The cost approach on a structure as new as the subject property, and where the site is improved to its highest and best use, can be given considerable weight. The only factor which tends to weaken the value indicated by the cost approach is the functional obsolescence present in the structure. This functional deficiency required considerable adjustment.

The comparable sales used in the direct sales comparison approach were very similar to the subject property. The adjustments required were moderate. It is my opinion that the direct sales comparison approach should be given most weight in this appraisal.

The ratio of land to buildings is typical for the area. The property fits well into the neighborhood and there are no inharmonious factors present which might adversely affect value. The high percentage of homeowners, when combined with the various amenities offered by this subdivision, result in a stable and popular neighborhood in which a typical homeowner will find a home offering the maximum amenities in his socio-economic class.

After careful analysis of the three approaches to value, and with particular emphasis on the direct sales comparison approach, it is the opinion of this Appraiser that the market value of the subject property, as of June 30, 1979, is $43,800.00.

Based on the information set forth in this report, general experience in the real estate business and appraisal experience, it is my opinion that the value, as defined herein, of the subject property as of June 30, 1979, is

FORTY THREE THOUSAND EIGHT HUNDRED ($43,800.00) DOLLARS

____________________________

Appraiser

**SUGGESTED FORMAT FOR CORRELATION (RECONCILIATION) AND FINAL VALUE ESTIMATE TO BE RETAINED IN PERSONAL FILES WHEN NOT MADE A PART OF THE FORMAL APPRAISAL REPORT**

The three value indicators by the three approaches are:

| | |
|---|---|
| *COST APPROACH* | $44,000 |
| *DIRECT SALES COMPARISON APPROACH* | $43,800 |
| *GROSS RENT MULTIPLIER APPROACH* | $43,900 |

Even though the value indicators are close, I feel that the cost indicator is weakened due to functional problems arising from inefficient design. While care was exercised in my estimate of functional obsolescence, I have some problems with the cost approach.

The gross rent multiplier approach is weak due to limited rentals of this type of house and a limited number of sales of similar homes which were rented at date of sale.

The direct sales comparison approach is very strong due to a very active market of extremely similar homes. There were several recent sales which required minimum adjustment.

THE VALUE BASED ON DIRECT SALES IS: $43,800

# 15

# How to Write the Appraisal Report for Residential Property

There are only two types of appraisal reports which are worthy of discussion and consideration. These two types of appraisal reports are the form report and the narrative report. Letters of opinion and oral value opinions are also used, but both of these should be carefully avoided. The time taken and the effort made on your part to arrive at a supportable value conclusion to put in a letter of opinion is almost equal to that required for a form report, saving you very little time and saving your client little or no money. In view of this fact, I recommend nothing less detailed than a form report giving a clear record of what you did and how you did it. Oral opinions of value should *never* be given. Such oral opinions are simply giving away your time and talent for free, and in many instances can place you in an embarrassing position with your clients and/or the professional appraisal organizations which forbid this practice. Even if you are employed by a medium to large real estate firm or a lending institution, you should insist on preparing a written report.

## TYPE OF RESIDENTIAL APPRAISAL REPORT USED MOST OFTEN

The most commonly used report format for residential appraisals is the form report. The standard form which is used in most residential appraisals where the form report is used is designed to provide a great volume of data in the least possible space. The data requirements and the amount of analysis you will have to do are no less for the form report than for the narrative report. The only time savings, and the reason for the fee for preparing a form report being less than that for a narrative report, is the actual time used to write the report. One word of caution about using the form report is that you should not fall into the trap of filling in every blank space, simply to complete the form, without proper analysis or adequate supporting data being made a part of your appraisal file. Even if the form does not provide adequate space to show your reasoning process, this should be shown on separate handwritten worksheets and kept in your permanent file. A discussion of the items which should be a part of any appraisal report will be included later in this chapter.

## WHEN THE NARRATIVE APPRAISAL REPORT IS APPLICABLE

The narrative appraisal report is used less frequently than the form report, primarily because the usual fee for appraising a residential property is not sufficient to compensate the appraiser adequately for the additional time required to write such a report. The narrative report is preferable to the form report in that the appraiser can explain his rationale much better in the narrative form, and the client or others who use the report can follow his reasoning process and more readily accept his final value conclusion.

If you work primarily in the same city and are very active in appraising residential properties, it is possible to provide your client with a narrative report for very little more cost to him than would be required for a form report. There are many pages in a narrative report which are standard for all such reports and simply require instructions to your secretary to copy and include in each report. Beginning at the front of the report and moving through it, you will find that the letter of transmittal, table of contents and summary of salient facts and conclusions will require only minor changes from one narrative report to another. The city data will be identical for all reports until an update is required. The section on neighborhood analysis for each neighborhood in which you do appraisals will remain the same until an update is required. The site analysis and improvement analysis format will remain the same, with only minor changes required to fit the particular property. If you are active in making residential appraisals, you will find that site sales within a particular neighborhood can be utilized with only an occasional update. The same would be true for cost data in the cost approach, sales data in the direct sales comparison approach, and rent multiplier and rent comparable data in the gross rent multiplier approach. It should be obvious to you that the data must be kept current and that the analysis must be made of the particular subject property. The format for correlation (reconciliation) and final value estimate would be the same, with minor changes required to fit the particular subject property. The appraiser's certificate, contingent and limiting conditions, and his qualifications should be the same for most narrative reports.

By utilizing data which you already have available, you can furnish your client with a narrative report for little more than the cost of doing a form-type report. The secret here is to utilize what you already have available in your files plus some good secretarial help and copying machines to furnish your client with a detailed narrative report rather than a simple form which may only partially explain your reasoning process. You may have to completely change five or six pages in a typical narrative report, and even here the format remains the same. The remaining pages will either require minor changes or none at all. Those of you who work for a large firm will have plenty of clerical and secretarial help available.

## UNDERSTANDING THE ESSENTIAL ELEMENTS OF A RESIDENTIAL APPRAISAL REPORT

Certain items must be included in all appraisal reports, regardless of whether they are presented to the client on a pre-printed form or in a formal narrative style. Some elements which would be included in a narrative report would obviously be omitted from a form report. I will discuss these essential elements in the order in which they would most likely be presented in a narrative report, and I will note those which would not be part of a typical form report. Most of the essential elements listed are required by the ethics of the American Institute of Real Estate Appraisers and the Society of Real Estate Appraisers. The few items listed which are not specifically required by the major appraisal organizations are essential to good appraisal practice. These essential elements are as follows:

1. *Title page.* This item is not part of a form report. It is the first thing seen by the client in a narrative report. It should be clear and attractive in appearance.

2. *Letter of transmittal.* This item is not part of a form report. It is the second item your client will see in a narrative report. It should be a neatly typed, concise summary of what you appraised, the date and the purpose of the appraisal, and your final value estimate.

3. *Table of contents.* This item is not part of most form reports. The table of contents should be neatly typed, preferably in all caps and double spaced. It should list the contents of the report by page

number, in the order in which they are included in the appraisal report, so that the client can easily find those items of particular interest to him.

4. *Summary of salient facts and conclusions.* This item is not part of most form reports and is normally included only in the more complicated narrative reports. This page simply summarizes the most important items in the report, such as property description, date of appraisal, value indicated by each approach and final value estimate. For most narrative appraisal reports of a residential property, the data furnished in a good letter of transmittal are sufficient.

5. *Appraiser's certification.* This item should be included in all appraisal reports. It simply certifies that the appraiser has no present or contemplated interest in the subject property. This assures the client that the value estimate is free of any bias or self-interest.

6. *Purpose and date of appraisal.* This item must be included in all appraisal reports. The purpose of almost every residential appraisal is to estimate market value, but the purpose of the appraisal must be clearly stated. The date of the appraisal must be shown, and will usually be the date of last inspection unless there are compelling reasons which require some other date.

7. *Definition of value sought.* This item must be included in all appraisal reports. The form report usually has it pre-printed. I recommend using the definition most commonly accepted in your area, but be sure to show the source from which it came.

8. *Identification of property appraised.* This item must be included in all appraisal reports. I recommend that you obtain a legal description of the property to be appraised and type it in here. The legal description can be abbreviated if necessary, but it should show where the documents (plat and deed) are recorded.

9. *City and neighborhood analysis.* These items should be included in all appraisal reports, although most forms provide very limited space and may require a written supplement if there are some important data you feel the client should have beyond that which the form will provide. When furnishing this data in narrative format, don't simply list the Chamber of Commerce type of data, but furnish conclusions about how this data affects the subject property.

10. *Site analysis and valuation.* This item should be included in all appraisal reports. The form report usually provides very limited space and may require a written supplement if the appraisal problem is complex. In the narrative form, I recommend a concise description and analysis including zoning, whether the present use fits the permitted use, and your opinion of the highest and best use of the site.

Site sales should be listed in sufficient detail to enable your client to understand each sale and how it was adjusted to the subject site in forming your estimate of site value.

11. *Cost approach.* This item should be included in all appraisal reports, unless the subject property does not lend itself to this approach. If the approach is not applicable you should explain why. The form report may not provide sufficient space for the more complicated appraisal and you may need a written supplement. For the narrative report, I recommend that the approach be complete, with any explanatory remarks kept as concise as possible, toward the ultimate goal that the reader will understand what you did as well as how and why you did it.

12. *Direct sales comparison approach.* This item should be present in all appraisal reports, unless the subject property does not lend itself to this approach. Full explanation should be furnished about why the approach is not applicable if you arrive at that conclusion. Most form reports will not provide sufficient space for you to do an adequate job on this approach. I recommend that you furnish the client with an additional written supplement, where necessary, for his full understanding of the approach. You should also retain your handwritten worksheets in your files for later reference, when and if needed. For the narrative report, I recommend furnishing essential details on each sale, a grid showing each sale adjusted to the subject property, an explanation of each adjustment and also an explanation of your reasoning process in arriving at the value indicated for the subject property by this approach.

13. *Gross rent multiplier approach.* This item should be included in all appraisal reports when applicable to the subject property. If the approach is not applicable, then an explanation should be furnished. Most report forms will either fail to provide any space at all for this approach or, if space is provided, it will be minimal. When doing a form report on a residential property where this approach is applicable, you will most likely have to provide a written supplement. For a narrative report where this approach is applicable, I recommend the same care in handling comparables as is exercised for the direct sales comparison approach. If you are going to use the gross rent multiplier approach, it deserves your best effort.

14. *Correlation (reconciliation) and final value estimate.* The form report provides a space for showing the final value estimate but usually does not provide sufficient space for explanation of your reasoning process. If you feel that the property is sufficiently complex, you should provide a written supplement for the client and you

should keep any handwritten data in your file. For the narrative report, I recommend a listing of the values indicated by each approach, a concise discussion of the strength and/or weakness of each approach and an explanation of how the final value estimate was derived, as well as the amount and date of the estimate.

15. *Contingent and limiting conditions.* This item should be included in all appraisal reports. Many report forms have these items pre-printed, but you should not hesitate to add items not included on the form or to furnish the complete list as a supplement if it is not included on the form. This form can usually be prepared in advance and simply inserted in the narrative report. If there are unique problems involved with the appraisal, it may be necessary to change the standard form for that particular assignment.

16. *Appraiser's qualifications.* The form report does not provide space for this, but I recommend a written supplement when you submit the first form report to a new client. You will probably want to update this periodically as you gain additional experience or obtain professional recognition. The qualifications sheet should be neat and concise, listing only the most important items. Most clients will be turned off by too long a listing (more than one page is too much). The qualifications page should be included in all narrative reports.

17. *Addenda.* The form report does not provide space for including addenda items. There may be space provided on the form for a plot plan, improvement sketch and one or two photographs of the subject property. This data will very likely be adequate for most appraisals where the form report is used, but I suggest that you supplement it where necessary. For the narrative report, I recommend a city map with the subject neighborhood clearly shown, including location of schools, shopping and other essential services. The map should also show the location of the subject property and all sales and rent comparables used. The report should include a carefully prepared plot plan of the subject site and a sketch to scale of the subject improvements. I recommend that you obtain a good quality 35 mm camera with a wide angle lens, and include clear color photographs of the subject property, as well as at least a front view of all sales and rent comparables used.

## SUMMARY

Remember that the first and perhaps the most lasting impression your client will have of you as an appraiser will be derived from the appraisal report. The appraiser who wishes to succeed in this most interesting and challenging profession will give each report his very best effort, always seeking to improve his ability. The fact that you may currently be on salary as part of the staff of a real estate firm or a lending institution does not lessen the importance of preparing a quality appraisal report. Even if you have to put in some overtime for which you are not immediately compensated, you will be well paid in the long run for the extra effort required to write a report that you can regard with pride.

## EXAMPLE OF FORM REPORT FOR RESIDENTIAL PROPERTY

| NAME OF OWNER(S) | MAIL ADDRESS | TELEPHONE NO.(S) |
| --- | --- | --- |
| John N. Doe | 1348 Pine Ridge Road<br>Anywhere, U.S.A. | (205) 263-2319 |

| ADDRESS | | AREA OR SUBDIVISION |
| --- | --- | --- |
| 1348 Pine Ridge Road | | Lot 9-Block E<br>Highpoint Estates<br>Plat #1 |
| CITY<br>Anywhere | STATE<br>U.S.A. | |

### PURPOSE OF APPRAISAL

To estimate Market Value in fee simple as of August 27, 1979

"Current fair market value" is defined as the amount that a buyer would be willing to pay for the property in its present condition and location, after time for negotiation, which is reasonable for the area, and not based on an immediate sale due to pressures on the seller to transact a quick sale.

### APPRAISAL SUMMARY

| | |
| --- | --- |
| APPRAISED VALUE—LAND **and Site Improvements** | $ 9,600 |
| APPRAISED VALUE—IMPROVEMENTS | $34,400 |
| TOTAL | $44,000 |

(Emphasis was given to market approach unless otherwise noted)

### CERTIFICATION

I do hereby certify that I have made a personal inspection of subject property and an analysis of those factors affecting its value, that I have no interest, present or contemplated, in the property, that neither the employment to make the appraisal nor the compensation, is contingent upon the value of the property reported, and to the best of my knowledge and belief, all statements and information in this report are true and correct, and no important facts have been withheld or overlooked.

APPRAISER'S SIGNATURE

DATE August 27, 1979 John E. Green, MAI-SRPA

FIRM NAME *(Please Print)*

### LIMITING CONDITIONS

This appraisal is subject to the following limiting conditions:

The legal description furnished us is assumed to be correct.

We assume no responsibility for matters legal in character, nor do we render any opinion as to title, which is assumed to be marketable. All existing liens and encumbrances have been disregarded and the property is appraised as though free and clear under responsible ownership and competent management.

The sketch in this report is included to assist the reader in visualizing the property. We have made no survey of the property and assume no responsibility in connection with such matters.

Unless otherwise noted herein, it is assumed that there are no encroachments, zoning violations or restrictions existing in the subject property.

Information, estimates and opinions contained in this report are obtained from sources considered reliable; however, no liability for them can be assumed by the appraiser.

Possession of this report, or a copy thereof, does not carry with it the right of publication, nor may it be used for any purpose by any but the applicant without the previous written consent of the appraiser or the applicant, and in any event only with proper qualification.

We are not required to give testimony or attendance in court by reason of this appraisal, with reference to the property in question, unless arrangements have been made previously therefor.

The division of the land and improvement values estimated herein is applicable only under the program of utilization shown. These separate valuations are invalidated by any other application.

DETAILS OF PROPERTY *(Describe by Marking "X" Where Possible)*

| CHECK TYPE OF HOUSE | | | | | | # DWELLING UNITS | # STORIES | TOTAL # ROOMS | # BEDROOMS | # BATHS |
|---|---|---|---|---|---|---|---|---|---|---|
| Spl. Level | Cape Cod | Colonial | Ranch | English | Other-Describe | | | | | |
| | | x | | | | 1 | 2 | 8 | 4 | 2½ |

| TYPE OF EXTERIOR | | | | | | | PLOT SIZE | | | | |
|---|---|---|---|---|---|---|---|---|---|---|---|
| Stone | Brick | Wood Shingle | Asb. Shingle | Clapb'd | Stucco | Other | Front | Rear | Side | Side | Year Built |
| | x | | | | | | 85 | 85 | 145 | 145 | 1970 |

FIRST LEVEL-(List each room, include center hall, powder room, porches, etc. state if modern kitchen.)
**Foyer, Living, Dining, Den, Built-in Kitchen, Laundry, Storage, Bedroom, Full Bath w/Dressing area, ½ Bath**

SECOND LEVEL-(List each room, state if baths are tiled-with shower.)
**Bath (Tile wainscot & floor—shower & tub), Hall, Bedroom, Bedroom, Bedroom**

THIRD LEVEL-(List each room, state if attic is full, finished, etc.)
**Attic partially floored (Storage Only)**

ADDITIONAL LEVEL(S)

BASEMENT: Yes ☐ No x — LIST LAUNDRY, PLAYROOM, ETC. **Laundry**
TYPE OF FOUNDATION: Stone ☐ Concrete Block ☐ Poured Concrete x Brick ☐
TYPE OF ROOF: Compos. x Shingle ☐ Other ☐

PLUMBING: Brass ☐ Copper ☐ Iron ☐
INSULATION: Yes x No ☐ Type- Rockwool, **Fiberglass**, etc. x
SCREENS: Yes ☐ No x Aluminum ☐ Copper ☐ Other ☐
STORM WINDOWS: Yes ☐ No x Aluminum ☐ Wood ☐

WATER SOURCE: Town x Well ☐
SEWAGE SYSTEM: Septic Tank ☐ Sewer x
HEATING SYSTEM—TYPE: Warm Air x Hot Water ☐ Steam ☐
FUEL: Gas x Oil ☐ Coal ☐
ELECTRIC WIRING: 110V x 220V x

GARAGE: No. of Cars **None** TYPE-Detached ☐ Attached ☐ Built-in ☐ Carport **None**
IF PERMANENT SWIMMING POOL IS INCLUDED: Yes ☐ Heated ☐ No ☐ Size
ANNUAL TAXES **$204.75**

ASSESSMENTS
**Land—$600 Imps—$500**

ANY EVIDENCE OF TERMITES ☐ DRY ROT ☐ DAMPNESS ☐ SETTLEMENT ☐ NO EVIDENCE ☒

CHARACTER OF NEIGHBORHOOD IS — **Good** NEIGHBORHOOD ACTIVITY **DEVELOPING**

| MAJOR STRUCTURES | CONSTRUCTION | TYPICAL CONDITION | BUILT-UP | AGE TYPICAL BLDG. | OWNER OCC. | VACANCY | ZONING | TRANSITION TO— |
|---|---|---|---|---|---|---|---|---|
| NEIGH. | **Good** | **Good** | **80%** | **6 mos.** | **99%** | **5%** | **R-85** | |
| BLOCK | **Good** | **Good** | **100%** | **2 yrs.** | **99%** | **0%** | **R-85** | |

| UTILITIES | AVAIL. | CON-NECTED | STREET IMPS. | CONVEN-IENCES | BLK. | MI. | TYPICAL INFLUENCES | IS SUBJECT TYPICAL OF NEIGHBORHOOD? (DESC.) |
|---|---|---|---|---|---|---|---|---|
| WATER | | X | WALKS X | G. SCHOOL | 9 | | OCCUPN. **Exec.** | SUPERIOR ☐ TYPICAL ☒ INFERIOR ☐ |
| SEWER | | X | CURB X | H. SCHOOL | | 2 | INCOME **20M-30M** | |
| GAS | | | PAVING X | STORES | 12 | | RENTALS **None** | |
| ELECTRIC | | X | ALLEYS | CHURCH | 12 | | VALUES **35M-50M** | |
| SEPTIC TANK | | | FIRE PROTECTION X | TRANSPN. | | | | |

REPAIRS *Show Repairs Needed to Place Property in Good, Marketable Condition* *(APPRAISED VALUE IS TO BE BASED ON "AS IS" CONDITION)*

| EXTERIOR REPAIRS | ESTIMATED COST | INTERIOR REPAIRS | ESTIMATED COST |
|---|---|---|---|
| **A minor touch-up of paint trim would be helpful in selling house but is not needed badly enough to be considered mandatory.** | $ | | $ |
| | | TOTAL INTERIOR REPAIRS | $ **None** |
| TOTAL EXTERIOR REPAIRS | $ **None** | TOTAL EXTERIOR & INTERIOR REPAIRS | $ **None** |

NON-REAL-ESTATE ITEMS INCLUDED IN THIS APPRAISAL WITH DOLLAR VALUE.

| | | | |
|---|---|---|---|
| 1. | $ | 5. | $ |
| 2. | $ | 6. | $ |
| 3. | $ | 7. | $ |
| 4. | $ | 8. | $ |
| | | TOTAL *(To Be Included in Cost Aproach)* | $ **None** |

MARKET APPROACH TO VALUE*

| ADDRESS | 1340 Pineridge | + or − | 1387 Pineridge | + or − | 1536 Pineridge | + or − |
|---|---|---|---|---|---|---|
| DATE SOLD | 3-16-79 | + 800 | 1-26-79 | +1,400 | 7-13-79 | + 200 |
| LOT SIZE | 85 x 145 | | 85 x 165 | + 100 | 85 x 155 | |
| STYLE | Modern | +1,000 | | +1,000 | | +1,000 |
| CONDITION | Good | | Good | | Good | |
| BEDROOMS | 4 | | 3 | +2,000 | 4 | |
| BATHS | 2 | + 500 | 2 | + 500 | 2 | + 500 |
| OTHER: | Double garage | −1,000 | | | | |
| | No fireplace | + 800 | Fireplace | | Fireplace | |
| | Comb. Dining Room | +1,500 | Comb. Dining Rm | +1,500 | Sep. Den & Dining | |
| | | | Covered Patio | − 100 | Patio | |
| | | | | | | |

| | | | |
|---|---|---|---|
| TOTAL + or − | + $ 3,600 | $ 6,400 | $ 1,700 |
| SALE PRICES OF COMPARABLES | $ 38,292 | $ 35,256 | $ 44,000 |
| INDICATED VALUE(S) BY MARKET APPROACH | $ 41,900 | $ 41,700 | $ 45,700 |

| ADDRESS | 3412 Woodhill | + or − | | + or − | | + or − |
|---|---|---|---|---|---|---|
| DATE SOLD | 2-27-79 | +1,400 | | | | |
| LOT SIZE | 90 x 160 | + 450 | | | | |
| STYLE | | + 500 | | | | |
| CONDITION | Good | | | | | |
| BEDROOMS | 4 | | | | | |
| BATHS | 2 | + 500 | | | | |
| OTHER: | | | | | | |
| | Fireplace | | | | | |
| | Sep. Den & Dining | | | | | |
| | Double Patio | | | | | |
| | | | | | | |

| | | | |
|---|---|---|---|
| TOTAL + or − | + $ 2,850 | $ | $ |
| SALE PRICES OF COMPARABLES | $ 40,730 | $ | $ |
| INDICATED VALUE(S) BY MARKET APPROACH | $ 43,600 | $ | $ |

COST APPROACH TO VALUE* (Use attachments if necessary)

1. Main Building
   2351 sq. ft. @ $ 15.00 per ft. — $ 35,265
2. Extras—list at right with values. — $
3. Garage or carport—replacement cost new. — $ N/A
4. Other buildings Shed — $ 224
5. Total Replacement Cost New say — $ 35,500
6. Depreciation: Physical 3% — $ 1,065
   - Functional Obsolescence — $ N/A
   - Economic Obsolescence — $ N/A
   - Location or Overimprovement — $ N/A
7. Total Depreciation. — $ 1,065
8. Depreciated Replacement Cost (5-7) — $ 34,435
9. Non-real-estate items — $ Nil
10. Land

85 front ft. @ $ 90 per ft. — $ 7,650

Improvements: Patio, Porch, Drive, Walks — $ 1,200

Landscaping & Fence — $ 800

Total Land — $ 9,650

Indicated Value by Cost Approach say $ 44,000

*Enter your final estimate of value under "APPRAISAL SUMMARY"

*REMARKS* — General condition, adequacy of layout and functional utility. Describe any positive or adverse influences that will affect marketability. Include any other comments or helpful information, i.e. probable means of financing (FHA, Conventional) discount points prevalent, if any, etc.

*The subject is located in a new section of a well established area of Anywhere known as Dalraida. This is a very desirable area, and this new section should develop quickly. The house was built by a reputable builder and is efficiently designed. Due to the scarcity of mortgage money and the high discount points, the time for marketing could be increased somewhat. However, equity sales are still common.*

Front View of Subject Property

Plot Plan and Photographs of Property

Show street names, location of subject property on plot. Show dimensions of lot. Indicate northerly direction.

Paste Upper Edge of Photographs here.

Sketch outline of subject, giving outside dimensions.

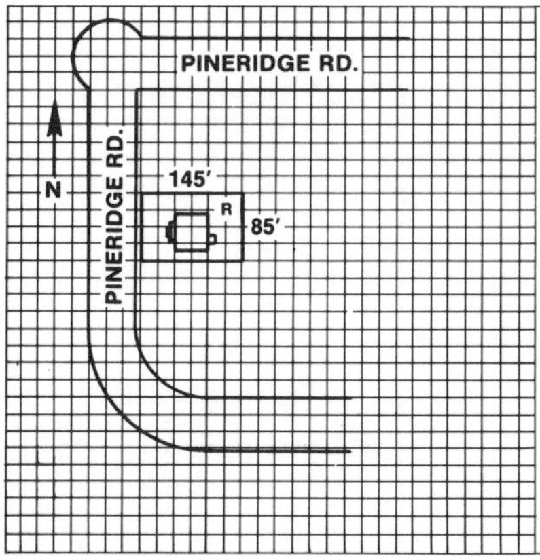


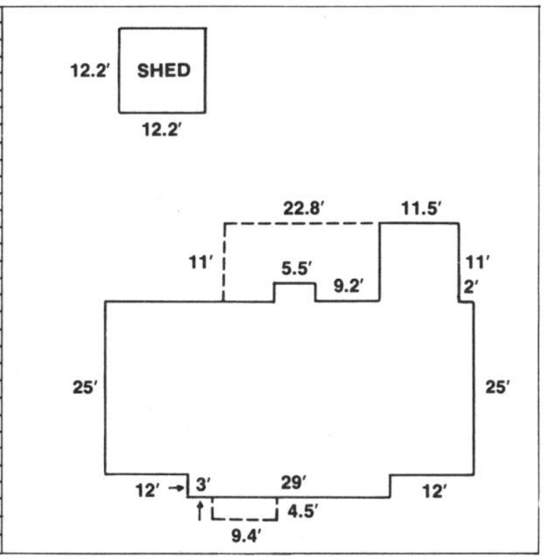

**EXAMPLE OF SIMPLE NARRATIVE APPRAISAL REPORT OF SINGLE-FAMILY RESIDENTIAL PROPERTY**

AN APPRAISAL
OF
A SINGLE-FAMILY RESIDENCE
AT
608 PARK AVENUE
ANYWHERE, U.S.A.
AS OF JULY 18, 19--
FOR
XYZ CORPORATION

REAL ESTATE APPRAISER

**JOHN E. GREEN** / M.A.I. / S.R.P.A.

104 CENTRAL BANK ANNEX • MONTGOMERY, ALABAMA 36104 • PHONE 205-263-2319

July 18, 19____

Mr. Asa B. Johnson, Jr.
Assistant to the Vice-President
XYZ Corporation
233 Main Street
New York, New York 10007

RE: J. E. Hungerpiller Property
608 Park Avenue
Anywhere, U.S.A.

Dear Mr. Johnson:

In accordance with a request received from your Company, I have made an appraisal of the property located at 608 Park Avenue, Anywhere, U.S.A.

This property is legally described as: All of Lots 4 and 5, Block 9, of Re-Subdivision of Blocks 9, 14, 15 and 16, of the Plat of Cloverdale, as recorded in the Office of the Judge of Probate of Metro County, in Plat Book 3 at page 35, except that part previously conveyed by Florence Davis Lobman to Alma H. Lobman by deed dated April 12, 1921, recorded in Deed Book 114, page 91, and to John P. Monsky and Joan C. Monsky by deed dated August 8, 1952, and recorded in Deed Book 350 at page 596.

I am furnishing two copies of the appraisal report. This report describes the process used in reaching a final value estimate.

I hereby certify that I have inspected the property; that all information is from sources believed to be reliable; that I have no interest, present or prospective, in the property; and that, to the best of my knowledge and belief, this appraisal has been made in conformity with the professional standards of the American Institute of Real Estate Appraisers of the National Association of Realtors.

It is my opinion that the market value of the subject property as of July 18, 19____, was:

FORTY-SEVEN THOUSAND, EIGHT HUNDRED ($47,800) DOLLARS

Very truly yours,

John E. Green, MAI-SRPA

## TABLE OF CONTENTS

## APPRAISER'S CERTIFICATION AND RESTRICTION UPON DISCLOSURE AND USE OF THIS APPRAISAL REPORT

The undersigned does hereby certify that, except as otherwise noted in this appraisal report:

1. I have no present or contemplated future interest in the property that is the subject of this appraisal report.
2. I have no personal interest or bias with respect to the subject matter of this appraisal report or the parties involved.
3. To the best of my knowledge and belief, the statements of fact contained in this appraisal report, upon which the analyses, opinions and conclusions expressed herein are based, are true and correct.
4. This appraisal report sets forth all of the limiting conditions (imposed by the terms of my assignment or by the undersigned) affecting the analyses, opinions and conclusions contained in this report.
5. This appraisal report has been made in conformity with and is subject to the requirements of the Code of Professional Ethics and Standards of Professional Conduct of the American Institute of Real Estate Appraisers of the National Association of Realtors.
6. No one other than the undersigned prepared the final analyses, conclusions and opinions concerning the property as set forth in this appraisal report.
7. Disclosure of the contents of this appraisal report is governed by the By-Laws and Regulations of the American Institute of Real Estate Appraisers of the National Association of Realtors.
8. Neither all nor any part of the contents of this report (especially any conclusions as to value, the identity of the appraiser or the firm with which he is connected, or any reference to the American Institute of Real Estate Appraisers or to the M.A.I. designation) shall be disseminated to the public through advertising media, public relations media, news media, sales media or any other public means of communication without the prior written consent and approval of the undersigned.

______________________________

John E. Green, MAI-SRPA

## PURPOSE OF THE APPRAISAL

The purpose of the appraisal is to estimate the market value of the unencumbered fee simple title to the subject property. The date of the appraisal is July 18, 19____.

## MARKET VALUE DEFINED

Market value is defined as the highest price estimated in terms of money that a property will bring if exposed for sale in the open market, allowing a reasonable time to find a purchaser who buys with full knowledge of all the uses to which it can be put and for which it is capable of being used.

## TAXES AND ASSESSMENTS

| | |
|---|---|
| Total Ad Valorem Assessment: | $5,760.00 |
| Tax Rate per $100 of Assessed Value: | $ 3.35 |
| Ad Valorem Tax: | $ 192.96 |
| Less Homestead Exemption: | $ 13.00 |
| Net: | $ 179.96 |

There is a homestead exemption claimed on this property. It is my opinion that both the assessment ratio and tax rate will show some increase in Anywhere within the next few years.

**CITY DATA—ANYWHERE, U.S.A.**

*LOCATION:* Anywhere is the capital city of the State, the County Seat of Metro County, and is the State's third largest city. The city has an estimated population of 168,550 at July 1, 19___ with a metropolitan population of approximately 190,000. The 1970 census showed a city population of 154,393. The city is located in the central region of the State. Anywhere is 100 miles south of Steel City, the State's largest city, and it is 190 miles north of Watertown, the State's second largest city.

*GOVERNMENT:* The city government is composed of a Mayor and two Commissioners. The quality of government is above average and efforts are continuously made to improve the service and public relations. The Police Department is slightly above average and is constantly being upgraded. The Fire Department is well equipped and is classed as one of the best in the nation. Generally, taxes are low in comparison with other cities. Assessments on property are generally at 15 to 30 percent of market value. The city has a 1 percent sales tax but does not impose a gross income tax. The State imposes a 4 percent sales tax in addition to the 1 percent sales tax.

*TRADE AREA:* Anywhere's trade area includes at least 13 counties with an aggregate population of approximately 571,000 people. Income from this area is derived from manufacturing, agriculture, retail and wholesale distribution, and extensive State and Federal government activities.

*AGRICULTURE:* The diversification of agriculture is apparent around Anywhere. The city not only serves as a market distribution point for cotton and other crops, but is a livestock

| | |
|---|---|
| | center as well. This city is considered the largest livestock market in the region. The agricultural industry contributes greatly to the economic stability of Anywhere. |
| *MANUFACTURING:* | Anywhere has some 400 manufacturing plants with an employment of approximately 8000 employees and an annual payroll estimated at $80,000,000. The industry is diversified, ranging from glass container plants and meat-packing plants, to brick and furniture manufacturing. The industrial growth of Anywhere has been at a steady pace rather than occurring as an industrial boom. It appears that the future industrial growth will follow the same pattern. |
| *GENERAL BUSINESS:* | In addition to the above-mentioned two sources of income, the city is the State Capital and has two permanent Air Force installations, at Maxwell Air Force Base (Staff Command and Air War College) and Gunter Air Force Base (Aero School of Medicine and SAGE Center). The State Veterans Administration is located at Anywhere, and a large V.A. hospital serves the southern part of the State. Anywhere has approximately 1000 motel rooms and over 740 hotel rooms available. |
| *TRANSPORTATION:* | The transportation system is above average. A modern airport offers connections with all major airlines. The city is served by both major bus lines. Twenty trucking firms offer freight hauling services. Rail transportation is above average. An excellent highway system connects with the Midwest and the East Coast. |
| *PURCHASING POWER:* | It is estimated that the Anywhere trade area has a population of approximately 571,000 people. The population and general business conditions are of a very stable |

nature, being built on a large number of white-collar workers, skilled labor, and an integrated and diversified agricultural industry. The large governmental installations contribute greatly to this stability.

| | |
|---|---|
| *EDUCATION:* | The educational system in Anywhere is above average, with some 38 grade schools, five high schools and four colleges. These schools are, on the whole, staffed by competent teachers of above-average ability. Several excellent private and parochial schools are found in addition to the public schools. There are two state-owned trade schools and four privately-owned business schools located in Anywhere. |
| *RECREATION:* | Four social clubs, five golf courses, several city-owned community centers, Y.M.C.A, Y.W.C.A., one baseball stadium, one football stadium, the Garrett Coliseum, three beautiful, large artificial lakes within 35 miles, and many hunting opportunities offer excellent and varied recreational facilities. |
| *CULTURAL:* | There is a very active Little Theatre group in Anywhere. This group offers several stage presentations each year. There is a county library and a city library. The cultural facilities offered by Anywhere would be considered fair for a city of this size. |
| *CLIMATE:* | The general climate is mild. The normal annual rainfall for the city is 52 inches, with an average temperature of 64 degrees. |

## CONCLUSIONS AND SUMMARY

The steady industrial growth, the trend toward a stable agriculture built around beef and dairy cattle, the large number of federal and state civilian employees, the two military bases with a large number of military personnel, and the employment in wholesale distribution activities result in a bright economic future for Anywhere.

The city offers opportunities for residents to obtain desired education, to enjoy religious, cultural and social activities, and to own homes and businesses with moderate taxes.

All of the above factors combine to make Anywhere an attractive city with an excellent economic future. The residents are financially able and eager to buy good-quality residential property with the predominant demand being for single-family houses.

## NEIGHBORHOOD ANALYSIS

The subject neighborhood is known as Old Cloverdale. It is one of the more stable residential areas in the city of Anywhere. There is a definite pride of ownership, which is evident from the general degree of maintenance given to properties within the neighborhood. There is no evidence of demand for change in use from the present single-family homes.

Most of the homes within the neighborhood range from 30 years old to some which are 50 to 60 years old. There are a few residences which have been constructed within the past 8 to 15 years. The price range within this neighborhood is from $35,000 to $60,000. The real estate market within this neighborhood appears to be very good.

The neighborhood is very convenient to churches and schools. It is located within a reasonable distance of the central business district. It is convenient to both neighborhood and regional shopping centers.

All of the properties within this neighborhood have received good maintenance and give the neighborhood an overall good appearance.

**DESCRIPTION OF SITE**

The subject lot is located at the corner of Park Avenue and Ridge Avenue. It is an excellent corner lot, with very good lawn and landscaping. There are good shade trees located all over the lot. The St. Augustine grass lawn shows excellent care.

The lot is at approximate street grade with moderate slope in a northeasterly direction.

The lot fronts 141.33 feet on the southeast side of Park Avenue. It has a depth of 233 feet along the east side of Ridge Avenue. This is considered to be one of the better lots in the neighborhood.

In arriving at an estimate of the land value of the subject property, consideration was given to 19___ sale of a lot directly across Park Avenue from the subject property. This lot sold for $11,500 and was approximately the same size as the subject lot. An analysis of lot sales in similar areas indicated that this was an excessive price for this lot. Lots of the size of the subject property in the high-price subdivisions such as McGehee Estates would sell for from $12,000 to $14,000. However, due to the location of the subject property in an older neighborhood, it is my opinion after analysis of the market for such lots, that the market value of the subject site is $9500.

Front View of Subject Property. Taken July 18, 19___.

Detached Garage and Workshop. Taken July 18, 19____.

J. E. HUNGERPILLER RESIDENCE
608 PARK AVENUE
ANYWHERE, U.S.A.

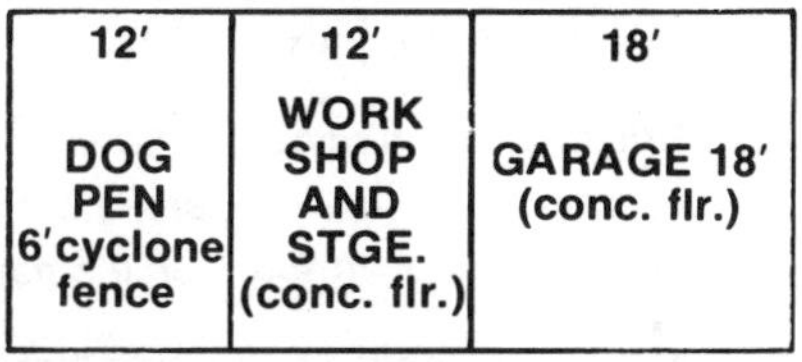


| | | |
|---|---|---|
| GARAGE AREA | = | 324 S.F. |
| W.S. & STGE. | = | 216 S.F. |
| FENCED AREA | = | 216 S.F. (42 LIN. FT. FENCE) |

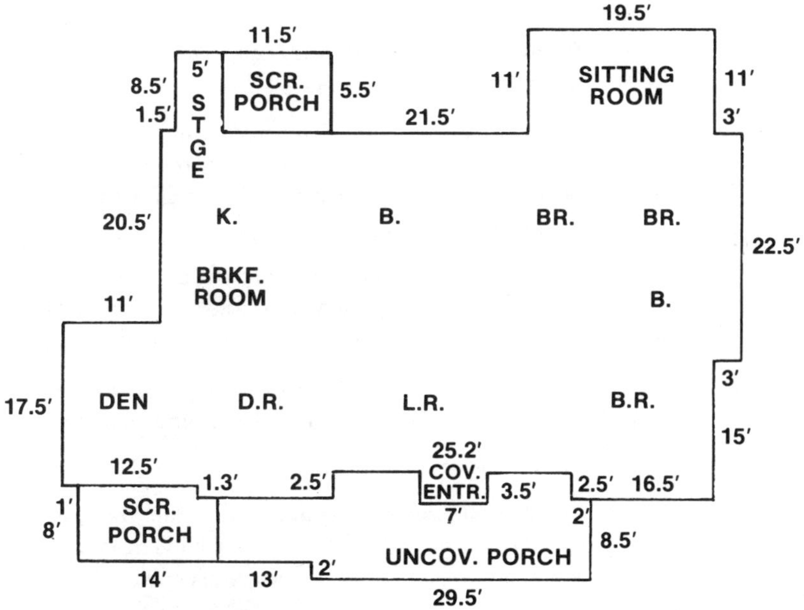


| | | |
|---|---|---|
| LIVING AREA | = | 2,830 S.F. |
| SCREENED PORCHES (2) | = | 206 S.F. |
| COVERED ENTRY | = | 25 S.F. |
| UNCOVERED PORCH | = | 375 S.F. |
| BASEMENT AREA | = | 384 S.F. |

SCALE 1″ = 20′

**DESCRIPTION OF IMPROVEMENTS**

| | |
|---|---|
| *Foundation:* | Conventional with crawl space. |
| *Exterior Walls:* | Stucco. |
| *Roof:* | Asbestos Shingles. There are three roof dormers on the subject property. |
| *Basement:* | Brick wall with concrete floor. There is a two-fixture servant's bath in the basement. This bath appears to be inoperable without some small amount of repair. |
| *Windows:* | Metal casement and double-hung wood sash. |
| *Floors:* | Some oak and some pine. Both in good condition. Some of the floor is covered with vinyl tile. The floor on the back porch is painted pine. |
| *Interior Walls and Ceilings:* | Plaster. Some covered with wallpaper. All walls in good condition. |
| *Plumbing:* | There are two full baths in the main living area of the house. The plumbing appears to be in good condition. There is an automatic electric dishwasher installed in the kitchen. |
| *Heating:* | Gas forced warm air. The window air-conditioners which are used for cooling are considered personal property and are not included in this appraisal. |
| *Electrical:* | The electrical wiring appears to be of very good quality. The light fixtures are also of good quality. |
| *Bath Finish:* | Both baths are ceramic tile. |
| *Attic:* | There is a floored storage area in the attic. This area could be converted into living space if the need were sufficient to justify the necessary expenditure. |
| *Other Improvements:* | There is a detached, two-car garage. There is an additional workshop and storage area which are part of the garage building. This building has wood shingles on exterior walls, asbestos shingle roof. The interior of the garage is not sealed. The storage room and workshop has pine walls and ceilings. All |

floors in this building are concrete. In addition, there is a dog pen fenced with 6-foot cyclone fence.

*Effective Age:* An inspection of this property indicates that, if the structure were new, it would have an economic life of approximately 50 years. It is my opinion that, as of the date of the appraisal, the remaining economic life is 30. Thus, the effective age is 20 years, indicating 40 percent accrued depreciation. In addition to this accrued depreciation, there is an item of deferred maintenance which will require performing this work in the near future. The exterior wood and metal should be scraped and painted.

**COST APPROACH**

*Reproduction Cost New:*

| | | | |
|---|---|---|---|
| Living Area | 2830 sq. ft. × $20.25 | = | $57,308 |
| Screened porches | 206 sq. ft. × $ 4.00 | = | $ 824 |
| Covered entry | 25 sq. ft. × $ 3.25 | = | $ 81 |
| Uncovered porch | 375 sq. ft. × $ 1.50 | = | $ 563 |
| Basement | 384 sq. ft. × $ 3.50 | = | $ 1,344 |
| Garage | 324 sq. ft. × $ 3.50 | = | $ 1,134 |
| Workshop and stg. | 216 sq. ft. × $ 4.00 | = | $ 864 |
| 6′ cyclone fence | 42 ln. ft. × $ 2.25 | = | $ 95 |
| Kenmore automatic dishwasher | | | $ 225 |
| Walks, drives, paved area, landscaping | | = | $ 600 |

TOTAL REPRODUCTION COST NEW: $63,038

*Depreciation:*

| | | | | |
|---|---|---|---|---|
| Economic Life if New | 50 Years | | | |
| Remaining Economic Life | 30 Years | | | |
| Effective Age | 20 Years | | | |
| Accrued Depreciation | 40% | | | |
| $63,038 × 40% | | = | $25,215 | |
| Add: Deferred Maintenance: | (Scrape exterior wood and metal, and paint) | | $ 250 | |
| Total Depreciation: | | say | | $25,438 |
| Indicated Value of Improvements | | | | $37,600 |
| Add: Land Value | | | | $ 9,500 |
| INDICATED VALUE BY COST APPROACH | | | | $47,100 |

**SALE NO. 1**
**409 THORN PLACE**

| | |
|---|---|
| SALES PRICE: | $40,000 |
| DATE OF SALE: | May 19 |
| LIVING AREA: | 2,825 Square Feet |

This house was 36 years old at date of sale. It is in good condition considering its age. A substantial part of the living area is upstairs. The overall quality of construction is not as good as subject. Subject lot and location are considered to be better. The sale property is centrally air conditioned.

*ANALYSIS:*

| | | | |
|---|---|---|---|
| Sales Price | | | $40,000 |
| Size Adjustment | | Nil | |
| Construction Quality | (+ 5%) | +$2,000 | |
| Lot and Location | (+10%) | +$4,000 | |
| Condition | (+ 1%) | +$ 400 | |
| Air Conditioning | | −$ 800 | |
| Date of Sale | (+ 6%) | +$2,400 | |
| Net Adjustment | | | +$ 8,000 |
| INDICATED VALUE OF SUBJECT PROPERTY | | | $48,000 |

Photograph of Sale No. 1. Taken 7-18-____.

**SALE NO. 2**
**3549 CLOVERDALE ROAD**

| | |
|---|---|
| SALES PRICE: | $38,000 |
| DATE OF SALE: | October 19____ |
| LIVING AREA: | 1,388 Square Feet |

This house was eight years old at date of sale. It is much newer than subject and is in better condition. The subject is substantially larger, has a much better lot and a better location. Comparable is better as to construction quality.

*ANALYSIS:*

| | | | |
|---|---|---|---|
| Sales Price | | | $38,000 |
| Size Adjustment (2,830 − 1,388 = 1,442 × $7) | | +$10,094 | |
| Construction Quality | (− 6%) | −$ 2,280 | |
| Lot and Location | (+20%) | +$ 7,600 | |
| Condition | (−20%) | −$ 7,600 | |
| Date of Sale | (+ 4%) | +$ 1,520 | |
| Net Adjustment | | | +$ 9,334 |
| INDICATED VALUE OF SUBJECT PROPERTY | | | $47,334 |

Photograph of Sale No. 2. Taken 7-18-____.

## SALE NO. 3
## 3606 CLOVERDALE ROAD

| | |
|---|---|
| SALES PRICE: | $38,000 |
| DATE OF SALE: | February 19____ |
| LIVING AREA: | 1,260 Square Feet |

This house was 14 years old at date of sale. It is much newer than subject and is in better condition. The construction quality of this house is better than the subject. This house is centrally air conditioned. Subject is much larger and has a much better lot and a better location.

*ANALYSIS:*

| | | | |
|---|---|---|---|
| Sales Price | | | $38,000 |
| Size Adjustment | (2,830 − 1,260 = 1,570 × $7) | + $10,990 | |
| Construction Quality | (− 10%) | − $ 3,800 | |
| Lot and Location | (+ 20%) | + $ 7,600 | |
| Condition | (− 15%) | − $ 4,700 | |
| Air Conditioning | | − $ 800 | |
| Date of Sale | (+ 2%) | + $ 760 | |
| Net Adjustment | | | + $10,050 |
| INDICATED VALUE OF SUBJECT PROPERTY | | | $48,050 |

Photograph of Sale No. 3. Taken 7-18-____.

## CONCLUSIONS—DIRECT SALES COMPARISON APPROACH

There are very few sales of properties similar to the subject. The sales which have occurred in the neighborhood are generally of smaller and lower-quality dwellings than is the subject. I was able to locate one sale which is considered an excellent comparable to the subject property. This is sale no. 1 which precedes. The remaining two sales were of smaller structures which are of better-quality construction and are newer than the subject. However, the subject is much better in terms of lot and location.

After giving careful consideration to each of the comparable sales and giving primary weight to sale no. 1, which is considered most comparable, it is my opinion that the value indication from the direct sales comparison approach is:

FORTY-SEVEN THOUSAND, EIGHT HUNDRED ($47,800) DOLLARS

## GROSS RENT MULTIPLIER APPROACH

The typical single-family residence is not considered to be an income-producing property. This is particularly true of homes in the price class of the subject property. The owners of property similar to the subject find that it is not economically wise to use a property such as this for rental purposes.

In view of these facts, the gross rent multiplier approach is not considered applicable to this appraisal.

## CORRELATION (RECONCILIATION) AND FINAL VALUE ESTIMATE

Consideration was given to the applicability of the three recognized approaches to value in this appraisal. It was my conclusion that the gross rent multiplier approach was not applicable to the subject property.

The two applicable approaches show value indicators as follows:

| | |
|---|---|
| COST APPROACH | $47,100.00 |
| DIRECT SALES COMPARISON APPROACH | $47,800.00 |

There is a difference of slightly over 1 percent between the two value indicators. This is certainly within an acceptable range.

The cost approach is considered to be the least reliable in this appraisal. The structure has an effective age of 20 years, which means 40 percent accrued depreciation. The older the structure, the less weight normally applies to the cost approach.

While truly comparable sales are very limited within the subject neighborhood, there was one excellent comparable plus two additional sales which tended to support comparable no. 1. I examined a number of sales in competing neighborhoods and am convinced that the value for the subject property as indicated by the three sales included herein is proper. The value indicated by the direct sales comparison approach is most meaningful in reaching a final value estimate.

After considering all factors known to me which would affect the market value of the subject property, it is my opinion that said market value, as of July 18, 19____, was:

FORTY-SEVEN THOUSAND, EIGHT HUNDRED ($47,800.00) DOLLARS

______________________________

John E. Green, MAI-SRPA

## CONTINGENT AND LIMITING CONDITIONS

The covering letter, certificate of appraiser, and this entire report are made expressly subject to the following conditions and stipulations:

1. No responsibility for matters legal in character nor as to title is assumed.
2. Existing liens and encumbrances have been disregarded, and the property is appraised as though free and clear of any encumbrances; however, the appraisal is made subject to any existing easements of which the appraiser has knowledge for public roads, transmission lines, pipe lines, and other public utilities.
3. It is assumed that all information furnished by the client and/or employees and agents of said client and incorporated in this report is correct.
4. The appraiser has made no survey of the property. Sketches submitted are believed to be substantially correct. Absolute accuracy is not assumed.
5. Information in this report has been carefully checked and is believed to be reliable. The appraiser assumes no responsibility for the accuracy of information obtained from the client and/or employees and agents of said client, from other informed persons, and from other sources of information available to the appraiser.
6. Neither all nor any part of the contents of this report, or copy thereof, shall be used for any purpose by any but the client without the previous written consent of the appraiser and/or the client; nor shall it be conveyed by any including the client to the public through advertising, public relations, news, sales, or other media, without the written consent and approval of the author, particularly as to value conclusions, the identity of the appraiser or a firm with which he is connected, or any reference to any professional society or institute or any initial designations conferred upon the appraiser as stated in his qualifications attached hereto.
7. The appraiser, by reason of this appraisal, is prepared to give testimony or to be in attendance in Court or at any hearing with reference to the property in question and the interest therein, provided satisfactory arrangements have been made for payment of services.
8. The sales prices of any comparable sales which are shown in this appraisal report were verified by contacting the grantor, grantee, agent, or other informed persons who were familiar with the transactions. The sales prices and other data regarding the transactions are believed to be correct since they were obtained from informed persons.

## QUALIFICATIONS OF JOHN E. GREEN

*APPRAISAL EDUCATION*

1. Completed Real Estate Appraisal I of American Institute of Real Estate Appraisers at University of Georgia in March 1960.
2. Completed Real Estate Appraisal II (Urban Properties) of American Institute of Real Estate Appraisers at University of Georgia in April 1961.
3. Completed Real Estate Appraisal IV (Condemnation Appraising and Court Testimony) of American Institute of Real Estate Appraisers at University of Miami in April 1962.
4. Completed Real Estate Appraisal III (Rural Properties) of American Institute of Real Estate Appraisers at University of Chicago in March 1963.
5. Completed Real Estate Appraisal VI (Ellwood Method—Income Property Capitalization) of American Institute of Real Estate Appraisers at Yale University in June 1964.
6. Completed course in Appraisal of Industrial Property sponsored by Society of Real Estate Appraisers at University of Georgia in January 1967.
7. Attended Instructor's Seminars presented by Society of Real Estate Appraisers.

*APPRAISAL EXPERIENCE*

1. From April 1959, to October 1967, Supervisor in Franchise Tax and Public Utility Division, Alabama Revenue Department. Appraised and/or supervised others in the appraisal of residential, farm, timberland, commercial, industrial, special purpose property and public utility property. Included major commercial and industrial properties in most of the counties within State of Alabama.
2. Established own appraisal firm in October 1967, and since that time have made fee appraisals of residential, farm, commercial, industrial, special purpose property, electric companies, REA Electric Co-Ops, telephone companies, freight car equipment leasing, railroads, water companies, and pipeline properties. Appraisals in Alabama, Florida, Mississippi, Texas, New Jersey, Kansas, Arizona, Indiana, Iowa, Tennessee, New Mexico, California, Wisconsin, Arkansas, Illinois, Louisiana, Missouri, Nebraska, North Dakota, Ohio, Oklahoma, Michigan, Oregon and New York.

3. Acquisition and re-use appraisals, rehabilitation studies, L.U.M.S. reports, and appraisal reviews for various Urban Renewal agencies.
4. Completed appraisal and/or sales ratio studies in Rice County, Marion County and Stafford County, Kansas.
5. Qualified as an expert witness in circuit courts of Alabama, Florida, Mississippi, Arizona, Kansas and Indiana; in state courts of Florida, New Mexico, Wisconsin, Arizona and New Jersey; in federal courts in Alabama, and before Tax Appeals Board or Tax Commission for the States of Kansas, Arizona, Indiana, California and Texas.
6. Prepared Alabama Appraisal Manual for Alabama Revenue Department.
7. Appraised four utilities for Mississippi Tax Commission and testified before Sub-Committee of Ways and Means Committee of Mississippi House of Representatives.
8. Consultant work for Tennessee Public Service Commission and for Nashville-Davidson County.

*PROFESSIONAL AFFILIATION AND RELATED ACTIVITIES*

1. M.A.I., Member of American Institute of Real Estate Appraisers.
2. S.R.P.A. (Senior Real Property Appraiser), Member of Society of Real Estate Appraisers.
3. Member of Montgomery Real Estate Board.
4. President of Montgomery Chapter No. 127 of Society of Real Estate Appraisers.
5. Now serving or have served on national and local committees of both the American Institute of Real Estate Appraisers and the Society of Real Estate Appraisers.
6. On faculty of Society of Real Estate Appraisers and have taught appraisal courses at Auburn University, University of Alabama and University of Nebraska.
7. Member of Public Utilities Taxation Committee of National Tax Association/Tax Institute and have been on program on appraisal of utility properties at Wichita State University.

# 16

# How to Be a Successful Appraiser of Residential Property

All of the preceding portion of this book concerned itself with how to go about making an accurate, supportable appraisal of a residential property. The ability to make such an appraisal is one of the three essential ingredients for becoming a successful appraiser. Another essential ingredient is to be recognized by fellow appraisers, other professionals engaged in the various areas of real estate activity, and your clients, as a person of absolute integrity. The third essential ingredient for success as an appraiser is the ability to defend your value estimates as an expert witness in court or in other adversary proceedings. If you follow the procedures outlined in the first 15 chapters, you should be able to make accurate appraisals of residential property, so no further discussion of this essential ingredient to being a successful appraiser will be included in this chapter. The other two essentials will be discussed now in this chapter.

## THE SECOND ESSENTIAL INGREDIENT—INTEGRITY

In making residential appraisals, you will encounter considerable pressure from a number of sources. The pressure will be for you to arrive at either a high or low value estimate depending on the particular self-serving interest of the party applying the pressure. The ability to withstand pressure, regardless of who is applying it, will be a major factor in your being able to establish yourself as a successful appraiser. The few self-serving people you alienate by being a person of absolute integrity will be replaced tenfold by clients desiring a longstanding business relationship with you. Other appraisers, as well as people active in other fields of real estate, will soon recognize you as a professional appraiser who can be depended upon to render an absolutely impartial appraisal.

## HOW TO HANDLE PRESSURE FROM CLIENTS, EMPLOYERS OR OTHER INTERESTED PARTIES

I have encountered pressure from builders who wanted to impress me that they "built only the best quality" homes and, according to their stories, anything they built deserved an add-on to value in recognition of this superior quality construction. If you observe quality differences, and if this fact is recognized in the market, then you can take it into account, but only if you are convinced by your own independent analysis. Another pressure from builders is to overlook certain structural defects on the theory that a minor item probably won't even be noticed by the average buyer. Just remember that you are deeply involved in what is probably the most significant investment the buyer will ever make, and you owe him a fair and impartial value estimate.

I have encountered pressure from real estate brokers who had a signed sales contract in hand and who wanted to be certain that I knew the sales price so that the appraisal would support this figure. I make it quite clear that I don't want to know what the sales price was nor even what the property was listed for if it had not sold at the date of the appraisal. Even if the appraiser should learn the sales price or listing price of a property he is appraising, it should in no way affect his value estimate. I have witnessed cases in which the sale price agreed upon in a sales contract was substantially far from being at market value because one of the parties was uninformed or was under undue pressure. The successful appraiser will arrive at a completely independent and unbiased value estimate. Those of you who are employed by real estate firms or lending institutions may encounter pressure from your superiors to support their preconceived ideas of value. The pressure can also come from fellow employees in the sales or construction department. If you can't maintain your professional integrity in such a setting, I suggest that you look elsewhere for employment.

I have encountered pressure from lenders who were eager to keep all available funds in active mortgage loans. Such lenders would have already reached an agreement with the project developer regarding the amount of money they would loan and the ratio of loan value to appraised value. The "appraisal" was therefore made, and all they needed was some cooperative appraiser to formalize it by making an appraisal to fit the predetermined appraised value. This situation was the cause of the failure of many of the real estate investment trusts. The smart developers of many projects were able to borrow at least 100 percent of the funds needed to build the improvements, including a nice profit from building with their own construction company. Such developers didn't care if the projects ever succeeded, since they made their money up front, and the lenders were stuck with the losers. An appraiser of integrity would never accept an assignment to arrive at any predetermined value. I routinely refuse such assignments and only agree to do an appraisal if I can do a detailed feasibility analysis to determine the probability of success. This type of client usually will turn to some "appraiser" who will cooperate, and losing such a client is really a blessing.

## HOW TO HANDLE STUDIES MADE BY OTHERS AND GIVEN TO YOU BY THE CLIENT TO USE IN A RESIDENTIAL APPRAISAL

I have encountered clients who will bring feasibility studies made by others and want me to accept these studies rather than make my own independent analysis. I have found some of these studies to be good and have accepted their findings, but *only* after a thorough review to convince myself of the accuracy of the conclusions contained in them. I strongly recommend that you give absolutely no weight to studies you have not personally reviewed. You will find little comfort or protection in blindly accepting studies done by others and presented to you, nor will such practice build your reputation as a person of absolute integrity.

## HOW TO HANDLE PRESSURE FROM PARTIES TO CONDEMNATION PROCEEDINGS

I have received substantial pressure from condemnors, condemnees and/or their attorneys to arrive at values which would serve their particular interests. I have been asked to accept studies, plot plans and other items intended to influence my final value estimate. Attorneys are advocates by profession and, unfortunately, many of them have the attitude that the end justifies the means. The appraiser of integrity must not and will not be an advocate of any one party's position. You should do appraisals for both the condemnor and the condemnee, and the identity of the client should make absolutely no difference in the final value estimate. The "appraiser" who will advocate the position of any client who hires him may make substantial money for a short time, but he will never establish an enduring appraisal practice. When it becomes generally known that your values are absolutely impartial, regardless of who the client is, I'll assure you that you will be swamped with all the work you can handle.

## HOW TO HANDLE REQUESTS FOR LOW APPRAISED VALUES FOR INHERITANCE TAX PURPOSES

I have also been under pressure to arrive at low values when making an estate appraisal for inheritance tax purposes. I first try to convince the client that such an appraisal is poor business practice and that the appraisal should be made at market value. If my effort to convince the client fails, I simply refuse to accept the assignment. If you will only do the appraisal for inheritance tax purposes if you can estimate market value, you will find that the Internal Revenue Service auditors will soon become aware of this fact and will seldom question your value estimates, and this will usually make the client happy.

## HOW TO HANDLE OTHER TYPES OF PRESSURE

You will encounter pressure from some clients to appraise a property for a use other than that to which it is presently devoted. As an appraiser of integrity, you will consider a change in use only after having made your own study and formed your own independent judgment. You will often find that some fancied change in use just won't pass the tests which must be applied.

The preceding paragraphs provide only a partial list of some of the pressures you will encounter as an appraiser. It would be impossible to list them all. The personal satisfaction dervied from being a truly independent appraiser is one of the major attractions of this business. The ability to face yourself, as well as everyone with whom you come in contact, and to be able to truthfully state that you have never violated your code of absolute integrity, is extremely satisfying. It is also the second essential ingredient for being a successful appraiser.

## THE THIRD ESSENTIAL INGREDIENT—ABILITY AS AN EXPERT WITNESS

Many of the appraisals you make will require your appearance as an expert witness in court or in other adversary proceedings. Many appraisers will not accept an appraisal assignment if there is a likelihood that testimony will be required. Most such appraisers probably have good reasons (such as health) for taking this position, but this does tend to severely limit the number of appraisal assignments available to them. I strongly recommend that you accept, and indeed welcome, appraisal assignments which require expert testimony. This part of the appraisal business is the most challenging and financially rewarding if you prepare yourself adequately.

It doesn't matter how fine an appraisal report you write, how accurate the value estimate is or how much personal integrity you have applied, if you are unable to explain and defend what you did on the witness stand. The appraiser who has the ability to explain and defend his appraisal, in understandable terms, in any adversary proceeding is almost assured of success in his chosen field. The rewards—both personal satisfaction and financial—are worth your best efforts.

Having done appraisals in at least 28 states, and having appeared as an expert witness in most of them, I offer several personally-tested guidelines toward becoming a successful expert witness. These tips are as follows:

1. Review your appraisal report carefully as soon as you know that a trial or other adversary proceeding is imminent. This includes reinspection of the subject property and review and updating of underlying data, including reinspection of comparables if necessary. You want your mind to be fresh about the property and your appraisal report.

2. Insist on adequate time with your attorney for pretrial preparation. The time taken to thoroughly review the appraisal report and the questions the attorney plans to ask you on direct examination is essential and will increase chances of success. Never accept an assignment where the client won't agree to pay for adequate pretrial preparation. The pretrial preparation should also include a review and rehearsal of probable cross-examination and your responses. Remember that your reputation and probable future success as an appraiser are at stake, so prepare carefully for the testimony. You will frequently find it necessary to prepare most of the questions, if your attorney lacks experience in the particular area, and to assist even the most experienced attorney in such preparation.

3. Discuss with the owner any statements he and/or his associates may have made, or any existing agreements of which you may not previously have been aware. Try to avoid surprises, since something sprung on you unexpectedly can be disconcerting. If you are surprised with something while testifying, the best procedure is to state that you were not aware of the particular circumstance, rather than trying to bluff an answer.

4. Be sure to present a neat appearance. You want the judge, jury, tribunal or whomever is hearing your testimony to be concerned

with what you say, not how odd you look. Always wear a neatly pressed suit of a single dark color, with a conservative matching shirt and tie. Your hair should be neatly trimmed and you should be clean-shaven, unless you live in an area where facial hair is normal and readily accepted. You must remember that you aren't the one making the decision, and you don't want your appearance to make a negative impression on those who will decide the case.

5. Answer questions politely and in as few words as needed to adequately answer the questions. Speak slowly and distinctly so that you can be understood. Never use technical terms without explaining their meaning in simple lay language. Remember that the people you have to convince of your position will be turned off by your use of difficult words they don't understand. Your testimony should be directed toward the lowest denominator of understanding among those to whom you are testifying. Your task as a witness is to convince your listeners of the correctness of your appraisal and not to show off your large vocabulary.

6. Always look at the person or persons to whom you are testifying, rather than at the attorney, if the physical arrangement of the hearing room permits it. This does not mean that you should stare at anyone, but rather casually shift your glance from one person to the other so that they have the feeling you are talking to them on a one-to-one basis.

7. Do not engage in an argument with the attorney or anyone else in the hearing room. Do not visibly show anger, regardless of how stringent the questioning may be. The cross-examining attorney will try very hard to get you angry and put you at a disadvantage. Never give a flippant answer, since your function in the hearing is as an appraiser and not a comedian.

8. Never hesitate to say, "I don't know," "I don't remember," or, "That is outside my area of expertise," if such is the case. Any cross-examining attorney worth his salt can tell when you are bluffing an answer. If you know the answer to his question, you should answer it truthfully. The liar will never be a successful appraiser.

9. If the cross-examining attorney asks you a question that can't be answered with a simple "yes" or "no," and yet insists that you do so, you should turn to the judge or other chief hearing officer and say, "Your Honor, the question as asked simply can't be answered yes or no." In almost every instance, you will be permitted to answer in full. You may be instructed to answer "yes" or "no" but to proceed with explanation of your answer. If you are not given permission to explain the yes or no answer, your attorney can ask a follow-up question later on in the proceedings.

10. Beware of the question which quotes from some publication such as a magazine or newspaper article or perhaps from the company's annual report. A favorite cross-examination trick is to quote such a statement out of context and then form a question. Don't attempt to answer such a question until you look at the document from which the quote was taken. This can be accomplished by simply saying, "I can't answer that until I have examined the source document from which the statement comes."

11. If either attorney or the court asks you a question you don't fully understand, don't even attempt to answer it until it is read back to you.

12. If the cross-examining attorney asks you a question and you aren't certain of the answer, you should ask that the question be read to you out of the record or ask the attorney to repeat it. This gives you time to think over your answer and many times the attorney will simply drop the question. You have every right to have the question repeated, but don't abuse the privilege by requesting it too frequently.

13. Have all of your reference material neatly organized before taking the witness stand. Bring only essential items to the stand with you since any item you refer to may be examined by the opposing attorney. I have found it helpful to outline the key parts of the appraisal on summary sheets, to avoid having to look through several documents. The person or persons hearing your testimony will be favorably impressed if you are well-organized.

14. If you follow the preceding 13 tips, you should have no reason to be nervous while on the witness stand. Remember, if you have done a good appraisal and have properly prepared yourself to testify, you will know more about the subject property than anyone else involved in the matter. This does not mean that you should act cocky and all-knowing, but neither should you appear to be nervous or unsure of yourself. The witness who is calm, sincere and self-confident will most likely make a favorable impression.

## SUMMARY

If you make certain that all three of the essential ingredients are present in your appraisal work, you will almost always be guaranteed success beyond your wildest dreams. The appraiser who makes every effort to prepare a neat and well-supported appraisal report, who is recognized by all as being a person of absolute integrity, and who can present expert testimony in a sincere, honest and clearly understood manner is a unique individual who can be very certain that he will indeed be successful in every sense of the word.

Those of you who are employees of real estate firms or lending institutions, and who perform only in-house appraisals, differ from the self-employed appraiser only to the extent that you have one client instead of many clients. The three essential ingredients for being a successful appraiser apply as well to the staff appraiser or other salaried real estate professional as they do to the self-employed fee appraiser.

# APPENDIX A

# How to Appraise a Mansion or Luxury Home

The real estate terminology, appraisal principles and the discussion of the three recognized approaches to value contained in the preceding 16 chapters also apply to the appraisal of the mansion or luxury home. The purpose of this appendix is to point out the additional items you should consider in appraising this unique type of single-family residential property. Each additional item beyond those which apply to the appraisal of the typical single-family residential property will be discussed under separate headings.

## HOW TO IDENTIFY THE MANSION OR LUXURY HOME

Most mansions or luxury homes were built during various economic boom periods by extremely wealthy individuals to gratify their personal desires, whims or personality traits. You will generally find that these wealthy individuals gave little or no consideration to the fact that it would be virtually impossible for them to ever recover their capital investment through a sale of the property. The home built or subsequently owned by a famous person will sometimes bring a premium price, when sold for its "snob appeal" to certain wealthy people who will pay a high price in order to bask in the "reflected glory." You will find that the mansion or luxury home will range in size and cost from the large, expensive, custom-built residence, to the huge and ornate mansion with landscaped gardens.

One extreme example of a mansion is the 250-room Biltmore House, which was built in North Carolina in the 1880s by George W.

Vanderbilt. This home is now operated as a tourist attraction and is thus a commercial venture. Another example is the elaborate 1916 mansion built in Miami, Florida by James Deering, at a cost of $20,000,000. For many years after the owner died in 1925, the home stood vacant and was finally sold to Dade County, Florida in 1952, for $1,000,000.

These two mansions are extreme examples. However, you should be aware of the fact that the high tax burden, the unique design of the mansion or luxury home, and the high cost of staffing and maintaining such homes tend to severely limit the market to the extremely wealthy, such as cash-rich oil magnates.

## HOW TO APPLY THE COST APPROACH TO THE APPRAISAL OF THE MANSION OR LUXURY HOME

When your appraisal assignment is to estimate the market value of the very large and ornate mansion or luxury home, or one which has a unique design, you may find that the cost approach is the most important approach and, occasionally, the only approach you can use. The very large and ornate mansion or luxury home, as well as the uniquely designed structure, may have little useful relevant market data available.

### STEPS TO BE TAKEN IN ESTIMATING REPRODUCTION COST NEW

You may be unable to arrive at a good estimate of reproduction cost for some of the more ornate structures. I recommend that you attempt to arrive at reproduction cost if at all possible. If you are unable to arrive at a good reproduction cost estimate, then estimate the cost in current dollars to replace the number of square feet of area, excluding the unique design features. If the nature of the assignment permits it, I would suggest employing a good cost estimator. You should be satisified that you have a good site value estimate from market analysis and a good estimate of reproduction cost or replacement cost before proceeding to the estimate of depreciation.

### STEPS TO BE TAKEN IN ESTIMATING DEPRECIATION

In appraising the normal single-family residence, the amount of accrued depreciation can be verified by market analysis. The difference between the value contribution of the improvements to the total sales price of a residential property and the reproduction cost new of the improvements is the amount of accrued depreciation as measured by market reactions. This procedure can also be applied to appraisals of the mansion or luxury home if sufficient market data are available.

There are usually very few meaningful comparable sales for the mansion or luxury home. If you have estimated reproduction cost, you will very likely have all three types of accrued depreciation present within the structure. If you have estimated replacement cost, you will have eliminated functional obsolescence but will still have a great deal of physical deterioration and economic (locational obsolescence) present. You may be able to adequately estimate accrued depreciation by using the observed condition method, in which you estimate economic life when new, remaining economic life and effective age. If you follow this procedure, be sure to take into account the economic obsolescence which arises from the very limited number of market participants for this type of residential structure. You can check the accuracy of your value estimate for the subject improvements if you have no useful comparable sales by looking at the value contribution per square foot for relatively large older homes which met no market resistance, to see that your value per square foot is quite a bit lower than that of most such homes. Sales prices of mansions or luxury homes, when sales can be found, will often show that the value contribution of the improvements may be no more than 20 to 30 percent of cost new.

## HOW TO STRUCTURE THE COST APPROACH IN THE APPRAISAL OF MANSIONS OR LUXURY HOMES

I suggest the following format for the cost approach for the mansion or luxury home using reproduction cost.

## HOW TO APPLY THE GROSS RENT MULTIPLIER OR INCOME APPROACH TO THE APPRAISAL OF THE MANSION OR LUXURY HOME

The mansion or luxury home is rarely rented. This eliminates the use of the gross rent multiplier approach. The only instance in which the normal income approach would apply would be where the property has been converted to a tourist attraction, allowing the capitalization of net income.

## HOW TO APPLY THE DIRECT SALES COMPARISON APPROACH TO THE APPRAISAL OF THE MANSION OR LUXURY HOME

Just as is true in appraising the normal single-family home, the direct sales comparison approach is the most meaningful approach when adequate comparable sales are available. However, unlike the normal single-family home, which usually enjoys an active market, the mansion or luxury home seldom sells. You may find it necessary

| | | | |
|---|---|---|---|
| Total Sq. Ft. Living Area | | 9,000 | |
| Total Sq. Ft. Auxiliary Area @ 50% (2,000 × 50%) | | 1,000 | |
| Total Effective Area | | 10,000 | |
| Reproduction Cost New (10,000 × $150) | | | $1,500,000 |
| Less: Accrued Depreciation: | | | |
| Economic Life When New | 50 Yrs. | | |
| Remaining Economic Life | 10 Yrs. | | |
| Effective Age | 40 Yrs. | | |
| Percent Accrued Depr. (100 ÷ 50 = 2 × 40) | | | 80% |
| Amount of Accrued Depr. ($1,500,000 × 80%) | | | $1,200,000 |
| Indicated Value of Improvements | | | $ 300,000 |
| Add: Land Value from Market | | | $ 100,000 |
| VALUE AS INDICATED FROM COST APPROACH | | | $ 400,000 |

NOTE: (1) The value estimate shown above is based on observed condition and takes into account the limited market participants, but the value conclusion should be verified by comparison to whatever market data may be available.

(2) If replacement cost had been used, the cost figure would have been reduced perhaps to $1,000,000, thus removing functional obsolescence and decreasing the percentage of accrued depreciation to 70 percent and the final value estimate would not be affected.

to search your entire state, or maybe even some adjoining states, to find any meaningful sales of mansions or luxury homes.

It is my conclusion that the further away from the subject property you have to range to find comparable sales, the less meaningful they will be. I strongly recommend using the direct sales comparison approach as an indicator of value as well as an aid to estimating accrued depreciation if you can find sales occurring within the past year. The relative weight you assign this approach in reaching a final value estimate will be a matter of judgment based on the quantity and quality of comparable sales data. It is preferable to research a wide geographic area to find sales of luxury homes rather than to simply explain away the use of the direct sales comparison approach by stating that there were no meaningful sales.

## ITEMS TO CONSIDER IN ADJUSTING COMPARABLE SALES OF MANSIONS OR LUXURY HOMES

The typical adjustments to comparable sales to be made when appraising the normal single-family residence have been previously discussed and are equally applicable here. There are several additional items which you should consider and adjust for if necessary:

1. Was the comparable and/or the subject property built by or subsequently occupied by a famous personality? If so, you must consider the possible prestige or "snob appeal" effect on value.
2. Does the comparable and/or the subject property have historical significance? If this exists, you must adjust for its effect on value.
3. Does the comparable and/or the subject property have a facade easement or other use limitation easement imposed upon it? If such easement exists, it may have a significant impact on value.
4. Does the comparable and/or the subject property have unusual cost of ownership and occupancy associated with it? Where such items exist, they must be adjusted for the effect on value.
5. Were there any abnormal finance terms or payment conditions associated with the comparable sale? You may find that unusual terms may have a great effect on value and this requires adjustment.
6. Was the comparable and/or the subject property designed by some famous architect? You may find a certain "snob appeal" here which will affect value.

7. Is there a trend within the area where the comparable or the subject property is located to buy and restore mansions or luxury homes? If this situation exists, you may find that the price will be affected.
8. Look for anything unusual while interviewing market participants in the process of sales verification, so that adjustments may be made where necessary.

The adjustment process should use the sales grid format which was previously illustrated. Be certain to take time to document your sales data and the amount and direction of adjustments.

## SUMMARY

The appraisal of the mansion or luxury home is certainly more difficult than the normal residential appraisal. If you apply standard appraisal principles and techniques, plus the additional procedures outlined herein, you will do a good job.

# APPENDIX B

## How to Appraise a Condominium Residential Unit

In Chapters 1 through 16, the material presented was primarily concerned with the appraisal of the free-standing single-family residence. During recent years there has been very rapid growth in the individual ownership of single-family residential units within a condominium structure. All of the material presented in the preceding 16 chapters also applies to the appraisal of individual residential units within the condominium complex. The purpose of this appendix is to acquaint you with the condominium type of ownership, its advantages and disadvantages, and additional items you should consider in appraising this unique type of single-family property.

### DEFINITION OF CONDOMINIUM

The 1975 joint publication, *Real Estate Appraisal Terminology,* by the American Institute of Real Estate Appraisers and the Society of Real Estate Appraisers, on page 47, defines condominium as follows:

> *A form of fee ownership of whole units or separate portions of multi-unit buildings by statute which provides the mechanics and facilities for formal filing and recording of a divided interest in real property, where the division is vertical as well as horizontal. Fee ownership of units in a multi-unit property and joint ownership of the common areas. Not to be confused with Cooperative.*

The type of condominium ownership which you will normally encounter and the one which we will discuss here is the fee ownership of a unit in a multi-unit property, and joint ownership of the common areas. I will also discuss briefly the proper procedures for appraising an entire condominium complex prior to sale of the individual units.

## IMPORTANT ITEMS TO CONSIDER BEFORE STARTING THE APPRAISAL OF A CONDOMINIUM SINGLE-FAMILY UNIT

The following preliminary steps are essential for the condominium appraiser:

1. Obtain and carefully study the condominium law in your area. The enabling act may be complicated and may justify having an attorney review it with you.
2. Obtain and carefully study the condominium document for the particular complex in which the subject unit is located. You may find that the legal description of each unit within the complex will also document the number of square feet in each unit. Such details are very helpful, not only as they relate to subject property, but also for sales of units used as comparables.
3. Know which method is used to calculate the percentage of ownership interest in common areas. One of three methods may be used. The three methods are ratio of one unit to total, ratio of value of one unit to total value of all condominium property, and square foot ratio of one unit to total. This is important for allocation of taxes on common areas as well as allocation of special assessments by the owners' association.
4. What is the amount of the monthly maintenance charge, what does it include, how stable has the charge been and to whom is it paid?
5. What has been the past history regarding special assessments?
6. How complete is the insurance coverage?
7. Look at the bylaws of the owners' association. Also determine if the association is well managed and financially solvent.
8. Learn who has title to and assesses charges for use of recreation areas. Be very careful if the developer did not relinquish this ownership, for he may use it as a strangle hold on the owners of the individual units.

9. Determine adequacy of parking space and recreational facilities for present owners and, if further construction is planned, you should see if these items will be expanded in proportion.
10. Look at services provided by employees of owners' association to unit owners. The quality and relative cost of these services will affect the desirability and resale value of each unit.

## HOW TO APPLY THE COST APPROACH TO THE APPRAISAL OF A CONDOMINIUM UNIT

If you are appraising a recently constructed property you can get much valuable cost data from the developer's records, if he is willing to cooperate. You can also use data from other recently constructed complexes to obtain square foot cost of living area and allocated cost per square foot of common area cost. This data can be used to arrive at the reproduction cost new for the subject unit or for the entire complex, if your appraisal entails this. The total reproduction cost new for the complex can also be broken down into cost per room or cost per unit for each of the various types of units.

## HOW TO ESTIMATE ACCRUED DEPRECIATION FOR THE CONDOMINIUM RESIDENTIAL UNIT

Most condominium units are relatively new and modern and thus will have little or no functional obsolescence. Assuming that there are no major problems regarding monthly maintenance charges, excessive special assessments, ownership of the recreational facilities by the developer, etc., there will be little likelihood of there being economic (locational) obsolescence present. This leaves an estimate of physical deterioration which can be done on an observed condition basis and verified by market analysis. For example, if you felt that the economic life of the unit was 50 years when new and that, in spite of a chronological age of 10 years, it had an effective age of 5 years, then the percentage of accrued depreciation would be 10 percent ($50 - 45 = 5$, $5 \times 2\% = 10\%$).

## HOW TO APPLY THE GROSS RENT MULTIPLIER OR INCOME APPROACH TO THE APPRAISAL OF CONDOMINIUM RESIDENTIAL UNITS

You will find that many owners of condominium residential units use them as occasional vacation homes for their families, but most of the time the units are rented to vacationers. Such units are managed by employees of the owners' association for a percentage of the rent collected. One word of caution here is that if your subject property has been rented on a regular basis, it may require more current repairs and also may have more deferred maintenance than the owner-occupied units. You should obtain a schedule of net rent paid to the owner of the typical rental unit in the complex and add to that figure the rental value of the unit while used by the owner. The projected net market rental for the subject can be capitalized by a market rate or converted to value by extracting a rent multiplier from sales of similar rented units. You will find very few condominium residential units being rented, other than in resort areas, so the gross rent multiplier or income approaches would not apply in such circumstances.

## HOW TO APPLY THE DIRECT SALES COMPARISON APPROACH TO THE APPRAISAL OF CONDOMINIUM RESIDENTIAL UNITS

Where you have an active market from which you can verify and analyze comparable sales, there is no doubt that primary weight should be given to the direct sales comparison approach. The basic areas of comparison and the grid format for sales adjustments were explained in detail in earlier portions of this book and are equally applicable here. There are several additional items which you must consider in appraising condominium residential units.

Try to find as many recent sales as possible in the same complex as the subject property. While they are not directly useable for the current appraisal, you will find it very helpful to study original sales and subsequent resales of units within the subject complex. If there are inadequate sales data within the particular complex, then you should look at similar facilities as nearby as possible. All sales should be verified and physically inspected. You should pay particular attention to the value contribution of any personal property which may have been included in the sales price. The ten items previously listed in this appendix should be considered and adjusted for any value effect. The important thing to remember here is that you should adjust for only those differences which are recognized by the market participants. All sales data should be carefully verified and all adjustments documented.

## HOW TO APPRAISE THE ENTIRE CONDOMINIUM COMPLEX PRIOR TO SALE TO OWNERS OF INDIVIDUAL UNITS

You will probably have very few occasions to make an appraisal of an entire condominium complex prior to sale of any units. If such an appraisal assignment comes, you will most likely be making a market value estimate of proposed construction from plans and specifications. Under this circumstance, or even if the construction is newly completed, you will find that the cost approach and the direct sales comparison approach are the only two applicable approaches. You should make a feasibility analysis for the proposed project before making the appraisal.

You can value the site by sales comparison with similar sites which sold recently. You can obtain the cost of the improvements from current bids if these are available, and verify the costs by comparison with recently completed similar units. You should remember that the cost figures thus obtained usually do not include carrying cost during construction, nor do they include the developer's anticipated profit, and will almost always be less than the market value indicated by direct sales comparison.

In applying the direct sales comparison approach, it will be necessary to estimate the sales price for each unit of each type by comparing them with recent sales of similar new units. The gross sales price for all the condominium units will have to be discounted for time to sell out, sales cost, advertising, legal fees and carrying cost on capital committed by the developer during the sell-out period. The probable cost of warranty repairs should also be deducted. The net figure is the indicated present market value of the entire complex as indicated by the direct sales comparison approach. I recommend making your own feasibility analysis and projection of sell-out time rather than accepting a study made by others or making blind assumptions.

I would suggest that you use those approaches to value which are applicable to the particular assignment. Reference to the last few pages of Chapter 1 will offer some guidance in this particular problem area.

# APPENDIX C

# How to Appraise a Cooperative Residential Unit

The appraisal principles and techniques which were covered in Chapters 1 through 16, although primarily directed toward free-standing single-family housing, are equally applicable to the appraisal of cooperative residential units. The material in Appendix B, while primarily involved with appraising condominium residential units, is also applicable in most respects to the appraisal of cooperative residential units.

The purpose of this appendix is to familiarize you with the cooperative type of ownership and to point out the advantages and disadvantages inherent in such ownership. I will also acquaint you with additional items beyond those usually applicable to the normal free-standing residential unit which you should consider in the appraisal of a cooperative residential unit.

## DEFINITION OF COOPERATIVE

The 1975 joint publication, *Real Estate Appraisal Terminology,* by the American Institute of Real Estate Appraisers and the Society of Real Estate Appraisers, on page 51, defines cooperative as follows:

> *A form of ownership whereby the owner of a stock in a cooperative apartment or housing corporation pays his proportionate share of the interest and real estate taxes paid by*

*the corporation. This proportionate share is based on the proportion of the total stock he owns, and the interest that is deductible can relate to any debit incurred by the corporation to acquire, construct, alter, rehabilitate or maintain the building or land. The cooperative must be bona fide; i.e., the stockholder's ownership must give him the right to live in an apartment or house on the property owned or leased by the corporation, though he need not actually live there.*

The type of cooperative ownership which you will usually be called upon to appraise, and which will receive most attention in this discussion, is that portion of stock ownership in the cooperative which equates to a single-residential unit within a multi-unit complex. I will also offer a brief discussion of the proper method for appraising an entire multi-unit complex under cooperative ownership. It is my conclusion that the condominium method of ownership is superior to the cooperative.

## ADVANTAGES OF COOPERATIVE FORM OF OWNERSHIP

1. Just as is true with condominium ownership, the land cost is less per residential unit.
2. With condominium and cooperative ownership, it is possible to provide more amenities and at less cost per unit than with a free-standing residence.
3. More security is provided than is possible with a free-standing residential unit.
4. The burden of exterior building and grounds maintenance is less per residential unit and is covered by the monthly maintenance charge.
5. Insurance cost and property tax cost are usually less per residential unit than for a free-standing residential property.
6. There may be some construction cost savings per residential unit in the larger complexes.

## DISADVANTAGES OF COOPERATIVE FORM OF OWNERSHIP

1. A cooperative unit is more difficult to sell, either by the original developer or by a subsequent owner, than a condominium unit or a free-standing residential structure.
2. Ownership of the individual unit and the proportionate share of the common areas, as well as the individual unit

share of the common mortgage obligation, are represented by stock ownership and are not as easily severable for transfer of ownership.

3. The cooperative is run by a committee who must approve purchase, sale, remodeling and most other aspects of occupying the individual unit and enjoyment of the common areas. Such committees can be very difficult to deal with in many instances. The owner has more control, particularly of his own unit, in a condominium setup.
4. All units in a cooperative tend to suffer more loss in value than do condominium units when the cooperative runs into financial trouble. The cooperative has a common mortgage, while a condominium has individual mortgages on each unit, and the default of one or two owners will have little or no effect on the other condominium units.
5. A major problem with both the cooperative and condominium type of complex is lack of privacy when compared with the free-standing residential property.
6. There is a tendency for developers of both cooperative and condominium complexes to provide insufficient parking and recreational facilities for the size of the complex so that overcrowding results.

## IMPORTANT ITEMS TO CONSIDER BEFORE STARTING THE APPRAISAL OF A COOPERATIVE RESIDENTIAL UNIT

The ten items listed in Appendix B are equally applicable here and will not be repeated. The only change is to substitute cooperative for condominium, articles of incorporation for condominium document, percent of stock ownership for percent of fee ownership, and stockholders' committee for ownership association. In addition to the ten items mentioned above, you should also study the common mortgage very carefully with respect to interest rate, payment terms and ease of transfer if and when a single unit sells. It is also a good idea to obtain information about the management efficiency of the stockholders' committee and the extent of their response to complaints and/or requests from stockholders who are not members of the committee.

## HOW TO APPLY THE THREE APPROACHES TO VALUE IN APPRAISING THE COOPERATIVE RESIDENTIAL UNIT

The procedures discussed in Appendix B also apply to the appraisal of the cooperative residential unit and will not be repeated here. I do recommend that you use cooperative construction cost to estimate reproduction cost, and an analysis of cooperative unit sales to estimate depreciation in the cost approach. Data relative to cooperatives, and not condominiums, should also be utilized in the other two approaches. A comparison of time required to sell and relative resale value, as well as the percentage of time rented and net rent received by the owners of comparable cooperative and condominium units will show you whether market participants recognize any value differential between the two types of ownership. Your own personal preference for type of ownership should not enter into your analysis or your final value estimate. Reference to the last few pages of Chapter 1 will offer some guidance on the applicability of the three approaches.

# APPENDIX D

# How to Appraise a Rental Apartment Building

A thorough discussion of appraisal principles and techniques for application of the three recognized approaches to value in the appraisal of a free-standing single-family residence was presented in Chapters 1 through 16. All of the data which was included in those 16 chapters are also applicable to the appraisal of a rental apartment building. The major difference in appraising a rental apartment building is that the motivation for owning it is for the production of income, thus making the income approach, utilizing the capitalization of net income, the most important approach to estimating value.

Regardless of the size of the rental apartment building, or even if a multi-building apartment complex is involved, the appraisal procedures are the same. I have concluded that the best way to explain the appraisal procedures involved in appraising a rental apartment building is to include several key pages from a 90-page demonstration appraisal report which I completed on January 3, 1966, showing a value estimate as of December 1, 1965. This report was submitted to the American Institute of Real Estate Appraisers as part of the requirements for the M.A.I. designation.

I would like to point out that, while the values relate to December 1, 1965, the procedures are equally applicable today. Most of your appraisal assignments won't require as much detailed explanation to be included in the report as is presented here, but the format should be followed and you should retain sufficient explanation in your files, even if it is in handwritten form.

You will note that I have not included explanation of some of the adjustments for the sake of brevity, but you have previously been furnished with information on how to document and explain adjustments. I have also eliminated city analysis, neighborhood analysis, site analysis, improvement analysis and other components for the sake of brevity, but refer you to the appropriate chapters within this book wherein full explanation and suggested format are furnished.

**DIRECT SALES COMPARISON APPROACH**
**VALUE OF SITE AS IF VACANT**

| SALE NUMBER | I | II | III | IV | V | VI |
|---|---|---|---|---|---|---|
| Grantor | Brewer | Graves Estate | Willard | Eckstein | Abraham | Augusta Corp. |
| Grantee | Haardt | Varner | Kreis | Aronov Realty Co. | Dickey | Killian |
| Date of Sale | April 1964 | April 1965 | Sept. 1963 | June 1963 | Jan. 1964 | June 1964 |
| Land: Frontage | 126.5 | 127.5 | 150.0 | 100.0 | 105.0 | 150.0 |
| Dimensions | 126.5 × 186.8 | 127.5 × 195 | 150 × 200 | 100 × 150 | 105 × 150 | 150 × 220 |
| Square Feet | 23,613 | 24,862 | 30,000 | 15,000 | 15,750 | 33,000 |
| Sales Price | $9,000 | $21,800 | $13,800 | $6,500 | $7,000 | $13,500 |
| Price per Square Foot | $ .38 | $ .88 | $ .46 | $ .43 | $ .44 | $ .41 |
| ADJUSTMENTS: | | | | | | |
| Time | + 1% | nil | + 2% | + 2% | + 1% | + 1% |
| Physical Characteristics: | | | | | | |
| Shape | nil | nil | nil | nil | nil | nil |
| Topography | nil | nil | nil | nil | nil | nil |
| Depth | −20% | −20% | −20% | −25% | −25% | −15% |
| Street, City Services and Utilities | nil | nil | nil | nil | nil | nil |
| Location | +10% | nil | nil | + 5% | + 5% | + 5% |
| Composite Percentage Adjustment | − 9% | −20% | −18% | −18% | −19% | − 9% |
| Indicated Sq. Ft. Value for Subject | $.3458 | $.7040 | $.3772 | $.3526 | $.3564 | $.3731 |

Land sales III, V and VI are considered most comparable to the the subject. Sales I and IV clearly support the value indicated by sales III, V and VI. Sale II is given little weight on a square foot comparison, since the square foot price is clearly excessive. The owner states that the fact that the site is approved for eight units substantially increased the price he was willing to pay.

It is my opinion that the above sales indicate a value of $.35 per square foot for the subject site.

SUBJECT LAND VALUE ESTIMATE: 26,855 Sq. Ft. @ $.35 = $9,399
say $9,400

FLOOR PLAN

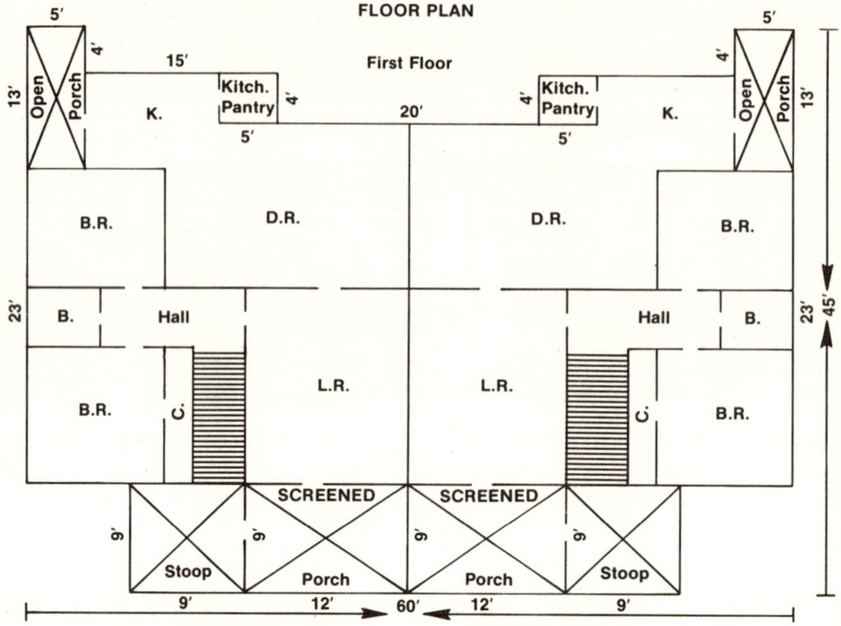


| Square Foot Area: | First Floor | Second Floor |
|---|---|---|
| Living Area | 1,750 | 1,912 |
| Stoops and Open Porches | 292 | 130 |
| Screened Porches | 216 | 216 |
| Total Sq. Ft. Area | 2,258 | 2,258 |

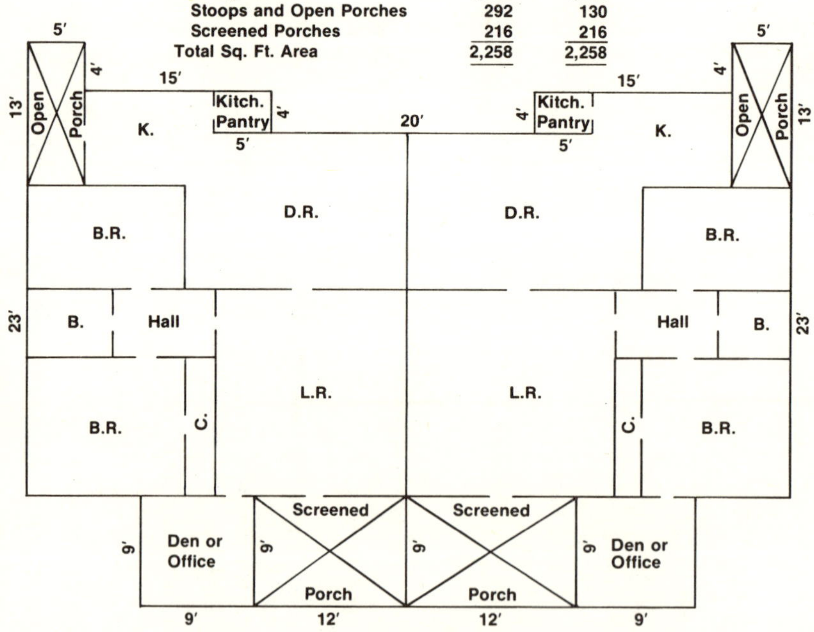


1" = 10' Second Floor

**COST APPROACH**
**REPRODUCTION COST BREAKDOWN**

| | |
|---|---|
| Excavation for Footings | $ 475 |
| Concrete Footings and Brick Piers | 667 |
| Exterior Walls (common brick veneer) | 5,693 |
| Framing | 695 |
| Roof Structure | 1,075 |
| Roof Covering | 668 |
| Interior Construction (walls, ceilings, stairs, etc.) | 8,227 |
| Floors: | |
| Wood Joists and Sub-floor | 561 |
| Tile Floor Covering (ceramic tile in baths) (linoleum in kitchen) | 620 |
| Varnished Oak Floors | 838 |
| Plumbing | 2,339 |
| Heating | 520 |
| Lighting and Electrical Wiring | 980 |
| Walks, Drives and Parking (concrete) | 875 |
| Landscaping | 300 |
| Direct Job Costs | $24,533 |
| Add: Indirect cost, architect fee, overhead and profit (22%) | 5,397 |
| TOTAL REPRODUCTION COST OF IMPROVEMENTS | $29,930 |
| say | $30,000 |

**COST APPROACH**
**DEPRECIATION**

**Physical Deterioration**

| | Replacement Cost | Percent Depr. | Amount Depr. | Total Depr. |
|---|---|---|---|---|
| Curable: | | | | |
| Ceiling: Fill Plaster Cracks & Paint | | | $ 200 | |
| Oak Floors: Sand & Refinish | $ 320 | 100 | $ 320 | |
| Outside Trim: Paint—2 coats | | | $ 375 | |
| Total Physical Curable Deterioration | | | | $ 895 |
| Curable Postponed: | | | | |
| Roof Covering | $ 668 | 50 | $ 332 | |
| Paint Interior Walls | $ 800 | 50 | $ 400 | |
| Plumbing (Water Heaters) | $ 300 | 80 | $ 240 | |
| Heating | $ 520 | 80 | $ 416 | |
| Screens (Windows & Porches) | $ 560 | 40 | $ 224 | |
| Total Physical Curable Deterioration (Postponed) | | | | $ 1,612 |
| Total Physical Curable Deterioration | | | | $ 2,507 |
| Incurable: | | | | |
| Excavation for Footings | $ 475 | 0 | Nil | |
| Concrete Footings & Brick Piers | $ 667 | 25 | $ 167 | |
| Exterior Walls—Common Brick Veneer | $ 5,693 | 50 | $ 2,847 | |
| Framing | $ 695 | 50 | $ 347 | |
| Roof Structure | $ 1,075 | 50 | $ 538 | |
| Interior Constr. (Balance) | $ 6,267 | 50 | $ 3,433 | |
| Floors: | | | | |
| Wood Joists & Subfloor | $ 561 | 50 | $ 281 | |
| Tile Floor Covering | $ 620 | 50 | $ 310 | |
| Varnished Oak Floors (Bal.) | $ 518 | 50 | $ 259 | |
| Plumbing (Balance) | $ 2,039 | 50 | $ 1,020 | |
| Lighting & Electric Wiring | $ 980 | 50 | $ 490 | |
| Walks, Drives & Parking | $ 875 | 40 | $ 350 | |
| Landscaping | $ 300 | 25 | $ 75 | |
| Sub-Total | | 50 | $10,117 | |
| Indirect Cost, Architect Fee Overhead, Profit Say | $ 5,467 | 50 | $ 2,733 | |
| Totals | $30,000 | | $12,850 | $12,850 |
| TOTAL PHYSICAL DETERIORATION | | | | $15,357 |

## COST APPROACH

### FUNCTIONAL OBSOLESCENCE

*Curable:*

There are no kitchen cabinets in subject property. The installation of 6 linear feet of base cabinets and 6 linear feet of overhead cabinets is necessary to satisfy tenant demands. These cabinets can be installed at $10 per linear foot.

| | | |
|---|---|---|
| Total Cost | $ 480 | |

Downstairs apartments are heated by natural gas floor furnaces, and upstairs apartments are heated by natural gas space heaters. The installation of more efficient heaters in the upstairs apartments is necessary to satisfy tenant demands. The cost of installing a natural gas blower-type heater in the upstairs apartments is approximately $225 for each unit.

| | | |
|---|---|---|
| Total Cost | 450 | |
| Total Functional Obsolescence—Curable | | $ 930 |

*Incurable:* (Functional Super-adequacy)

The typical gross square feet of living area per unit in apartments comparable to the subject property is from 800 to 825 square feet. The subject property has an average of 915 square feet of living area per unit. Analysis of rentals in comparable properties disclosed that the additional space in subject property would produce no additional rental income. Thus, subject property has approximately 100 square feet per unit which adds nothing to the rental value of the property.

| | | |
|---|---|---|
| Gross square feet of living area—subject | 915 | |
| Less: Gross square feet of living area—comparables—say | 815 | |
| Unproductive space per unit | 100 | |
| Number of units in subject | 4 | |
| Total unproductive square feet | 400 | |
| 400 sq. ft. × $4.91 (60% of $8.19 per S.F. Repro. Cost) | $1,964 | |
| Less: Physical depreciation charged elsewhere (50%) | 982 | |
| Total Functional Obsolescence—Incurable (Super-adequacy) | | 982 |
| TOTAL FUNCTIONAL OBSOLESCENCE | | $1,912 |

## COST APPROACH

## DEPRECIATION—NARRATIVE EXPLANATION

*Physical Curable:*

The physical curable items include rehabilitation or accrued maintenance which is needed at the date of the appraisal.

The ceiling plaster is cracked in all four apartments. The plaster cracks need to be filled, sanded to a smooth finish and painted. The estimated cost to cure is $50 per apartment or $200.

The oak floors require sanding and varnishing. The estimated cost to cure is $80 per apartment or $320.

The outside trim requires two coats of paint and, in addition, there are several rotted boards which should be replaced. The estimated cost to cure is $375.

*Physical Curable Postponed:*

The physical curable postponed items are ordinarily replaced during the life of the structure. These items are partially worn-out at the date of the appraisal but are not economically feasible to replace or to cure until the end of their useful life. These items are known as "short-life" building components.

These items were carefully inspected for physical condition in estimating accrued depreciation. Those items which were already depreciated under "physical curable" were deducted and the applicable depreciation percentage applied to the remainder.

The roof covering is a 20-year roof and is 10 years old at date of appraisal; thus, the roof is 50% depreciated.

The interior walls were painted two years prior to the date of the appraisal and should not require repainting for an additional two years; thus, interior walls painting is 50% depreciated.

The water heaters are considered to be the only short-life item in the plumbing costs. It is an opinion that the remainder of the plumbing will last the remaining 25 years economic life of the building. The water heaters are eight years old and it is an opinion that the heaters will last an additional two years; thus, the water heaters are 80% depreciated at the date of the appraisal.

The wood frame window screens and the screen wire used on the screened porches are four years old at the date of the appraisal. It is an opinion that the screens will last an additional six years; thus, the screens are 40% depreciated.

*Physical Incurable:*

The physical incurable items are all building components which have not been previously depreciated. Substantial portions of these items are hidden from view and cannot be observed.

The unit-in-place method of estimating reproduction cost allows the appraiser an opportunity to make a series of smaller judgments based on the observed condition of individual items. The portion of each component which has already been depreciated under "physical curable" or "physical curable postponed" is deducted from total cost of that component and the physical incurable percentage applied to the remainder.

The lighting and electric wiring component was not treated separately as a short-life item. It is an opinion that the lighting and wiring will last the remaining 25 years of economic life estimated for the structure. The plumbing component, with the exception of water heaters, was not treated as a short-life item for the same reason.

The indirect cost, architect fee, overhead expense and contractor's profit component was depreciated at the 50% rate which is applicable to the major portion of the building components. It should be noted that total physical deterioration of $15,357 is approximately 51% of total reproduction cost.

*Functional Obsolescence Curable:*

For a functional item to be classified as curable, the cost required to effect the cure must be economically feasible. If a functional item is economically feasible to cure, the amount of functional obsolescence is the cost to cure.

None of the apartment units in the subject property have any kitchen cabinets. Competing apartments were found to have an average of 6 linear feet of base cabinets and 6 linear feet of overhead cabinets. The tenants in subject property have reluctantly accepted the kitchen pantry in lieu of kitchen cabinets. While the addition of cabinets will not increase the rent which the apartments will earn, it appears that the substantial competition from apartments which offer kitchen cabinets makes it necessary to install the cabinets to maintain present rent schedules. The potential loss of tenants and/or the required compensating reduction in rent causes the item to be economically feasible to cure. The estimated cost to cure is $10 per linear foot applied to 24 feet of base cabinets and 24 feet of overhead cabinets, for a total cost of $480.

The apartments constructed in recent years in this city have central forced air, natural gas heating, as well as central air-conditioning. The room layout and building design of the subject property would cause the installation of central forced air heating and air-conditioning to be extremely expensive. The installation of the necessary vents, pipe and wiring would be very difficult and expensive. Due to the large costs involved and the fact that subject improvement had only an estimated 25 years remaining economic life, it was concluded that a central forced air heating and air-conditioning system was not economically feasible.

Interviews with tenants disclosed that the floor furnaces in the downstairs units did a satisfactory job of heating the apartments. The space heaters in the upstairs units were not considered satisfactory. It was found that apartments in the class which compete with subject property offered, as a minimum, a floor furnace heating system. Since floor furnaces could not be easily installed in upstairs units, it is an opinion that, in order to prevent loss of tenants and/or the required compensating reduction of rent, it is necessary to install a natural gas blower-type heater in each upstairs apartment. While the installation of these heaters would not result in an increase in rent for the upstairs units, it would enable the present rent schedule to remain in effect, thus causing the item to be economically feasible to cure. The estimated cost of the heaters is $225 per unit, resulting in a total cost to cure of $450.

*Functional Obsolescence Incurable:*

The measure of functional obsolescence incurable is generally the capitalized rent loss attributable to the functional deficiency, if such deficiency is not economically feasible to cure. If the functional obsolescence incurable is the result of super-adequacy in the structure, the measure of such obsolescence is the reproduction cost of the super-adequacy minus physical incurable already charged, plus the present worth of added expense caused by the condition.

In comparing the subject property with other similar apartments, the comparison was on a per room basis. It was found that, if the rooms were of sufficient size to be useable, the above-average size rooms, such as are found in the subject property, did not increase the rental value of the apartment. The typical tenant is interested in a room of sufficient size to accommodate a reasonable amount of furniture, plus enough additional space for normal foot traffic and assigns little or no value to exceptionally large rooms.

A study of several apartments similar to the subject property disclosed that the gross square feet of living area per unit is from 800 to 825 square feet. The subject property has an average of 915 gross square feet of living area per unit. The result of this study indicates that the subject property has excess space of from 90 to 115 gross square feet of living area which produce no additional income.

It is an opinion that the subject property has excess space of 100 gross square feet of living area per unit or a total of 400 square feet for which no additional rent could be obtained.

The cost of the excessive area is less per square foot than the overall reproduction cost per square foot. This is due to the fact that the cost of plumbing, heating, lighting and practically all the wiring would not be reduced by a reduction of 400 square feet in the size of the structure. It is an opinion that 60% of reproduction cost would be applicable to the super-adequacy. Therefore, the square foot cost applied to the 400 square feet of excessive space is 60% of $8.19, or $4.91 per square foot. This indicated a total reproduction cost of $1,964 for the super-adequacy. This amount was reduced by 50% physical deterioration already charged, thus leaving functional obsolescence incurable (super-adequacy) of $982.

The 400 square feet of super-adequacy was not considerd as adding any expenses that required discounting. Therefore, the $982 shown in the above paragraph is the total functional obsolescence incurable charged against subject structure.

## COST APPROACH

## ECONOMIC (LOCATIONAL) OBSOLESCENCE

Economic obsolescence is caused by factors outside the property. The amount of economic obsolescence is the capitalized value of the rent loss caused by the economic factor and is attributable to the improvements only.

In this instance, it initially appeared that the fact that subject improvements were built on a lot zoned for single-family residential use would cause some economic obsolescence. However, consultation with the officials of the City Planning Commission revealed that the present use was a legal nonconforming use and that the zoning waiver would not be withdrawn. The waiver has been in effect for 25 years and it is reasonable to assume that the waiver will continue for the remaining economic life of 25 years.

The subject property is well protected from encroachment by inharmonious uses on all four sides by substantial residential properties. The residents of the area are compatible and the entire neighborhood would be considerd above average in stability.

After careful analysis, it is an opinion that the subject property does not suffer from economic obsolescence. Consequently, there is no economic obsolescence charged against subject property in this appraisal.

**COST APPROACH—ESTIMATE OF VALUE**

| | | | |
|---|---|---|---|
| Reproduction Cost of Building | | | $30,000 |
| Depreciation: | | | |
| Physical Deterioration—Curable | $ 895 | | |
| Physical Deterioration—Curable Postponed | 1,612 | | |
| Physical Deterioration—Incurable | 12,850 | $15,357 | |
| Curable Functional Obsolescence | | 930 | |
| Incurable Functional Obsolescence | | 982 | |
| Economic Obsolescence | | nil | |
| Total Accrued Depreciation | | | 17,269 |
| Indicated Value of Improvements | | | 12,731 |
| | | say | 12,700 |
| Add: Land Value (from Market) | | | 9,400 |
| TOTAL VALUE INDICATED BY COST APPROACH | | | $22,100 |

## DIRECT SALES COMPARISON APPROACH

| | *Comparable Sale VII* | | *Comparable Sale VIII* | | *Comparable Sale IX* | | *Comparable Sale X* | | *Indicated for Subject* |
|---|---|---|---|---|---|---|---|---|---|
| Street Address | *3255-59 Norman Bridge Rd.* | | *509-15 Thorn Place* | | *517-23 Thorn Place* | | *3420 Norman Bridge Rd.* | | |
| Date of Sale | | 9-6-63 | | 1-4-64 | | 1-3-64 | | 9-14-64 | |
| Sales Price | | $22,500 | | $21,000 | | $21,000 | | $32,500 | |
| Gross Rental Income, Year of Sale | | $ 2,520 | | $ 2,400 | | $ 2,400 | | $ 3,780 | |
| Gross Annual Rent Multiplier | | 8.93 | | 8.75 | | 8.75 | | 8.60 | 8.75 |
| Adjustments: | | | | | | | | | |
| Time | +$ 900 | | +$ 420 | | +$ 420 | | +$ 650 | | |
| Location | equal | | +$ 500 | | +$ 500 | | equal | | |
| Physical Characteristics: | | | | | | | | | |
| Lot (Size & Condition) | +$1,000 | | +$1,000 | | +$1,000 | | +$ 500 | | |
| Kitchen Cabinets (Subject—none, Est. cost to install $480) | −$ 480 | | −$ 480 | | −$ 480 | | −$ 480 | | |
| Heating System | −$ 800 | | −$ 200 | | −$ 200 | | −$4,500 | | |
| Stove, Refrig., Blinds | −$1,500 | | −$ 750 | | −$ 750 | | −$1,800 | | |
| Physical condition of improvements | equal | | equal | | equal | | −$5,000 | | |
| Total Adjustments (Net) | | −$ 880 | | +$ 490 | | +$ 490 | | −$10,630 | |
| Adjusted Sales Price | | $21,620 | | $21,490 | | $21,490 | | $21,870 | |
| Number of Apartment Units | | 4 | | 4 | | 4 | | 4 | |
| Sales Price per Unit | | $ 5,405 | | $ 5,373 | | $ 5,373 | | $ 5,468 | $5,400 |
| Number of Rooms | | 20 | | 20 | | 20 | | 18 | 20 |
| Sales Price per Room | | $ 1,081 | | $ 1,075 | | $ 1,075 | | $ 1,215 | $1,075 |
| VALUE CONCLUSION: | | | | | | | | | |
| $2,520 Gross Annual Rent Income × 8.75 (Gross Annual Rent Multiplier) | | | | $22,050 | | | | | |
| 4 Units at $5,400 per Unit | | | | 21,600 | | | | | |
| 20 Rooms at $1,075 per Room | | | | 21,500 | | | | | |
| DIRECT SALES COMPARISON APPROACH, ESTIMATE OF VALUE (at Dec. 1, 1965) | | | | $21,500 | | | | | |

*NOTE:* Comparable sales were adjusted for differences between comparable and subject in physical condition and functional efficiency; therefore, no reduction from the value estimate for physical and functional curable items is indicated.

## INCOME APPROACH

The subject property is considered to be an income-producing property. Four-unit apartments similar to the subject have become popular in many areas of the United States. The two-unit or duplex apartment in many instances is purchased for owner-occupancy of one unit and the other unit is used to assist in loan amortization. Properties of four or more units are generally bought by investors for their income-producing potential and, as a result of this fact, the net income which the property will earn is given great weight by the investor.

The income approach is primarily concerned with the present worth of the future potential benefits to be derived from ownership of the property. The primary steps used in the income approach are:

1. Estimating the market rental value of the subject property based on an analysis of comparable rentals.
2. Estimating the percentage of vacancy and rent loss by comparison with other competing apartments.
3. From the conclusions reached in steps 1 and 2, estimating effective gross income.
4. Analysis of comparable sales for selection of capitalization rate.
5. Estimate of future expenses, including depreciation.
6. Estimate of net income before depreciation.
7. Process net income before depreciation into value indicated by the income approach.

The supporting data for each of the above steps in the income approach is shown on the following pages along with the appraiser's reasoning and value conclusion.

*Economic Rental Value of Subject Property*

The properties which are utilized in the market data approach were found to be most comparable to the subject property and are also utilized to estimate the economic rental value of the subject. The comparables are listed as sales VII, VIII, IX and X in the market data approach. These properties were selected as being most comparable to the subject property for economic rental analysis after a study of the rental market for four-unit apartments in this city.

The comparable rental data analysis is as follows:

| | SALE VII | SALE VIII | SALE IX | SALE X |
|---|---|---|---|---|
| Address | 3255-59 Norman Bridge Road | 509-15 Thorn Place | 517-23 Thorn Place | 3420 Norman Bridge Road |
| Gross Monthly Rent | $210.00 | $200.00 | $200.00 | $315.00 |
| Number of Rooms | 20 | 20 | 20 | 18 |
| Gross Rental: Per Room per Month | $ 10.50 | $ 10.00 | $ 10.00 | $ 17.50 |
| ADJUSTMENTS: | | | | |
| Location | equal | + 1.00 | + 1.00 | equal |
| Physical Features | − .10 | − .10 | − .10 | − 6.00 |
| Functional Utility | nil-see expl. | nil-see expl. | nil-see expl. | nil-see expl. |
| Utilities Furnished | equal | equal | equal | equal |
| Net Adjustment | − .10 | + .90 | + .90 | − 6.00 |
| Indicated Rental Value per Room per Month for Subject | $ 10.40 | $ 10.90 | $ 10.90 | $ 11.50 |

The comparable rental data analysis indicates a rental value for the subject property of $10.40, $10.90, $10.90 and $11.50 per room per month. Analysis of the above comparables with particular emphasis on the properties at 3255-59 Norman Bridge Road, 509-15 Thorn Place and 517-523 Thorn Place indicates an economic rental of $11.00 per room per month, or $55.00 per apartment per month for the subject property.

Thus, the indicated market rental value of subject is:

| | | |
|---|---|---|
| 20 Rooms | @ $11.00 | $220 per Month |
| 5 Rooms per Apt. | @ $11.00 | $ 55 per Month |
| 4 Apartments | @ $55.00 | $220 per Month |
| | $220 per Month × 12 = | $2,640 per Year |

In comparing the subject property with the comparable rentals, the adjustments which were considered are location, physical features, functional utility and utilities furnished.

*CAPITALIZATION*

Owners of property similar to the subject can generally anticipate a gradual decrease in net income during the economic life of the improvements. The improvements deteriorate or waste away with time, while the land is assumed to be imperishable. The land value for subject property as found in the market is considered to be reasonably reliable.

Considering the age of the subject improvements in addition to the facts stated above, the straight line method of capitalization, using the building residual technique, is regarded as most applicable to the subject property.

**INCOME APPROACH—VALUE ESTIMATE**

| | | | |
|---|---|---|---|
| Gross Annual Income | | | $ 2,640 |
| Less: Vacancy and Loss of Rent (5%) | | | 132 |
| Effective Gross Rental Income | | | 2,508 |
| Service Income | | | nil |
| Effective Gross Income | | | $ 2,508 |
| Less: Expenses and Reserves: | | | |
| Fixed Expenses | $298 | | |
| Operating Expenses | 485 | | |
| Replacement Reserves | 210 | | 993 |
| Net Income Before Depreciation | | | $ 1,515 |
| Loss: Interest on Land ($9,400 [from Market] × 5.25%) | | | 493 |
| Net Income to Improvements | | | $ 1,022 |
| Indicated Value of Improvements ($1,022 ÷ 9.25%) (5.25% Interest + 4% Recapture) | | | $11,049 |
| Add: Land from Market | | | $ 9,400 |
| Value Indicated by Income Approach if Functional Curable Deficiencies Are Cured | | say | $20,500 |
| Less: Cost to Cure Functional Curable Deficiencies | | | 930 |
| INCOME APPROACH, Estimate of Value | | say | $19,600 |

## CORRELATION (RECONCILIATION) AND FINAL VALUE ESTIMATE

The subject property is considered to be an income-producing property. The property is a single structure containing four apartments. The purpose of this appraisal is to estimate the market value of the unencumbered fee simple interest as of December 1, 1965.

The city data gathered and analyzed indicates that this city will continue its economic and population growth at a steady rate. Due to the continued growth, proximity of the city to Maxwell Field and Gunter Field military bases, and other favorable factors, the future rental and marketability of four-unit apartments similar to the subject are expected to be good.

The neighborhood in which the subject property is located would be considered above average in convenience to schools, churches, shopping and recreational facilities. The subject property is well protected by surrounding homes and by city zoning from encroachment of undesirable commercial or industrial users. The occupants of the neighborhood have a very harmonious relationship and the neighborhood is considered very stable.

In estimating the land value, consideration was given to vacant land market sales, as well as making a comparison of indicated land value from sales of properties improved with apartments. The subject site contained a substantial amount of excess land which could not be improved with an additional structure due to zoning restrictions. The indicated value of subject site is $9400.

The subject improvements were constructed in about 1940, and are very similar to other competing apartments constructed in prewar years.

The sales of similar apartment properties, when analyzed, indicate that the subject improvements may expect a remaining economic life of approximately 25 years.

The three recognized approaches to value were used in the appraisal of subject property. These three approaches are summarized as follows:

| | |
|---|---|
| Cost Approach, Estimate of Value | $22,100 |
| Market Approach, Estimate of Value | $21,500 |
| Income Approach, Estimate of Value | $19,600 |

The cost factors used in estimating reproduction cost new were checked with a reliable contractor and cost estimator. The reproduction cost new of $30,000 is believed to be reliable.

The subject improvements were in fair to good condition at the time of the appraisal. However, there were several items of deferred maintenance and several functional deficiencies which required estimates. In addition, the improvements were approximately 25 years old, thus there was a substantial amount of physical incurable deterioration which required an estimate.

Because of the substantial amount of estimating required, both in estimating reproduction cost and in estimating depreciation, the cost approach is considered to be the weakest approach and is used primarily as a check against the other approaches to value.

In estimating the value indicated by the direct sales comparison approach, three indicators of value were used: the gross annual rent multiplier, the sale price per unit and the sale price per room. Each of these indicators were relatively close and supported the value conclusion reached by the direct sales comparison approach.

Three of the comparables used in the direct sales comparison approach were very similar to subject in age, condition and remaining economic life. These three sales required very little adjustment and are given considerably more weight than the sale at 3420 Norman Bridge Road, which was much newer, more modern and offered many amenities not offered by the subject property.

The direct sales comparison approach is considered to be reasonably reliable as an indicator of value for the subject property. The direct sales comparison approach is not given as much weight as the income approach in the final value estimate.

Properties similar to the subject are generally bought for their income-producing ability. The income approach is normally the best indicator of value for this type of property. This is also true in this instance. The income approach is given most weight in the final estimate of value.

The rent analysis on subject property indicated an economic rent of $55 per unit per month. This rent schedule should be maintained if the functional curable deficiencies are cured at an early date.

The data available in estimating the vacancy and rent loss is adequate; therefore, the vacancy and rent loss allowance of 5% is considered to be reasonable.

The band of investment technique was utilized as a check against the interest rate indicated by direct comparison. The interest rate of 5.75% indicated by this technique is not considered to be as reliable as the rate of 5.25% indicated by direct comparison. Thus, the interest rate used in the income approach was 5.25% and is considered to be reasonable and well supported by market data.

The availability of owner's operating statements were of great assistance in estimating future expenses. However, the estimated future expenses are based on several sources rather than the owner's operating statement alone. The amount of estimated future expenses is considered to be reliable.

The value estimate by the income approach is considered to be the best indicator of value for the subject property. The value indication of $19,600 by the income approach is perhaps somewhat low due to a tendency of the appraiser to assure that estimates of future expenses and replacement reserves were fully adequate. While every effort was made to arrive at accurate estimates of future expenses and replacement reserves, the cautious tendency mentioned above could possibly have resulted in a slight overstatement of the expense and replacement reserve items.

Based on the information contained in this report, and considering the value estimates by the three recognized approaches to value, it is my opinion that the market value of the subject property as of December 1, 1965 is $20,500, divided as follows:

| | |
|---|---|
| Land | $ 9,400 |
| Improvements | 11,100 |
| Market Value | $20,500 |

______________________________

Appraiser

# Index